PENGUIN BOOKS

Unloved

Peter Roche lives with his wife and children in Hampshire. This is his first book.

Unloved

The True Story of a Stolen Childhood

PETER ROCHE

PENGUIN BOOKS

PENGUIN BOOKS

Published by the Penguin Group
Penguin Books Ltd, 80 Strand, London WC2R 0RL, England
Penguin Group (USA) Inc., 375 Hudson Street, New York, New York 10014, USA
Penguin Group (Canada), 90 Eglinton Avenue East, Suite 700, Toronto, Ontario, Canada M4P 2Y3
(a division of Pearson Penguin Canada Inc.)
Penguin Ireland, 25 St Stephen's Green, Dublin 2, Ireland
(a division of Penguin Books Ltd)
Penguin Group (Australia), 250 Camberwell Road, Camberwell, Victoria 3124, Australia
(a division of Pearson Australia Group Pty Ltd)
Penguin Books India Pvt Ltd, 11 Community Centre, Panchsheel Park, New Delhi – 110 017, India
Penguin Group (NZ), 67 Apollo Drive, Rosedale, North Shore 0632, New Zealand
(a division of Pearson New Zealand Ltd)
Penguin Books (South Africa) (Pty) Ltd, 24 Sturdee Avenue, Rosebank, Johannesburg 2196, South Africa

Penguin Books Ltd, Registered Offices: 80 Strand, London WC2R 0RL, England

www.penguin.com

Published in 2007
9

Set in 12.5/14.75 pt Monotype Garamond
Typeset by Rowland Phototypesetting Ltd, Bury St Edmunds, Suffolk
Printed in England by Clays Ltd, St Ives plc

ISBN: 978-0-141-03355-6

www.greenpenguin.co.uk

To All My Children

Contents

Acknowledgements

To my wife: my partner, mother of my children and my best friend, the one who pushed and prodded me in her own quiet, determined way until I stopped talking about writing a book and did something about it. I am the luckiest husband in the world, and I know it – even though I don't say it very often. I don't even want to think about where I would be without you.

To Vincent and Johnny: you were the only adults who showed me compassion and kindness when I was a child. I'm sure you would have done more if you could, and perhaps thought that what you had done wasn't enough. I can tell you that your humanity made all the difference to a confused, mistreated, starving boy.

To the big detective in Coventry: I remember your name – how could I forget it? But I wouldn't want to embarrass you in what I feel sure must be a well-earned retirement. All I can say is that I am more grateful than you may ever know for the break you gave a frightened, foolish kid when he really needed it.

To Miss Zils: thank you for all the kindness you showed me and for doing all that you could.

To all my children, big and small: I am proud of every single one of you, proud to be able to say that I am your father. You have taught me what family means. Without you, I could never have understood what people mean when they say blood is thicker than water.

To Pat Lomax, my dedicated agent; Cheryl Stonehouse, for helping me to turn my feelings into words; and Carly Cook, my editor at Penguin, who saw the book's potential right from the very beginning and allowed my voice to be heard: a tough threesome whose skill, compassion and sheer hard work got this book out of me. None of you ever stopped believing in me and my story for a minute, and that still amazes me. Thank you.

Finally, to Dave, my dump-yard soulmate, the person who first showed me friendship without any thought of what might be in it for him: I have never forgotten you, mate, and wherever you are, I wish you well.

1. 1971

The day my father died was just like any other. I was walking along my road in Lambeth where a row of tall early nineteenth-century houses stood set slightly back from the main road. Back then most of these old houses had been condemned by the council and a lot of them were boarded up with sheets of galvanized metal. Most of the front gardens were scruffy and full of rubbish, old furniture, bits of bikes and prams, any old junk.

I was heading back from the corner shop. An old bloke had seen me sneaking out from my safe place, the dump yard at the back of the condemned houses, and had asked me to run round and get him a loaf of bread. I'd done it because I never minded doing an errand like that. It was something to do, something with a purpose to it, and there was always a chance that I'd get a few pennies for doing it.

I'd delivered the loaf and got my tip, and as I turned back into my road I saw a little crowd gathered a bit further up where an ambulance was standing at the bus stop right outside my house. These were still the days when Sundays were deathly quiet in London, with most of the shops shut, not much traffic and very few people about, so there was obviously a bit of an event going on. I wandered up and had a look for myself.

My house didn't have its windows boarded up, even though it looked completely derelict. It was filthy from top to bottom and there was no glass in a lot of the windows, no paint on the woodwork. From inside the house I could hear screams and all kinds of commotion and the ambulancemen were just coming out of the front door carrying a man laid out on a stretcher. It was hard to tell whether he was alive or dead. He had thinning, greying hair and his skin was much the same colour. He looked rough, unshaven and half-pissed, a man who wasn't in the best of health even when he wasn't on his way into the back of an ambulance. His head was lolling back and his mouth was slack, hanging open, and although he was covered by a blanket you could see he was only wearing a vest. A boy standing next to me suddenly looked straight at me. He thought he recognized me but he wasn't sure. He was puzzled because I was standing with him, as if I was just another rubber-necking local kid like him who'd happened to come along to see what all the fuss was about.

He stared at me for a moment and then asked: 'Isn't that your dad?'

'No,' I said. I put my hands in my pockets and walked off in the opposite direction. I was almost nine years old and that was the last time I saw my father alive.

2. Family Ties

There can't be too many Londoners who grew up south of the Thames and have fond memories of police stations, but the one I visited in Lambeth holds a special place in my heart. I had one of the best days of my life with my best friend, John-John. We were both little more than toddlers when we ended up spending an afternoon at the station, being fed and made a fuss of by the officers on duty.

It was quite a new building and it seemed really posh. The staff there gave us sweets and, better still, took us to their swanky, shiny cafeteria with its clean, modern Marley-tiled floor and Formica-topped tables and gave us a hot dinner. They dug out a few toys from somewhere and played with us from time to time through the day. It was warm, everyone was friendly, the police station was great. I didn't want to leave. In fact, I didn't have a single thought about my mother or the rest of my family until Mum turned up with John-John's mother to take us home. We'd been there hours by then and it was already dark outside.

That was when I got upset. I asked the police officers whether I could come back to see them sometime, half hoping that one of them might say: 'Don't go home at all, stay here with us.'

All you know when you're that young is that life is as it is. The police seemed to find me easy to have around, so why wouldn't it be simpler for everyone if I lived there with them? In every possible way I could think of, the police station was a lot nicer than home.

On that wonderful day I spent at the police station, my friend and I had been found playing in the rubbish-strewn garden of a derelict house, a good half a mile away from our homes, which were in part of a complex of low-rise flats. It was a gloomy red-brick warren of flats, each block four floors high, with tiled concrete stairwells leading to the balconies that each front door opened onto. The three-bedroom flat we had there is the first home I can recall.

There was nothing out of the ordinary about wandering the streets to me. I was more comfortable in the alleys and walkways around the flats where I lived than I ever was in my home, and I wasn't afraid to go further afield. I was pushed out of the flat every day for hours on end by my mother and left to go where I wanted, and I was quite proud of knowing my way around. I quite often found myself crossing busy main routes into central London, but although I had never been taken there by my parents, I had at an early age worked out that traffic would stop if I stood at the zebra crossing between our flats and the park entrance. There was a playground there with swings and a roundabout, and there were ponds near to it that I could walk round and throw stones into. It was interesting and peaceful. I had no idea that it was also a place that could have been deadly for a toddler on his own and that no child that young should have been left wandering round it. No normal person would have done that to such a small child, of course. My mother and father wouldn't have thought twice about it, but they weren't normal. And, in any case, even at that age I didn't want to go home.

By the time Mum arrived, brought there with John-John's mother by an officer, it was dark outside. They put Mum and me in one car and John-John and his mum in another to take us home and I knew she wasn't happy. She didn't say much, just held my arm so tightly that it hurt. I should think the police officers probably said to themselves: 'Poor lad, he's going to get it when he gets home.' What they couldn't have known was exactly what I was going to get.

Once the police were gone, my mother started. She was shouting and swearing and dragging me by the arm as we walked along the balcony to the door of our fourth-floor flat. She paused to say goodnight to John-John's mother as they disappeared into their flat a few doors down, and once we were through our door the battering started.

Mum wasn't a tall woman, maybe only a few inches over five feet, but she was built like a bulldog. When she'd been a young girl back in Ireland her family had called her Big Bridget, but this described her width rather than her height. It wasn't that she was overweight, but she had broad shoulders and arms as powerful as a boxer's. She might have been quite a beauty when she was younger, with her fair skin and dark, straight hair, but I only ever saw the hair faded and greying and cut in a short bob and the face tired and mean-looking. She had a distinct smell that clung about her, a sweet, musty smell that seemed to get stronger when she was really angry. Her clothes were always shabby and often grubby, and the only feminine thing about her that I can recall from my early childhood was the red patterned headscarf, tied under her chin, that she almost always wore when she was out.

On this night she didn't stop to take off the scarf or her coat. She shut the door and began to batter me around the head over and over again, belting me so hard that each blow knocked me across the hall from one side to another and I was rebounding off the walls like the ball in a pinball machine. She wasn't the kind of mother who only used the flat of her hand. It was fists, feet, everything. As she battered me, she was screaming at me.

'You fucking little bastard, what did you think you were doing – you can disappear for good for all I care, but don't you ever bring the fucking police to my door again, you little shit.'

Her whole body was shaking uncontrollably and her brown eyes had turned black with sheer animal fury. She was putting so much force into kicking me that her hair looked wild, as if she'd been running through the rain, strands of it stuck to her face. She was so angry that fists and feet weren't enough. I saw her reaching blindly about her, as she always did when she'd completely lost it, for another weapon, anything that she could use to inflict more damage. Her hand found a pan on the floor just inside the kitchen door and she brought it down on my head again and again.

She was not beating me because I had wandered off. Not for frightening her to death. She was outraged that I had shown her up. Both Mum and Dad always made sure we knew that the worst crime we could commit was to get them caught out and embarrassed by their own neglect of their children.

The truth is that it was John-John's mother who had raised the alarm and called the police when she realized her son had wandered off the estate and was nowhere to be found. I don't know whether my mother had noticed. Maybe she hadn't. Maybe she had realized that I wasn't there and hadn't come back at bedtime, but couldn't be bothered to waste her time looking for me. I know she would have been thinking to herself: 'The little bastard can spend the night outside – that'll teach him.'

After all, she put me out of the door every day after my older brothers and sisters had gone to school and made it clear she didn't want to see me again until the others were back. I wasn't even called in for lunch. I suppose there must have been a time when she kept me in, but I couldn't remember it. By this time my baby sister Rosemary, eighteen months younger than me, had been born, and as soon as I could walk reasonably well that would have been the end of her interest in me. Maybe this was partly because I was a boy. My parents seemed to think that boys could bring themselves up and didn't need any special care, but it was also true that love and affection were not emotions I could ever have associated with either my mother or my father. All they cared about was what made life easier for them, and the only emotions they showed were the anger and violence that erupted out of them when their children made life difficult for them.

It certainly seemed that in my mother's mind, where boys were concerned, there was nothing between being a baby and being a man. It was out of nappies and out of the door. From the earliest days I could remember, it was as if I was a dog being let out for a pee. I knew not to come back until long after school was over and my brothers were back, unless I wanted a beating for bothering her, even if I was hungry – and usually I was already hungry when she shoved me out onto the balcony. 'Get out of my fucking sight, boy. Leave me in peace' was how she usually closed the door on me, without waiting to see where I went or what I would do next.

So it wasn't for having worried her sick that I was beaten from one end of the flat to the other after we got back from the police station. It was for bringing the authorities to her door, and this beating was so ferocious that I had, just for a moment, forgotten about Dad.

I should have realized that if she was this far out of control, Dad's reaction was going to be more violent than anything I'd ever suffered before at his hands. I had already had plenty of beatings from both of them, but I suddenly felt that Mum was being so vicious that I didn't know how it was going to end, or if it would ever end. So I made the terrible mistake of trying to run away from her fists into one of the flat's four rooms. I ran straight into the room where Dad was already getting to his feet to come and play his part in my punishment.

Dad was a big man, close to six feet tall, and I had no chance of escaping him. He grabbed me as I tried to dodge round him and then he reached for his belt. Sometimes he wore a belt, and sometimes he seemed to have nothing to hold his trousers up but a piece of string, but all through my childhood, wherever we lived, there was a leather belt hanging by the fireplace ready for him to use on us. Now he held me by a fistful of hair in one hand so that I couldn't get away while he whipped me as hard as he could with the buckle end of it.

'You little fucking bastard,' he snarled at me. 'I'll teach you to bring trouble to my door. I'll give you something to teach you a lesson you'll never forget, boy. You won't be able to get to the toilet to piss, never mind the fucking police station.'

I was screaming my head off with pain and fright. Dad's reaction to my distress was automatic, the phrase I heard him use over and over again, hundreds, maybe thousands of times.

'Crying, are you? I'll give you something to cry about,' he roared, and he gripped my hair tighter and laid into me with fresh energy. My hands went up in a movement that had become second nature to me, clamped to the back of my head underneath his hands, trying to hold my scalp on while I was lifted bodily into the air. With each lash of the belt, my body swung and juddered as if I was a rag doll being flung about by a rabid dog. The pain was gone. There was too much of it. Instead what I could feel was a sick, horrible, shivery feeling of heat rising from my stomach and spreading through my whole body. I knew this feeling well. It came every time I had a beating like this, when it had got so bad that I had given up begging him to stop, and I knew myself to be completely helpless, utterly powerless and in the hands of the Devil himself.

Dad would have been in his late forties then, but even allowing for the way a child thinks his parents are impossibly old, he looked a lot older than he was. Like my mother, he had been a looker in his youth, I think, tall for a man of his generation, with masses of dark, wavy hair and a fine, long, straight nose. Whatever he looked like now, unshaven, half drunk, his words slurred because he'd probably been in a stupor on the living room sofa, where he and Mum slept, when we'd come in, all that was insignificant as the pain he was inflicting on me made my vision blur. The whipping continued until every part of me was numb. I guess I stopped being able to process any emotion, any feeling. Whatever kicked in, I was grateful.

It did end and I didn't die. I found myself being thrown through the air into the dingy, squalid back room where I shared mattresses on the floor with my five older brothers. It was late and they were already in there. Some of them were still awake and had heard it all. If I expected sympathy I didn't get it. Pitch dark closed around me as the bedroom door was slammed shut and I landed on a body. The body sat up and thumped me hard. I heard sniggers in the darkness.

'You stupid little fucker,' said a voice. I think that was

Raymond, my oldest brother. The contempt in his voice was like another slap. 'Now shut up,' he said. I realized I was still sobbing. 'We want to get some fucking sleep.'

I felt around for a corner of mattress where I might be able to curl up, getting a few kicks from the feet that seemed to be everywhere. A blanket was out of the question. Any that there were would be wrapped tightly round someone else's body so that no-one could nick it. I didn't even bother to look. I lay in the dark, comforted just enough by the strange calmness that always crept over me like a blessing after I'd had a beating. It was over. That one was over, at least. I had survived. For today.

When my mother met Davie Roche he was in uniform and he must have looked good in it, a member of the Irish National Guard, the neutral army that acted as a home defence force in Eire during the Second World War. That would have been quite an achievement for a young man who had been born out of wedlock in the narrow-minded society Ireland was in the 1920s and 1930s, and I don't know why he wasn't able to build on that promising beginning.

He had had a tough childhood himself. His mother had become pregnant just a few months after the end of the First World War and left her close-knit village in the middle of Ireland to have her baby in Dublin, away from the gossips. Dad's birth certificate shows that his mother tried to pass herself off as a married woman, Mrs Louisa Roche, naming her child's father as David Roche, but it didn't work. She did manage to avoid having her baby taken from her for adoption, but she couldn't survive on her own, and when she came back to her parents' house Dad was brought up by her parents as if he were her youngest brother. Even after he knew the truth, relatives said, he insisted on calling her Auntie because he was so ashamed of her. She must have lived in shame all her life. She was in her sixties when she died and had never married. Dad never, ever talked about her.

I never knew him as anything other than a vicious-tempered drunken animal. He did manage to hang on to the only job I recall him having, working as a council lavatory cleaner at the public conveniences in Lambeth, but he drank constantly. Day and night, whether he'd just been out drinking or he was on his way out to work in the toilets in the shabby suit and tie he always wore, no matter how filthy the clothes were, he stank like a wet pub floor, a mixture of old beer and fag ash. Whether he was a disappointed man or just a vile one, I was never sure. That night there had been nothing I could do to stop him except wait for his temper to wear itself out on me, taking each stinging lash of the belt as best I could, praying that the beer he had inside him would eventually get the better of him and he would run out of steam.

This was a particularly vicious beating, but violence of this kind seemed normal to me. It was what parents were for, what they did to you. If I thought about it at all I believed it was no more than I deserved and that it was my fault I brought this kind of punishment on myself. I often thought that if only I wasn't so bad, I would get affection and sympathy. I was beginning to ask myself why I was always in trouble. There had never been a moment when being good got any reward, but I still tried hard to do what they wanted. Especially for my father. I wanted to be loved, but most of all, even from a young age, I wanted to make my dad happy. But I never, ever saw him happy, and whatever I did, I just seemed to cause bother.

I had been taught early on that there was no point looking to Mum for any comfort to make up for Dad's evil temper, because one of my very first memories is of lying in a cot in our Lambeth flat, and across the room my mother is sitting, sewing. I feel ill, I feel hot. I'm crying because I'm not well and I want it to stop. So does my mother – not my illness, but the crying. 'Shut up, for Christ's sake,' she shouts. But I can't stop crying. I feel so ill. I'm small and in pain and want my mum to make it better. So she gets up, walks across the room to where I'm lying and shoves a baby bottle at me with sweet cold tea in it. This doesn't stop me crying because I'm not thirsty and I'm not hungry, just ill, and the next thing I know she's flying back across the room screaming and swearing. She stands over me and rains blows down on me with her fists, hitting me and hitting me and hitting me. Maybe the shock of her attack stuns me into silence. Maybe I just shut down as soon as the violence starts. Maybe not. Did I have the sense after that to stay quiet and keep how bad I felt to myself? If I didn't learn that lesson at that moment, I did learn very quickly that there was no kindness to be found in the Roche house – far from it. And perhaps I've wiped what happened next from my memory because what happened next was even worse.

There are a lot of gaps in my childhood memories of that kind, like a black curtain that's been drawn across parts of my mind to conceal pain that I don't want to remember. Or perhaps I only remember this one scene because it was the first time that the surprise of getting more pain when I needed comfort really struck home.

I do think this was the moment when I began to learn the one lesson any child in our family had to grasp to survive. If you needed anything – anything at all, like food and warmth and clothes and a bed to sleep in, never mind affection or understanding – you kept your mouth shut. Even when I was older and Mum took us to jumble sales to get clothes, I knew better than to depend on her to look out for anything for me. I had to get in there between the sharp elbows of all the other women raking through the cast-offs piled high on the trestle tables in the church hall and grab anything I thought looked a good bet, a shirt or a pair of trousers, and find Mum and shove them into her bag so that she would pay the few pennies the church ladies wanted for them. Then I had to make sure I stuck to her like glue so that I could stake my claim to them before anyone else in the house got their hands on them. Throughout my childhood I would beg, steal, search through bins and make my bed in a rubbish dump sooner than ask my parents for anything. To ask for help, to be needy, was to ask for a beating that would leave you bleeding and battered and numb from the terror of not knowing when it might stop. These attacks were systematic, automatic, and they were relentless. The trouble was that there was never any logic to these punishments – I was told I asked for it, and yet most of the time I didn't know what I had done wrong. In the end I knew that everything I did, even breathing, was bad and that not a day of my life would go by without punishment and pain.

As I have said, my parents were not normal. All through my childhood I was surrounded by families who didn't have much more than we had, but I never saw a child being beaten the way I was. There was nothing nice about being with Dad and Mum. Apart from that one day when the police forced her to bring me home, I don't remember any other occasion when my mother came looking for me because she was worried about where I was. Because she was in a temper with me, yes, because she wanted to beat me up, yes, but never because she cared.

It couldn't even be said that she was simply a harassed woman with too many children, pushing her toddler out of the door for a bit of peace. She would frequently send me down the road on errands, to get bits and pieces from a shop down there. The roads were busy with double-decker buses and lorries, but off I would go, pleased to have a job to do and relieved to be escaping her temper. I was dimly aware of the odd looks I got from the grown-ups I passed, but I had the confidence of a boy who had been sent to the shops by his mum, so I avoided their eyes and got on with my mission. A lady called

Molly ran this shop, and I was usually sent there to get sugar and boxes of tea. Sweet tea was what kept us going, kids as well as adults. When we could, when there were no grown-ups around to belt us for doing it, us kids would eat the sugar straight out of the packet. I would come across my older brothers doing it and join in, and there was a desperate feeling about it because what we really wanted to do was eat the lot, but if too much disappeared we'd all be in big trouble. It was hard to watch a bigger brother putting the packet away, out of my reach, saying: 'That's enough, no more.'

Sometimes I would protest that I'd had hardly any, being the smallest and not able to push my way in through the arms and sharp elbows of the others. 'Fuck off, Dwarf,' was the usual reply from one of them. 'You'd better grow up fast, then' was another jeer I heard often. There was no sense of anyone looking out for the little ones.

It was outside the house, from the very start, that I found all my consolations. Molly's shop, for instance, sold fruit and vegetables too, and sometimes she would give me an orange or an apple, and that was an event. I would find somewhere quiet on the way home, a back alley or a factory yard, where I could carefully put it into the one safe place I owned, my stomach. If I'd taken it home it would have been taken away from me, either by Mum or by one of my brothers.

We must have been fed, but meals on plates almost never happened. To be fair, I don't know how it would have been possible to make a meal every day and serve it on plates to everyone who was living in that flat. It had only four rooms, apart from the bathroom and kitchen, and there were twelve people living in it, three adults and nine children. The third adult, if you can believe it, was our lodger, a drinking pal of my father's called Harry, who was there to help pay the rent. He may have been more than a lodger or a friend, perhaps a distant cousin of Dad's – it was never very clear what his connection to us was, but he always called Dad by his childhood nickname, Jacksaw, and he had known him when they were both boys back in Ireland. Harry worked as a gardener somewhere in south London. No matter how short of money he was he always wore a shirt, tie and jacket, even if they had seen better days, just as Dad did. The only time I saw Dad out of the house without a tie was on the day he died.

Harry was a gentler character than either of my parents, and sometimes when I was little he would take me with him into the centre of London to visit Westminster Cathedral, the centre of the Catholic faith in Britain, and we would light candles. I never recall Dad going to church, but Mum and Harry tried to keep up in their own way with the religion they'd been brought up in. What was best about these trips, though, is that Harry would take me to a café afterwards and we'd have sausage and chips. He was, as my parents called him, a simpleton. He wasn't very bright and he often looked confused, lost, when Dad or Mum waded into one of us, beating us like no normal person would have even beaten an animal. So I never saw him try to shield us from our parents' violence or stepping in to stop it. He didn't have the kind of understanding that might have made him attempt to calm either of them down. I bet Dad would have physically thrown him out onto the street if he'd tried it.

Certainly, when I was a little older and the hunger was really beginning to bite, I realized that he saw nothing odd in him and my Dad sitting down to a meal every day after work – a meal on a plate was something that happened only on a Sunday for us if we were lucky – while all the kids in the house, whatever their age, were scrabbling in the kitchen cupboards as the grown-ups ate with knives and forks. We were left to feed ourselves as best we could.

There were a lot of us to feed, of course. Our oldest sister, Kathleen, had been born in 1941, shortly after our parents first met. She must have been about twenty-one when I was born and wasn't living with us. While I was still little she went to Australia with her husband and children on one of those £10 tickets they were giving out to anyone who wanted to emigrate during the 1960s.

For some reason there were no more babies until my sister Christine was born in 1955, but after she appeared a new Roche child arrived pretty much every year for the next nine years. After Christine came Raymond, then a third sister, Alison. After her came five boys in a row: Paul, Terry, Francis, Laurence and then me. The final girl, Rosemary, was born eighteen months later. Up until the year I arrived my parents moved around a lot, but by the early 1960s it seems that they had finally given up any hope of finding a better life or better fortune somewhere else.

Being the last of the boys was, of course, very bad

news for me. Ours wasn't a family where children were taught to treat each other with respect. We were terrorized every hour of the day by our parents for causing them inconvenience or irritation, or maybe just because they felt like hitting something, but what we boys did to each other was regarded as our business as long as it didn't affect them.

I eventually realized that I was the only person in the house who didn't have someone smaller than them to pass the violence on to. I had a little sister, but the only rule you might call a moral that I can recall being handed down from my parents was that you didn't hit girls. For all the brutality they handed out to us boys, I never saw them doing anything like that to Christine, Alison or Rosemary. They weren't exactly nice to the girls, but none of them could ever have gone wandering off as I did and not been missed. They were looked after and watched over in a way that their brothers weren't. The girls still had to grab what food they could when it was there but if there were two of us going for the last slice of bread and one of them was a girl, the boy would get a beating if he didn't let her have it. It seemed that a boy, whether he was a teenager or barely walking, needed to be beaten into submission every moment of his existence.

While we weren't to touch a hair of the girls' heads, my brothers nevertheless put into practice what they had learned from our parents about how to deal with problems. They turned on each other, and beating the living daylights out of someone smaller than you was an acceptable outlet for any frustrations. I was too young to know what frustrations my older brothers were going through, but they had plenty to be angry about. We all did. They were going to school, and I don't suppose they were any cleaner, better dressed or better fed than I was to be when my turn came. I imagine that like me they were obvious targets for the bullies that liked to pick on neglected children who came to school dirty, unwashed, often smelly and scratching heads that were alive with nits. Nits were another everyday part of life for me. Mum's solution was a trip to the barber's for the lot of us every now and again, so that our heads could be shorn to the skin as if we were sheep. With skinhead haircuts and Charlie Chaplin clothes, we might as well have had the word 'victim' painted on our backs. So my brothers came home from school and took it out on each other, and as I got older all of them took it out on me.

Dad had nicknames for us but they weren't affectionate, just another form of bullying. I can't recall our oldest brother, Raymond, having one, but after him came Paul, who was Dunce, and then Terry, who was Deafty. There was something particularly cruel about his nickname because, as we agreed years later, the chances were that his deafness in one ear had been caused by a hammering that Dad or Mum had given him when he was little. After Deafty came Francis – Spindle-legs – and Laurence, known as Cabbage. I was Dwarf. In my early childhood I was very small for my age, probably because I wasn't being fed properly, and, being the weakest, I always lost out in the scrum for any food that appeared in the house. For a long time I believed Dwarf was my name.

I answered to it without really understanding what it meant. Forever afterwards I thought of myself as short, a pushover, a target, a born victim.

I never looked forward to seeing my brothers coming home from school. I knew I was only going to get pain from my parents, and I learned that pain was all I was going to get from my brothers too. At best I was pushed aside and at worst, if I'd done something they didn't like, they would punch and kick me and yank my hair until I backed off. They knew no better, but that didn't make it any less painful for me – emotionally, as well as physically.

I had no idea what my parents were doing for money. There was presumably some cash coming in from Harry, but I had no sense of Dad going out to work. I was usually pushed out of the flat in the morning before he got up, and sometimes I saw him much later coming back into the flat drunk, although more often, thankfully, we'd be in bed by then. If he came back before that I learned to watch the way he walked through the door. He was always ready to give us a hiding, but if he was pissed it was certain that he wouldn't need to find an excuse. He had a heavy, flat-footed way of walking that made him move around quite slowly, but if he stepped up the pace and started walking fast, I knew he was looking for a victim. He could march at the double even with a night's beer inside him, and the sound of those thumping footsteps coming swiftly, one after the other, was the sound of hate and cruelty on legs. It was the most terrifying noise I knew. If we were awake and heard him come home, we knew better than to make any noise.

He had a bike, and when he came in at night he would put it in the boys' bedroom. One night, after he'd brought the bike in after a night's drinking, he came back in again on fire with rage. One of us had been out of bed, switching the bicycle lights on and off in the dark. I'm fairly sure this would have been Paul, the second of the boys, because he was never able to stop himself doing what he shouldn't have been doing. Someone had been opening and shutting a drawer too, although heaven only knows how there was room in there for a bike, a chest of drawers and five boys aged between three and ten. He was furious and drunk, but this time he held off beating any of us. It turned out that he was also frightened, the only time when we saw fear get the better of his viciousness.

The older boys swore blind that the lights had switched themselves off and on, and that the drawers had opened and closed on their own. As it happened, my parents were convinced that there was a poltergeist in the flat making banging noises at night in the living room where they slept, and Dad was sure he'd seen a man standing in the kitchen one evening when he'd come through the front door. Dad had turned swiftly to ask who the fuck he was, and he had disappeared. The bike lights and the drawer noise in our room suggested to him that the ghost was taking over the whole place. In the end my mother called in the local Catholic priest and asked him to bless the flat to get rid of whatever it was that was supposedly haunting us. It was a strange episode, one that showed me how even a bully as relentless as he was could be overtaken by superstition.

It wasn't, however, as if there was ever a moment when the family I had been born into was sane or rational. Whenever anyone spoke in that flat, it was to have a row. No-one sat quietly and had a normal conversation. No-one talked to us, told us anything interesting or asked us what we liked or how we felt. Even when Dad was in the house and we younger ones knew that we had to be as quiet as mice, Mum and Dad would be yelling at each other or at one of us.

It was endless chaos and pandemonium, and I had to watch my back day and night. I was never asked to do anything, only ever told to get it done, with a curse and the threat of what would happen if I didn't do it quickly. There was always someone shouting and someone else shouting back, and always beatings and screaming. I never could stand commotion, and that was my bad luck given the family I'd been born into. All I ever wanted to do was get out of there, away from them all. I seemed to have been born knowing that there was no friendship to be found in this family. No-one was ever kind to anyone else. There were simply too many of us for us to forge the kind of bond of trust and mutual support that I've heard some abused and neglected children take refuge in.

One day, when I was on one of my outings with John-John, the two of us were walking down the road, minding our own business. It must have been a Saturday or a Sunday because my brothers weren't at school. About twenty minutes from John-John's house, there was a wooden hut, a newspaper stand, and the man who ran it also sold sweets. John-John and I were on the other side of the road when I looked across and saw one of my older brothers climbing out of it. Predictably it was Paul. He had a load of stuff in his hand, which I assumed were stolen sweets. He looked straight back across the road at me and, putting his finger to his lips, signalled that I was to keep quiet. I stood there looking at him going up the road for quite a while and then walked on. I'd had half a hope that he might turn back and give me some of what he'd stolen but he kept going. I kept quiet anyway, but not out of any sense of loyalty. Self-preservation kept my mouth shut as nothing else could have done. Paul was five years older than me and capable of giving me a hiding as bad as the one Dad would have given him if I'd told tales about what he'd done.

The turning at the end of the service road was my escape route out of the estate to freedom. A row of iron railings came to represent a small haven of peace for me. They separated the estate from the playground of the Victorian infants' school where Laurence, a year older than me, was in the baby class during the year before we moved.

I used to sit looking through the bars for hours and hours on end, waiting for the children to come out to play. It wasn't that I missed Laurence. But I did envy this new, friendly life he had been allowed to join. When all the children came out to play I watched them intently, feeling terribly sad. I wanted to be part of what seemed to be one big happy gang, but even then I felt as if I was a long way off from them, separated from those other children by more than my age and a line of railings. I had already half realized that for reasons I couldn't yet understand I would never be able to join in. It felt bad. I was the ninth of ten children and I already knew exactly what loneliness was.

3. The Photographers

We were a strange lot and I must have been a strange little boy. Despite the cruelty of home, I was still young enough to crave company and kindness and to be really happy if I found it. I'd talk to any stranger I met just to see if I could get them to talk to me. I have a vivid memory of chatting away to one of the dustmen on the estate as he collected the rubbish round the back of the flats, and he gave me a little blue plastic toy train. He must have found it in one of the bins on his round and perhaps he'd kept it to give to his own boy or some other child he knew, but he took pity on me. Toys were never a part of my childhood and we never saw a Christmas or a birthday present, so it was amazing to be given a toy that I could call my own. It had a piece of string already tied to it and I spent hours pulling it around the play area in the dingy concrete courtyard below our balcony. At the end of the day, when Mum leaned over the balcony with her usual bark of 'Peter? In here, now!', I picked it up and toddled up the stairs with it. I got as far as the living room door just inside the flat.

'What the fuck's that?' roared my father. He didn't wait for an answer. 'You fucking little bandit,' he snarled, pulling it out of my hand and giving me a hard slap on the side of the head, assuming that I'd taken it from some other kid. He hurled it out of the still-open front door, over the balcony, and I just about heard it land four floors down before the door was slammed shut. It seemed to me that I lay awake almost all night thinking about it, wondering whether it was broken, and it was the first thing I thought of when I woke next morning. I couldn't wait to get out there and see it again. I didn't have to be pushed outside that morning. I couldn't quite see over the balcony, so I ran down the four flights of concrete stairs as fast as I could. It was gone. I never saw it again, but I often thought about the day it was mine.

Then, out of nowhere, Batman arrived in my life. Batman was in fact a woman who wore a long cape, and what else would the local kids call her in an outfit like that? She had a funny accent and she would appear on the estate from time to time, visiting the families that lived there, chatting to the mothers and giving them bags of second-hand clothes for their children.

Eventually she became a regular visitor to our flat and seemed to take a particular interest in me. I liked her too. She was, after all, the only grown-up I had ever met who paid attention to me in a way that felt nice and friendly. She would often take me down to the play area and put me on one of the swings and ask me to smile while she took pictures. My mum didn't seem to mind about all this picture-taking and, although it made no sense to me, these were moments when I thought to myself: 'I'm having a good time here, this is okay.'

As a child all I knew about this woman was that she had a strange name – Miss Zils – to go with her strange accent. She was what the National Society for the Prevention of Cruelty to Children called a visitor, not one of their regular uniformed officers but someone who went round the roughest estates of south London befriending families living in poor circumstances.

A year or so before Miss Zils began to bring her camera with her when she visited us, there was one very special day when other pictures were taken. I knew it was special, because although she was there, there were a lot of other people around too and a lot of fuss going on. My home was never empty or peaceful, but it was usually full of children, not grown-ups. I was very confused.

Small as I was, I realized I was being followed around the flat by a man who kept hiding his face behind a strange black box. There seemed to be an enormous crowd of people behind him. Then several of them were standing around me, telling me to put my hands down from my face.

I'm trying to cover my eyes because of the great bangs of bright light that keep exploding from the man's black box, and I don't like them. Eventually someone – Miss Zils, I realize – takes hold of my arms and pushes them down by my side. My right hand goes straight back up again, but, presumably in the few seconds before my left hand gets to my left eye, this man has taken a picture of me rubbing one eye with one hand, looking desperately unhappy.

A few minutes later I was put on our sofa on a blanket and the man with the box knelt in front of me. I wasn't enjoying this. I looked at my mother, who was sitting on a kitchen chair behind him, writing on a piece of paper while a strange woman looked over her shoulder.

When these visitors first arrived I had been shoved into one of my brothers' shirts, to cover the vest that was all I was wearing. The shirt was so big on me that my mother's rough hands pinched my arms painfully, as she had to turn the sleeves up again and again. She had wrapped the front of the shirt over itself on my chest and pinned it together with a huge safety pin. My feet had been put into a pair of wellingtons.

But by the time I'm on the sofa the wellingtons are off and the shirt has fallen open. My bare legs are now in full view, as is the vicious bruising that marks them from just below my knees to the top of my thighs. This is what my mother has been trying to hide, and this is what the man with the box has seen. Mum doesn't seem to have realized.

'Come on then, smile – we're going to make you a star,' Miss Zils said to me a year or so later during one of our photographic sessions on the swings. 'Why won't you smile today, don't you know what we're doing?'

I was unhappy. She had brought a man with her, a man in a uniform, and I didn't like men. My mother was hardly gentle with me but a lot of the time she ignored me. Whenever my father or brothers were around I was constantly being punched and whipped and slapped and tripped up and banged over the head. It never stopped. Men and boys were trouble. I was stubborn and wouldn't play Miss Zils' smile-for-the-camera game that day. When she visited again and asked if I would like to come on a bus with her, she promised there would be no men at the place she was taking me to. I really played up on the top deck of the bus that day, cheekily calling her Batman every moment I could. She made the mistake of giving me a harmonica and I blew it hard all the way into central London, with her sitting beside me, saying quietly now and again: 'Keep the noise down, Peter. Softly, softly.' I might have been cute to look at, but my behaviour was wild. She took me into a building that seemed enormous and very posh. It had an old-fashioned lift with metal criss-cross gates that had to be opened and closed to make it work. I was fascinated by it, watching people going up and down in it while Miss Zils chatted to some women in one of the offices. She came out to check what I was up to.

'Can we go in that?' I asked.

'Would you like to go in the lift or would you rather have a hat?' she replied.

I thought hard about this. 'A hat,' I said in the end, deciding that having a hat of my own was a thrill that would last longer. Clothes were hard to come by, especially warm ones. I was often cold during my long solitary days outside and a hat would be a fantastic thing to have.

She took me downstairs to another office, where loads of women stopped working to gather round and make a fuss of me. A hat appeared and I put it on. Miss Zils took me to another part of the office and yet another woman appeared, and in her hand she held a small grey plastic box with buttons and a lens that by now I knew well.

'That hat is lovely, isn't it?' said this woman. I was a seasoned model now and I went straight into my cute pose while she took yet more pictures. They were all at it.

What I couldn't know then, what I wouldn't find out until many, many years later, was that Batman had changed my life, although not in the way that she and the NSPCC could and should have changed it. Her visits were bright moments in my existence, but apart from the brief ownership of a few new bits of clothing – they were always taken away from me and given to someone else the moment she was gone – the violence inside our flat and the long, neglected hours I spent outside it went on without interruption. When we moved just after my fourth birthday, she vanished from my life. It would be many, many years before I discovered that she hadn't been taking pictures of me just because she liked me.

'You were a lovely boy, but you were allowed to run wild. I would have liked to do more for you but my boss wouldn't let me,' Miss Zils was to tell me when I was a father myself, and had tracked her down in the hope of getting some answers to the many questions I had about my own childhood by then. 'There were homes, Barnardo's homes, where you might have gone, but there you would only have had the material things of life, none of the emotional input.'

She meant it kindly but I didn't know whether to laugh or cry. Emotional input. That was a good one.

4. The Mad House

At the north end of our old road in Lambeth, the row of maybe thirty quite grand-looking houses, each with three floors and a basement, are all that remains of an up-market housing estate built about two hundred years ago by an aristocrat. By the time my family moved there to our new house in 1967, there was nothing up-market about the area. All the houses in the triangle, which included our crumbling terrace and several streets of little terraced houses behind it, were owned by the council, and the whole area had been earmarked for demolition and redevelopment.

I was taken to see the house with my parents just before we moved in. My youngest sister and I were the only two children not at school by then, so they had to take us with them. It certainly wasn't because they wanted to, as if we were going on an outing. We didn't have outings, ever.

The houses were set a long way back from the pavement and there was a ten-foot-wide strip of what you might call front garden running the whole length of the terrace. In front of the house we were looking at the grass was strewn with rubbish and broken glass. What I spotted, though, that made the visit so memorable was an old toddler's tricycle that someone had dumped there. I wanted it.

'That's mine,' I thought, and suddenly I was really excited about moving into this house. My parents must have been pleased too, to be moving to a house that had six or seven rooms and a basement kitchen at the back, even though the whole place was falling apart. There was a basement room on the front that wasn't much more than a cellar, really, which we would quickly begin to use as a dump for old stinking mattresses and clothes that had become rags too torn even for us to wear. This was a part of the house we would get to know too well over the next six years. Beyond it there were two old coal cellars that stretched under the pavement outside. When we could afford a delivery, the coalman used to pour the coal through a manhole cover above them and we would have to go in there to fill the scuttle.

The floor of the basement room was screeded with filthy concrete and there must have been half a dozen old wooden rat traps scattered here and there, their spring catches rusted solid. The walls were plastered and painted, although it was impossible to tell what colour it was under the grime. An ancient net curtain, torn and almost black with soot and pollution from the main road outside, hung at the window, which was missing two of its panes. Near the ground the plaster all round the room was blistered with damp. Some of it had broken away, revealing the brick core of the walls. By the time we'd been there a few months the whole room smelt evil, stale and decaying, with an underlying stench that made me think of the alley behind one of the local pubs where men too drunk to get to the toilet relieved themselves. A cord hung from the ceiling, but I never saw a light bulb in it. The crucial thing about this room was that to get to it, you had to go down a short flight of steps that led in a straight line from the kitchen door. The stairs up to the ground floor and the back door that led out into the yard at the rear of the house were off to the side, round the bend of the banister, and when you were in the kitchen it was hard to get out and upwards to safety. The basement room was a dead end, and once you were in there, there was no escape. The only way of getting out was when whoever had cornered you had finished with you.

The whole house was in a terrible state even then and it had no bathroom, just a toilet that had been built onto the back at some point in its history. To us, at least in the early days after the move, it seemed luxurious. We needed space more than we needed a bathroom.

For my parents, though, there was a problem about the move. They didn't tell me what it was. I was just told that I must not say anything to our neighbours about us leaving, even though we weren't going out that far. It was a hard secret to keep. I was four. I was sure I was going to have a tricycle when we moved. I had to tell John-John.

He told his parents. They spoke to my father.

'We hear you're moving, Davie?'

'No, I'm not.'

'Your kid says you are. He's going to get a tricycle, he reckons. You come in to some money then?'

'None of your fucking business.'

I heard the heavy footsteps coming, and they were coming fast.

'Where is he, the little bastard?' he roared. 'Where the fuck is he? He'll wish he'd never been born, the little fucker. Telling the fucking neighbours my business.'

I wasn't sure he meant me because I didn't really know what he was talking about, but I tried to get behind something or someone and look as small as possible. His eyes met mine and I knew I was what he was looking for. I tried to make a dash for it, past him, out of the flat, but he put out a hand and grabbed a handful of hair. He hoisted me off my feet until my eyes were level with his, hard little slits of fury and hatred. His face was a dull, dark red, a sure sign that he was about to go right over the edge, and as he spoke, his face inches from mine, the suffocating beer fumes made me feel sick.

'You will learn to keep your mouth shut,' he said, very slowly, very deliberately, shaking me hard as he said the last word, making my legs flail about wildly. His grip on my hair tightened and I could almost feel the anger building in him, ready to explode. I had my hands in their usual protective position, holding tight to the top of my head, but nothing I could do was going to make much difference. He carried me over to the fireplace, still holding me by the hair, and got the belt down.

'You never tell anyone my business again,' he said. A lash for every word as he said it. Whack, whack, whack, whack . . .

'Don't, Dad, please don't. Please stop –'

The whipping went on for what seemed like hours until I was thrown, bloody and numb, into the bedroom, where I was locked in for the rest of the day. I learned my lesson well. I didn't even dare look for the tricycle as we moved in. It had already brought me too much grief, and even a tricycle wasn't worth the risk of more.

Things should have been better in the new house, because we all had a lot more room and I was aware that Dad now had a job. It's possible that this was something that the NSPCC and Miss Zils had done for us, and perhaps they had even helped find this house. He would put his suit and tie on and go off in the morning early. Before I had any chance to imagine that he was going to an office, I was hearing my older brothers talking about being chased down the street by boys who ran after them shouting 'Bogbrush!', and I discovered that he was working for the council, cleaning the public toilets in the area.

It wasn't all bad, I thought to myself. Raymond, being the eldest boy and almost twelve years old, had been given a room to himself, and although the other five of us were still in one room together, it was a big room, the one on the front above the living room that ran the width of the house. Even though several of the floorboards were missing it felt like a palace for a short while.

The two oldest girls had a room together, but I'm not sure where Rosemary, the baby of the family, was sleeping. She was still only two or three years old and the stairs in the house were steep, so perhaps for a while she was in with my parents. They had the ground floor room at the back of the house, which was separated from the front room only by folding doors, but it wasn't as if anyone would want to sit in the front room after our parents had gone to bed. We didn't sit around together as a family after tea watching telly. We didn't have a telly for a long time. By the time of the first moon landing, two years after we moved in, we had a rented black-and-white set by the fireplace and I did watch some of the landing, one of the few times when there was something going on in the world which was bigger than the fights that always broke out whenever a few of us were in the same room together.

We didn't have tea either, at least not in any way other people might recognize it. We lived there almost seven years, and I witnessed only one teatime, when one of my older brothers had the crazy idea of inviting the school bully round. He thought it might get this thug off his back, make a friend of him. The strangest thing was that Dad did the honours. We all hung around the kitchen table because there weren't enough chairs for us all. This was a very special occasion. Dad did the tea military-style, which meant that he put a load of cups – well, most of them were old jam jars – in a group on the table and then swung the milk bottle round them. Then he got the teapot and did the same. There was probably as much tea and milk on the table as there was in the cups. Then he buttered the bread and chucked it at us like he was dealing a pack of cards – 'Here, get on with that' – and the look on this kid's face was something else.

I died inside knowing that the school bully was seeing all this.

'What have you done?' I thought to myself, looking at

Francis and thinking that even though he was two and a half years older than me, I had more sense than he did. 'We're never going to live this down. How are we going to walk down the street after this?'

'You lot live like pigs, and you eat my shit' was one of the many insults I heard him shout at Francis and the rest of us in the street in the months afterwards. 'I shit in your dad's bog and he brings it home on his hands. That's what you get for tea. Bread and shit.'

Our house, as the kid saw with his own eyes, was a dump. There was no wallpaper on the walls, the floorboards were thick with dirt and the kitchen – well, you could see the grime on the floor, the surfaces, the doors. The place was unbelievably filthy.

I was keen to get what I could of this unexpected meal but at the same time I knew we were all in for grief once he got back to his mates and told them about our house and the way we lived. It was humiliating. We had all developed our own ways of surviving in this family, and mine was to be as invisible as I possibly could. To have boys shouting at us in the playground and the street about our kitchen, our dad and our house was terrible, worse than the kickings and punches they gave us.

Mum sometimes cooked meals, but this didn't seem to happen very often. It was hard for me to be sure when it might, because there was no pattern to our lives, apart from the routine of going to school. I started school very soon after we moved, and from then until we left the house, when I was almost eleven years old, daily life was a mess of chaos, fighting, violence and hunger, in no particular order. She probably cooked a meal on a Sunday. It would be something in one big pot, like stew, or mash and peas, or sausages and soup, something like that. But it was never very certain that she would, and more than likely I wouldn't get any of it anyway.

I still asked sometimes, when I felt brave. 'What is there to eat, Mum?' I'd say as cheery as I could, but making sure I was on the right side of the bend in the stairs outside the kitchen so that I could get to the back door first if she turned nasty. Generally I'd just get one of her nasty, foul-mouthed put-downs.

'Shit on a stick,' she'd snarl back, her eternal mug of tea in one hand and a fag in the other. It was if I'd asked her to walk to the other side of the world to get me something to eat.

We had to wait for the grown-ups to eat first, which meant Dad and Harry, who had moved with us from the old place, sitting down at the table for theirs as they had done in the flat, and then every child for itself. It was a chancy business, because if you wandered into the kitchen too early, you'd get a whack, and if you were too late it would all have gone and you'd get nothing. Sometimes Mum would dish it up for us and hand out bowls, and I took what I got. Protesting that someone else had got more was asking for trouble, even though it always seemed to me that I got less than anyone else. The older you were, as far as I could tell, the more food you got. This didn't make any sense to me, because us younger ones had no way of getting extra food. The older ones seemed to be able to get food of their own, because

I sometimes saw them eating it in the street, but I had no idea yet how they did that.

There were times when Mum would come in with shopping, usually from the local Co-op. There'd always be Co-op 99 tea in the house. Sometimes there'd be milk and cereal, bread and margarine. As I got older I could sense a kind of desperation that spread through the house whenever we knew there was any food in the cupboards. It was about not knowing whether there'd be any left when we were hungry, and frantically working out how we could get some extra and hide it away for later. Being at the bottom of the pile, not clever or strong or fast enough to play this game and win, was a real problem for me. I once had the nerve, or the stupidity, to say to Raymond, as some food was being divided up between the older ones, that I had a right to eat too.

'You've got no rights,' he snarled at me. Raymond was top dog in the house after our mother and father, the only one of the boys I never saw being beaten by Dad, although he must have had his share of that leather belt before I was born. He had left school and had a job, and was bringing money in, so he got a certain amount of respect from our parents, although this only meant that most of the time they left him alone.

'You have though, you've got just one right,' Raymond added, his face about an inch from mine. 'Air.'

He stood up, and as he walked away, his parting shot came over his shoulder at me. 'And even that's only temporary.'

When I began to realize that the older boys hid food

in all sorts of strange places, so that they could be sure of something to eat later, I learned to look a lot further afield than the kitchen cupboards. If I was lucky I found a curling piece of bread and marg here, a bowl of cereal there. They were often hidden in places that would have made most people gag at the thought of eating them, but I was hungry. Under the floorboards, on top of the toilet cistern, under soggy mattresses or a bit of carpet swarming with silverfish. The basement, strewn with all the festering rubbish that was too dirty even for our family, was a prime place. There was always a chance of finding a slice of bread down there, hidden under some filthy, stinking rags. To be found eating, for me at least, was to get a hell of a hiding and have whatever the food was taken away. I don't know if Mum and Dad knew that we all regularly stole and hid food, but once, Dad caught me in the basement with some bread that I'd been storing. He picked up a metal bar that happened to be lying on the floor and smashed it over my head. I had to be taken to the local children's hospital and stitched up.

He didn't say very much as he moved towards me silently but with as much force as an express train. I froze. He hit me over the head with the bar without a word and then took what was left of the bread from my hand as I lay on the floor.

'You will never take food again, Dwarf,' he said, with his back to me as he walked away towards the door. I couldn't believe that was the extent of the punishment. Usually once he had started bashing me, he found it impossible to stop. It must have been my lucky day.

After that, I would try to go looking for food only if the house was empty. If I found something to eat and I wanted to get it down me without being surprised, I would take it to the front door so that I could be sure I would know if someone was on their way in. Then I would cram it into my mouth as fast as I could. To be quite honest, I ate like a savage and I knew it. There was never a time when I didn't hate eating in front of people, even people I knew well and liked, because most people couldn't help staring at the way I did it.

Even now I find it difficult to sit down to eat with my own wife and children. There's a fear always at the back of my mind that I'll forget myself and start shovelling food into my mouth as fast as I can. When I was a young man I went out for a meal with a girl and I have never forgotten the way she asked: 'How do you get that much food into your mouth all at once?' I've never eaten out since, not even in McDonald's.

5. Crime and Punishment

It wasn't only food we were short of. There were arguments just after we moved in between the older boys about who would have the blankets that had been left behind by the removal men who had shifted the bit of furniture we had from the old house. There was no other bedding, not then or later. We had bare mattresses on the floor, and there were a few old coats and bits of raggy clothing that we could sleep under if we could get our hands on them. I'd often wake up shivering because one of my brothers had taken whatever it was I was using as a cover while I was asleep.

There was no heating in the house and the bedrooms were like fridges in the winter. Quite a few of the window panes were broken and some had no glass in at all. They were the original nineteenth-century sash windows and the cords were broken, so when, in the summer, the room got hot and unbearably smelly, we'd have to prop them open with sticks. The truth was, though, that even in the coldest winter the bedroom stank to high heaven because it was filthy and so were we. The mattresses and the things we used as bedding were always infested with fleas and lice, and getting bitten at night was just a fact of life. It may have been the late 1960s, the second half of the twentieth century in Britain's capital city, but the place was crawling with insects, silverfish, earwigs, cockroaches and God knew what else, any creature that liked damp and dirt, and at night, when it was quiet, I could always hear mice scuttling about somewhere in the building. The spiders were like something out of a horror film, huge hairy things that lived for years, it seemed to me, undisturbed in the corners of every room. From time to time there were rats too. I swear that one night I woke and looked into the darkness and some beast winked at me. I shut my eyes tight and hoped it would go away. It wasn't as if I could put on the light to scare it away. It was a room no-one in their right mind would go into unless they were exhausted and wanted only to close their eyes, so what was the point of having a bulb in the light fitting? I was obsessed by the idea that while I was asleep some bug would crawl into my ear from the mattress or the floor and I would never be able to get it out again. Every morning I would wake up and bang each side of my head in turn, hoping to dislodge anything that was in my ear canal.

Dirt was ground so deeply into the floors all through the house that the paths worn by our feet were a shiny black. I got used to this and took it for granted, in the same way that I stopped noticing the smell if I'd been inside for a while. But if I'd been out at school the stench hit my nose the minute I walked through the door. It was a smell that had everything foul in it, not just the rotting, damp smell of the house but also unwashed bodies, stale cooking smells, beer, fags and old wee.

The disgusting sweet-sour smell of ancient urine in the

bedroom was always enough to knock you sideways, summer and winter. The idea of bed as a refuge was alien to me. If I was tired, that bedroom was where I had to go, but it was revolting. Bed-wetting by one or other of us turned the mattresses a patchy dark brown, marked from edge to edge with countless rings of urine stains. Something about the way urine seeped through the mattresses made them stick to the floors, and if you tried peeling one of them up, there'd be a mess of evil-smelling gluey stuff underneath them. As soon as warmer weather arrived masses of flies, big and small, feasted on this stuff, infesting every room in the house.

I was sharing a mattress with Laurence and Francis, the two brothers closest to me in age, but I seemed to have the worst bed-wetting problem of all of us. Eventually they got fed up with waking to find themselves lying in a wet bed. There were some nights when I would try to pretend it hadn't happened, curling round the wet patch, trying to sleep, hoping to God that my brothers wouldn't notice. But the mattresses were already so damp that any extra fluid spread through them like blotting paper.

'You filthy bastard,' one of them would yell, sitting up like a jack-in-the-box when he realized that he was lying in my wee, and thumping hard down on me with his fist where I lay next to him.

They thumped me a lot, but that didn't help stop me doing it. When we had a relatively new mattress – new to us, that is, but never a clean, new, unmarked mattress – we would try turning the mattress over each morning in the hope that it would dry out by the night. It never did. Often the underneath was more disgusting than the top. In the winter there was no hope. In the end Laurence and Francis flatly refused to let me in the bed with them, threatening me with serious violence if I tried it, and for a while I had to sleep on the bare floorboards next to the mattress.

It amazed me that I could sleep like this, even though there were nights when every part of my body was numb with cold. I did shiver for hours sometimes, awake and longing to sleep. Every cloud has a silver lining, and this did at least mean that my brothers would fall asleep before I did and I could sneak up to them and steal a coat one of them was using as a blanket. Once I'd got a coat, I could wrap myself tightly in it and mentally make the dirt, the cold, the bugs go away. I developed a very useful ability to wipe my mind clean and forget where I was, what I was lying on. Exhaustion and lack of food would do the rest, and I'd sleep until I'd wet myself and the cold had half frozen my clothes to my body. The struggle for sleep would start all over again. I would try to wrap the upper part of myself in the dry bit of the coat, waiting and longing for my body to warm the wet patch underneath me enough for me to forget about it. For years on end, it seemed, all my nights were spent wet and cold and exhausted, praying for sleep.

The only break I got from my brothers came when we realized that Paul was wetting the bed regularly too, even though he was five years older than me. Paul had a particularly hard time at my father's hands. He was the one Dad called Dunce and he didn't seem quite as nimble in his thinking as the rest of us. He wasn't exactly slow, but he was often excitable and likely to do stupid things on impulse. He was also desperate to be thought of as devious and clever. He was always tapping the side of his nose confidentially, while saying: 'Never let the right hand know what the left hand's doing.' It would have been comical if it hadn't been so dangerous. He was always getting found out by Dad and was always on the receiving end of terrible beatings. The rest of us were a bright bunch, really, and I have sometimes wondered whether Paul's mind was damaged by the violence that was regularly dished out to him. For most of his school life he went to special schools.

There was one attack on Paul I never forgot. I came into the house one afternoon after school and heard screaming, really awful screaming, a high-pitched animal sound, and I shot downstairs to the dreaded dead-end basement, where the sounds were coming from, to find Paul tied to a door handle by the hands, naked from the waist up. My father was standing over him with the leather belt.

By now we all knew that the basement room was bad news. If Dad or Mum went for us while we were in the kitchen, that was where we were going to end up. With Dad, we were grabbed by the arm or the hair and pushed out of the kitchen door, straight down the steps and into the dank, stinking room at the bottom of them, where he had all the room he needed to swing us around by any bit of the body he had gripped in his big fist, and to really swing his belt arm back so that he could make every lash count. Mum's tactics were different. She would come at us with a flurry of punches and kicks, maybe picking some weapon up as she passed a handy plate or a broom, or even waiting until she'd backed us into the basement and picking up an old tool from the floor. She didn't usually get hold of her victim. What she did, to stop us dodging round the corner and escaping up the stairs, was keep up the barrage of blows and then, once in the room, back us into a corner from which we couldn't escape.

We weren't always in the kitchen when either of them lost their temper, obviously. That was why there was a shouted sentence that never failed to make your blood run cold and make your mind race, wondering whether it was worth taking the risk of making a run for it out of the front door. They both used it. It would boom and echo through the carpetless, curtainless house. Just four words.

'Get down here, now.'

Even though it was a place to be very, very afraid of, I didn't hesitate when I heard that high, wailing screaming coming from down those steps.

'What's the time?' Dad was shouting at Paul over and over again, whacking him across his bare back with the buckle end of the belt each time he got it wrong or didn't answer.

Dad had taken the brass spider clock down from the living room wall and hung it above Paul's head. He was pissed out of his mind, I could see that, and every inch of his hands, his forearms, his face and neck were flushed dark red. A vein in his neck was throbbing. I never had any difficulty understanding what people meant when they said a man's blood was up.

Paul was supposed to be looking at the clock and working it out, but even if he had been able to tell the time, his mind seemed to have shut down completely with the fear and the pain of what was being done to him. The only sound he could make was that terrible animal noise. I felt desperate. Although my parents had been hurling every swear word in the dictionary at me since the day I was born, this was the first time I heard the word 'bastard' inside my head.

'You bastard!' I thought.

I don't why I thought I could help. I certainly wasn't able to tell the time myself, but I took a wild guess in the hope that it would make my father stop what he was doing.

'Quarter to four,' I shouted.

Dad whipped Paul again.

'Quarter to four, Dad, quarter to four. Please, please. Stop, Dad. Quarter to four, Dad.'

I was on the floor. He'd turned round and hit me so hard on the side of the head with his free hand that I just dropped full-length from the spot where a moment ago I'd been on my feet. He kicked me and whipped me with the belt, and by this time he was gasping with the effort he'd put into attacking Paul and me. When he paused, I heard movement upstairs. Brothers and sisters coming back into the house from school, a little later than Paul and I generally did. Paul got back at about three because the special school he was at finished earlier than mine did, and that was about the time Dad came back from work if he didn't go straight to the pub.

Dad heard the movements too. He grunted something I couldn't make out, and went over to Paul and undid his hands from the coal cellar door. The second his hands were free, Paul shot out of the room screeching like a wounded animal and was out of the back door and gone. Dad didn't try to stop him. He just picked up his belt and stepped over me, and I heard his heavy, slightly unsteady footsteps going back upstairs.

My nose was bleeding, and I sat up and looked around for a rag that wasn't too dirty to wipe the blood away with. That was it, then. Until the next time.

It wasn't something I could talk to Paul about, even when a few days had passed and he was a bit more like his old self again. For a couple of days he flitted through the house like a ghost, a figure I just caught sight of before he scuttled away into some dark corner. Much later I did ask him about it, how it had all started. He insisted his hands were tied behind his back, but I know I saw him tied up with his hands in front of him. I realized this was something that must have happened more than once, when he and Dad were alone in the house together. He wouldn't say any more about it, not then, not ever. None of us ever talked to the others about our beatings. We knew better. It was like asking for sympathy, and we all knew we would get none of that from each other.

So Paul started wetting the bed and the next brother down, Terry, who had been sharing with him, moved to the dry mattress with Laurence and Francis, or at least the mattress that wasn't as wet as his. This meant that I was able to sleep on a mattress again with a fellow bed-wetter.

At one time there was a metal tank standing in the middle of the room that had been put there to catch a leak that was coming through the roof. No workmen ever came to our house to fix anything. Paul would use the tank in the bedroom as a toilet rather than make the trip all the way downstairs, past Mum and Dad's bedroom, to the bottom of the house in the dark, to the lean-to where the only lavatory in the house was. He might have been afraid of waking them, but I think he also thought it was funny. I looked into the tank from time to time and saw live things swimming in there. God knows what they were.

Before I had fully learned the lesson that asking for help was a stupid thing to do, I would wake wet in the night and go downstairs crying to my parents' bedroom door. I would always end up curled as tight as I could manage into a little ball on the landing while my father beat me over and over again for having dared to wake him up.

'Stop, Dad. Stop. Please, Dad. I'm sorry. Stop, please.'

I would say it over and over again, not yet having worked out that to beg him to stop was somehow to put fresh energy into his arm. It went on and on. When your clothes are wet, a beating hurts a lot more. After a while, though, the numbness comes and the pain of each new blow seems to be no big deal any more. After beatings like these I would sometimes sit and look at my arms where I'd tried to protect myself, and watch the blood seeping up under the skin. Then I'd do my best to find something to wear to put over the sore bits to protect them, and to make sure that no-one outside the house would see the marks. They were evidence of the shame and punishment I'd brought on myself.

In the daytime, as he whipped us, he called us every name under the sun. Even when he was sober and calm, every second word he spoke was an obscenity. But in the small hours of the morning, beating me senseless in the dark, he never spoke, not even to curse. He just whipped and whipped silently until he had finished, and then kicked my body with his foot to get it out of the way of his bedroom door. He'd go back inside and close the door, leaving me there.

One night he did something different. I had come down once too often. He groped around in the dark when he'd finished beating me and dragged me down the stairs by the hair to the back door. It was raining outside.

'If you want to be fucking wet, fucking get out there,' he growled and he pushed me out, closed the door and locked it. It was like he'd put the cat out.

I sat on the stump of a dead tree in the garden in the rain, not daring to move. My parents' bedroom window looked out over the garden and I didn't want to make a sound in case my father heard me. I sat there for what seemed like hours, until the sky started to get light, before I decided I would try to creep back inside. I got in okay but there was nothing else in the house I could wear and

I had to go to school in clothes damp with urine and rain. Eventually I learned that I just had to live with my bed-wetting, be wet and stinking, and keep quiet.

Clothes were always a problem for all us boys, but because of the bed-wetting the problem for me was even worse. Every winter was an ordeal. On the one hand I wanted to go to bed in as many clothes as I could find because it was so cold in the bedroom at night. On the other, if I went to bed in the clothes I had on there was every chance that they'd be wet in the morning. It wasn't as if you could get up and put some dry clothes on. There weren't enough clothes to go round. I couldn't win. If I took my clothes off before I went to bed, one of my brothers would wake up before me and steal them. They would even steal my trousers, which, although they might be dry, were nearly always reeking of urine from many previous nights of bed-wetting. That was how desperate we all were.

There were many times when I had to go down to the basement wearing nothing but a grubby shirt and poke around in the stinking rags that had been dumped down there, looking for something, anything, to cover myself with. There was really no way out for me except to be almost always damp at the start of the day and to always be smelly.

There wasn't such a thing as washday. There was no immersion heater in the house and the electric geyser in the kitchen didn't work, so the only way to get hot water was to boil it in pans on the gas stove. Sometimes there'd be a trip to the launderette at the bottom of the road next to ours but that didn't happen very often, because Mum usually didn't have the money for it. If we did go there we certainly didn't put the washing in the dryer, because that would have cost too much. We'd have to bring it back wet and Mum would hang it out on the line in the bit of garden at the back. In the winter you could see the clothes going stiff as they froze. Being the one who took the washing to the launderette was embarrassing. A woman once looked in my machine and said: 'Blimey, your clothes are dirty, aren't they?'

I realized that the suds in my machine had turned black. In everyone else's machines they were white. So I stood in front of the machine until the wash had finished, trying to stop anyone else seeing.

I was always ashamed about never having any underwear, although it was hardly my fault. Jumble sales didn't often have underwear for sale except for big old men's pants. Even when there'd been a jumble sale and for a short while we had clothes that were reasonable, not too dirty or smelly, we never looked right. Everything was too big or too small. Often they weren't even children's clothes, but men's with the sleeves and legs cut off short to make them wearable. Shoes were worn out before we got them. It seemed normal to feel the pavement through the holes in a pair of shoes that had been falling apart when I first started wearing them, and to come home with my feet bleeding from where I'd stepped on something sharp. There were never enough clothes, certainly never enough coats.

I used to dread winter coming because I knew I would

be cold day after day, night after night, even in the house. There was only one room in the house where a fire was ever lit, and that was in the front room next to my parents' bedroom. It was a hard thing to have to decide whether you were really so cold that it was worth going in there. The first thing I looked at whenever I decided to go in was the fireguard. When the fire was lit, that was where Dad's belt always was, warming. He reckoned it worked a lot better when it was warm. He would sit in his chair and threaten us constantly. You had to sit absolutely still when you were in there.

'If you speak, boy, you won't sit down for a week.' He would get the belt, double it up and snap it together. 'You understand me, boy?'

You didn't know if you'd get a beating for not answering him, or for speaking if you did.

Sometimes he'd look at one of us and say: 'Don't look at me like that, boy.' If we avoided his eyes, he'd say: 'Fucking look at me when I'm speaking to you.'

It didn't much matter whether you answered him or not, whether you looked at him or not. Maybe whoever he'd picked on would try to defend himself, protesting that he hadn't done anything, or hadn't meant to. Sometimes, if I was near the door, it seemed worth trying to make a run for it. Sometimes I made it and sometimes I didn't.

'Don't give me that, boy,' Dad would yell, and he'd have you by the hair and be on you with the buckle end of the belt. He had simply been overtaken by the need to beat hell out of someone and we all knew he was a crazy,

crazy man. The only solution, we knew, was not to be around him, yet there were times when it was so cold everywhere else in the house that the chance to get a bit warm in front of the fire made it seem worth the risk. There were two ordinary chairs in there which were reserved for Mum and Dad, or for Raymond if either of them weren't in, and although they were stained and torn, they seemed to be the height of luxury. If the rest of us wanted something to sit on we had to bring orange boxes back from the shops. When there wasn't much coal those would get burned too. There had been holes in our bedroom floor upstairs where floorboards were missing and from time to time another one would disappear, used for fuel. One night we were sitting in the front room when a leg came through the plaster above our heads from the room above. My mother leapt up, screaming: 'Look what that bastard's done to the ceiling!' and she ran upstairs with her Sally, as she called the three-foot-long switch she used on us. Francis, who had stepped in the wrong place and put his foot through a gap in the floorboards, got a stinging whipping to go with his bruised leg and groin.

Mum was almost as violent with us as Dad, but a little more predictable. She would use one of those heavy old-fashioned wooden brooms on us like a hammer if she lost her temper, hitting us on the head with the brush end. If you were in the kitchen when you said something she didn't like, she'd pick up a plate and smash it over your head. Then she'd pick up a rag and shove it at you to put on the bit that was bleeding and say: 'Here's a cloth, you fucking whiner, there's nothing wrong with you. Shut your racket, you little bastard.'

Brutal beatings were so much a part of our lives that we knew there were only two things we could be certain of. One was that every day we would be beaten. The other was that we would go to school come hell or high water. Although nine times out of ten we couldn't predict what we would be beaten for, there was one crime we knew would always bring down the full fury of Mum and Dad on our heads. That crime still was and always would be bringing authority to the door. They did not want officials, and that included truancy officers, asking them questions. In Dad's eyes officials were never there to help, only to cause trouble. This was why, although we must have seemed a wild and strange bunch to an outsider's eye, the Roche children very rarely stayed away from school.

All through those early years of my childhood it seemed to me that I was constantly being forced to choose between one horrible thing and another that was just as horrible. Like the business of whether to take off my trousers at night or not, whether to face the next day with peed trousers or no trousers at all. This problem of whether or not to go to school tormented me every day for years. If I didn't and I was found out, my parents would torture me. If I did, I would spend six hours of the day, every day, being taunted by the other children and often mocked and humiliated by teachers.

Still, even though I knew that not going to school might be as deadly as lying down in the middle of the road at rush hour, there were still times when I just couldn't face any more bullying. On one of these days I was seen walking about the streets quite a long way from home – I had at least had the sense to get out of the area. I didn't know I'd been seen, or that this busybody had knocked on our door on the way home to tell my mother that I hadn't been anywhere near a classroom that day. I wasn't old enough to tell the time and I set off home once I'd started to see other children who had obviously just come out of school about the streets.

'Where have you been?' she demanded to know when I walked through the door.

'At school.'

'Walking around the streets all day? On your fucking way to school all bloody day, you lying little bastard?'

She got down the big metal bowl that Dad and the lodger used for their shaving water and ordered me to stand in it.

'Look at the state of you,' she said grimly. 'You'll get yourself cleaned up.'

She put a big pan of water on the gas stove, talking on and on while it heated up about how she'd give me walking the streets when I should have been at school and how I'd find it hard enough just walking to school by the time she'd finished with me.

The kitchen walls were painted with shiny blue gloss paint and I stood with my feet in the bowl watching the pan on the gas, and watching the condensation from the slowly heating water running down the walls. This was something that had never been done to me before, but I had already worked out what was coming. I was terrified, so terrified that I even dared say to her a couple of times that I thought the water must be hot enough now. All the time I was thinking: 'How can I get away from here?'

'It isn't hot enough yet,' she said, quite calmly, and that was more terrifying than any of her rages.

When it *was* hot enough for her, she poured it into the bowl. She tried to hold me there, clamping her hand on my shoulder while I screamed and hopped about trying to get out of the water. The metal of the bowl took the heat of the water away from the soles of my feet, but the skin on top of them was red-raw in seconds and already blistering. The pain was so terrible that even she couldn't hold me down, and I screamed and kicked so hard that I managed to overbalance the chair, the bowl slid off and I slid out from under my mother. Never mind my scalded feet, I was up like a flash and out of the room, swerving round the bend to get on the upwards flight of stairs before she could corner me and back me into the basement, and away as fast as I could towards the back door, out into the safety of the garden and the derelict wasteland of condemned houses behind it. If nothing else, the ground out there was cool and gave me some relief.

I didn't go to hospital with my burned feet. We went to hospital only for blood and even then there had to be lots of it. There was no question of being off school ill, and I did the best I could to ignore the pain and get there. The shoes I had at the time were too big for me, and that was a blessing for once, but even so the tops of my feet were sore for weeks. I tried everything to lessen the pain of the shoes rubbing on the burns, short of going to school barefoot, including sitting with a needle the night after the scalding, piercing and draining each huge blister. Beyond that, there wasn't much I could do except walk very slowly and make sure that I didn't miss school. I didn't miss it for a good while after that.

Their cruelty, though, wasn't always as calculating as this. Often it was casual, almost a habit. Sometimes, by comparison with how sadistic they could be when they had good reason to be annoyed, it seemed almost comical. On the backs of the doors in the house were big metal hooks, the really strong ones that were often seen in old houses, and sometimes, just because I happened to be in the way when he was passing, Dad would pick me up and hang me on one of them.

'Dwarf,' he would sneer. 'You can stay up there, you little bastard,' and I'd hang on the hook trying to keep as still as possible, hoping that even though I was up in the air at his eye level I could somehow make myself invisible and not tempt him to do worse to me. I'd be wondering how I was ever going to get down, but I wouldn't dare say a word.

Since everyone in that house was everyone else's enemy, I knew that my brothers' reaction would simply be relief that it wasn't them. That was survival. It was no surprise to me that my brothers would crowd round the door I was hanging on, laughing at me and pushing the door backwards and forwards, watching me swing helplessly one way and then another, enjoying my humiliation.

They would wait until Dad was well out of the way, of

course, but then it would be: 'Dwarf! Look at the Dwarf! You'll have to stay up there until you're twenty. And even then you won't be able to get down. At least you're getting a ride, Dwarf, and it's free.'

And so on. There was no-one who was interested in getting me down. I was just the Dwarf and it was funny that I was so small that I could hang by my clothes on the back of a door. Eventually they would all drift off, still laughing, thinking it was even funnier to leave me there on my own, stuck four feet off the ground. When I was alone, that was when I could stop trying to be invisible and begin trying to wriggle my way free without having to put up with the indignity of being watched while I did it, and being jeered when I finally hit the floor hard.

And yet, in spite of it all, for a good year after we moved house I liked to stand and watch at the front window after school to see if I could spot Dad coming home from work or the pub. Stupidly, I looked forward to seeing him. He was my dad and I wanted him to be pleased to see me. The hopefulness that very young children have hadn't quite been bashed out of me. I don't know what I expected, but I would run to meet him when he came in. Every single time he'd walk in and lash out at me for being too near the door.

'Get out of the way, you little bastard!' he'd yell, hitting me and often sending me sprawling.

I can't understand why I ever did it more than once.

6. School: Part 1

I came home from school one day and hung about in the kitchen, where my mother was making tea in the big stained, white enamel teapot which was the piece of kitchen equipment that got the most use in our house. Neither of us spoke. No-one in my family ever said hello or asked how you were. Eventually she looked at me.

'What are you hanging about here for?' she snapped.

I decided I'd try it. No harm in asking, surely. My class was going on a school trip to Richmond Park and I needed some money or even just some food that I could take with me. A slice of bread and margarine would have done, but she told me in a few choice words that there was nothing to eat in the house and I wouldn't be getting anything from her.

'What do think, I'm made of money, you bastard? Now fuck off and leave me alone.'

I couldn't help it, the words just came out. 'But I'll be the only one without anything to eat,' I said.

She picked up a plate and smashed it over my head. She would probably have followed it up with more of a beating, but she had just made a pot of tea and wanted to sit down with a cigarette.

I stood stupidly in the middle of the kitchen surrounded by broken china.

'Pick up that fucking mess, now, you little shite,' she barked as she half turned and reached for the teapot. 'And get out of this fucking kitchen as fast as you like, if you know what's good for you. Don't come to me talking about your sodding school trips. If you don't get your school dinner, you'll like it or you'll feel the end of my Sally if you come whining to me again.'

Almost before she'd finished I had picked up the bits of plate and was gone, intent on getting out of there before she changed her mind about letting me off so lightly.

I went on the trip, of course, because not going wasn't a choice for quite a while after Mum scalded my feet. Even not going on a school trip like this one would be classed as playing truant, and although the teachers for once might not have cared whether I was there or not, it wasn't worth the risk.

I got by, as I always did, by hanging round the kids who weren't as aggressive as the hard core of bullies in my class and looking into their packed lunches, asking them what they had. Some of them weren't so bad, really, and I got half a sandwich here and a bite of an apple there. I really missed the free school dinner that day. For a long time those five free dinners a week during term-time were the only regular meals I could count on. A hot drink was certainly a luxury way out of my league, even though I knew it was something most people took for granted. I don't know why, but I became fixated on being 'normal' and there is nothing more normal than having a coffee, so one day I helped myself from the cupboard. The only problem was that I left the dirty cup on the side. Dad came in from work and saw it. He knew he hadn't had a cup of coffee.

'What's this?' he said, in the very calm, controlled way he had that was a warning as clear as thunder clouds that something bad was coming. He put the cup under my nose. 'Smell it,' he ordered.

I smelt it.

'What is it?'

'Coffee,' I answered.

Bang. His fist came at my face like an iron ball out of a cannon.

'You're not fucking allowed any coffee,' he said, quite calm again and turning away to put the cup in the sink as I lay on the floor groaning, my nose spouting blood.

While life inside the house was bad, life outside it was no easier. There was no escape for me from the daily struggle for survival. I am still not sure how I got through the years between starting school and getting to the point, when I was about eight, where I'd begun to be a bit more savvy about the dodging and wheeling that even a small child could do to fill his stomach, and also to fill the miserable, dreary days that had no meaning or purpose. There was rarely any breakfast before school, school itself was a torture, and after school it was hardly worth going home because there wasn't even good company to be found there. I was always tired in class because my bed-wetting and the conditions in our bedroom made a proper night's sleep impossible, and because I wasn't getting enough to eat. One day followed another and nothing made any difference.

If I had hoped that school would open up a new life to me, one with friends and a purpose, I soon discovered it did nothing of the kind. My primary school was a ten-minute walk away across a busy main road and along a kind of death alley, a long straight rat-run through the tenement flats that were the next buildings along the road from our terrace. Even in 1967 it wasn't a street you would want to walk down after dark. I quickly learned that if one of the bullies wanted to get you on the way to or from school, this was one of their favourite places to ambush you, because there was no escape except running like hell as fast as you could for the other end of it. Often they were quite happy just to see me run for my life even if they couldn't catch me to give me the beating they'd have liked to.

There was no relief in the playground from abuse and violence – in fact I only got more of it there. Of course, very quickly I was walking to school on my own. A couple of my older brothers were supposed to take me with them, but we all avoided each other whenever possible. It was partly that we were afraid of each other – I was certainly afraid of all of them – and partly because I think we all had this mad hope that if we could keep the others away we might be able to make some kind of a place for ourselves. We didn't want other people to know we were associated with kids that scruffy and smelly. It was embarrassing enough to be a stinky, raggy kid. We didn't want to make it even worse by letting on that we were related to other stinky, raggy kids. I suppose I must have been excited about going to school for the first time, but if life with my family had taught me anything, it was that belonging was about more than getting through the door. To belong you had to have all the things I didn't have. You had to have a good home, and have the right clothes, and they had to be clean. You had to know how to eat your school dinner in front of other people in a way that didn't make them laugh at you and want to beat you up. You had to have the kind of parental guidance that told you what the right way to behave was, with teachers and especially with other children. I hadn't a clue. You had to be washed and not always trying to hide the cuts and bruises. I was a browbeaten kid, a bit cheeky when I was off-guard, but mystified by what teachers were trying to do with us and always afraid of them, of the other kids, of my own shadow.

The only thing in my favour was that I had learned not to be a bully myself. Our parents had taught us how to be violent, but they had also beaten into us a terrible fear of getting physical violence back in return, and whether we realized it or not, they'd taught us that it was always safer to pick on someone smaller. Of course, being the smallest and youngest of the boys, I had never had that option. I was always the easy target – Mum, Dad, brothers and now teachers. Once I started school I began to see that my brothers were brave at home when they only had each other and me to intimidate, but over the years I watched them being chased down the road by the school bullies again and again, and taking the ridicule that we all got because of the way we looked and smelt, without fighting back, and I realized that outside the house they were always victims too. I did at least learn that what they and the school bullies did to me and to each other couldn't be called bravery and I think that's why I never did it myself. Despite what they did to me, I decided early on that I wouldn't inflict such behaviour on my worst enemy. Somewhere in the chaos of my early years I learned what empathy was, and strange as it sounds, I decided early on that I didn't ever want to be like that. I even felt a bit sorry for my brothers. I always had a sense that behaving like this wasn't right. The only weapons I had were cheekiness, looking keen, trying to please. They didn't get me very far at that point in my life. As one of the nastier teachers put it, at school I was just another Roche. Laurence, a year older than me, was there too, and although he usually wouldn't say boo to a goose, there were times when he got into a fight.

Predictably, Laurence was no friend of mine in the playground, and Terry, who was three or four years older and in the senior part of the school by then, was so distant from the likes of me in the infants that I can hardly recall him being there. Francis, two and half years older than me and perhaps the gentlest of us, might have been a friend of sorts but he had literally stopped talking when he was about seven years old and, as I started school, he was sent to a special school that was a bus ride away. I was quite worried about him, but I think now that he came up with the most sensible survival strategy of any of us. He just opted out of his life, our life, and even Dad couldn't really get to him. He could threaten him and make him cry, but he couldn't make him speak.

For the rest of his school life he got on a bus every morning and left the area, and for a good part of the day he was well out of the hell of our life – in fact I was almost jealous. He started speaking again when he was nine, but he was always a bit switched off. Not because he was slow, but because that was how he chose to be, how he chose to survive.

Of course, the other children in my class noticed very quickly that I had holes in my shoes and that my clothes smelt really bad and didn't fit, and I was called names on a daily basis – tramp, stinky, whatever they fancied. They would put their hands up in class if they ended up next to me: 'Miss, Roche smells, I can't sit next to him, don't make me.'

I suppose I must have smelt terrible. We didn't even brush our teeth. The first time I saw toothpaste was when a tube of it came into the house in a delivery from some kind of weekly savings club that my mother sometimes paid into. I found it lying around somewhere and had a taste and thought: 'Crikey, this is different,' and then I ate the lot.

I always had third- or fourth-hand shoes and they were nearly always too big for me, so I would get newspaper and screw it up and push it into the toes so that they fitted better, pushing my heels to the back of the shoe. This worked fine until it was wet outside and then the paper would get soggy, my toes would push forward into it and the shoes would flap on my feet like flip-flops.

We never had underwear, and that led to a humiliation which I hadn't expected, because in those days very young children did PE in their underwear. Even at the age of five and six I had enough sense of modesty to be certain that no way was I going to take my trousers off in front of anyone at school, so there was nothing I could do except pretend to be very ill or just not go to school. This was one issue that made me not care what anyone did to me, teachers or parents. PE day was the one day that could now and again make me choose the risk of feeling Mum's fists and stay away from school. Of course, after a while the teachers refused to believe that I was ill every time PE came around and they started ordering me to go into the hall and get on with it. I would go in but refuse to get undressed. In the end I spent most PE lessons sitting outside the deputy head teacher's office, waiting to be told off about my disobedience. PE looked like fun and I wanted to do it, but I could never bring myself to explain to the deputy head why I wouldn't take my trousers off. It was too shaming.

Eventually, in the second year, we were allowed to wear shorts, and at that point one of the teachers, Mr Wood, the only one I liked, came to my rescue with a pair of shorts out of a lost-property box he had in his classroom. They were long, quite faded, and made out of heavy cotton material and looked like something Stanley Matthews might have worn in the 1950s, but they didn't have any holes in them and they were mine. Mr Wood was all right. He seemed to be the only teacher there who was able to use his imagination and guess what was going on for me. He took art classes and he would come round the classrooms from time to time to ask whether any of us would like to do some painting or drawing. Almost every hand shot in the air, and he would pick a few and take them off to the school's art room. After the first time I got picked I didn't bother putting my hand up because I assumed I wouldn't get another go, but he picked me anyway. Once he got me to lie down on a big piece of paper so that he could draw round me. Obviously I was worried about the state of my clothes, but if I smelt too awful and was hard to be near, he never showed any sign of horror. I painted myself in the outline he'd drawn and for a while my picture was pinned up in the school hall. This was the highlight of all the years I spent in classrooms – I had achieved something. I barely learned to read and write and sums were beyond me. The inside of my head was a mess. I couldn't concentrate on anything for more than a few minutes. It was as if I was jumping inside my own skin all the time, and even sitting down quietly was more than I could manage. It wasn't as if I'd ever had much practice at sitting down. There was no calm at home, nowhere peaceful to sit and play, and most of my waking hours outside school were spent roaming around the streets. School did nothing to make up for that lack of peace. Every day there seemed to be a new trial that had to be survived. There was even a pointed dunce's hat in the school, like the ones you see in comics, and now and again I had to wear it, standing next to the teacher's desk facing my class. I tried hard to make my sums add up, to behave and be like all the others, but I wasn't like everyone else. They knew how to take the chances school gave them, it seemed to me, while I was just a target. It was just one more humiliation. I got through it.

Eventually I had no clothes, really, and it was winter and my mother found me a pair of granny boots, those boots with zips up the front and furry bits round the ankles. I knew they weren't right for a kid of my age. I wanted to say to her: 'Mum, I can't wear these, I'll be slaughtered,' but I knew it was out of the question. She would have slaughtered me.

'Be grateful for what you fucking get – you don't know you're born' was one of her favourite sayings.

So I had to put them on knowing that this outfit was the final straw. I knew I would now be a permanent target in the playground, but the thing was, they were warm and they had no holes in the soles, so for once my feet weren't going to be cut to ribbons. It was another horrible decision that had to be made, no shoes or these things. Mum gave me a coat too, and she had a rare smile on her face.

'There you go, son, you'll be warm in that. It's one of mine, but you can have it.'

She spoke for all the world as if she was a fine, proud mother telling me how lucky I was to have her. My brothers couldn't stop laughing. I went to school trying not to look anyone in the eye, being ashamed, but being warm. Of course, everyone at school laughed at me. 'So what?' I told myself. This time there was no choice to make, not really. They were all going to laugh at me anyway, so I might as well be warm.

School dinners should have been the one simple and easy moment in the day, but because I hardly even knew how to eat with a knife and fork, and I was always so desperate to get the food inside me, I was always being taunted about the way I ate. One day the kid sitting next to me spat in my food. Hunger won over disgust and I ate it because it was the only meal I was going to see that day. A few years later, when I got older and I'd had enough of the bullying, I just used to go into the dinner hall and get a bread roll and then go outside to a corner of the playground where I could eat it in peace. I was starving, but at least everyone left me alone.

Dad's job was, of course, yet another problem. All the kids were local, and they certainly knew the public toilets, and it wasn't long before they worked out the drunk cleaning them was our father. That gave them loads of ammunition. Your dad's a bog cleaner.

'We went down there and had a good shit and your dad had to clean it up,' they would say, dancing round me in the playground.

'We stuck his head down the toilet.'

'Your dad smells of shit, just like you.'

'Bogbrush, bogbrush, your dad's a bogbrush.'

Even if they hadn't known that, they would have seen him stumbling back home drunk because he nearly always went to the pub after he'd finished work. Even if he hadn't gone to the huge pub almost opposite our house, he would still be seen coming home on the bus pissed. As bad luck would have it, the bus stop was right outside our house and several times he got off his bus and fell down senseless on the pavement. The older boys would have to go out and help him in. It wasn't as if you could pretend he didn't live with us, although I did try.

'No,' I would say when kids asked me if that was my dad, just like I did on the day he died. I don't know who I thought I was kidding.

So in the playground at break-times I was taunted, never picked for any games and usually beaten up. Four or five of them would get me into a corner and sometimes I'd get down on my knees, like I did with my dad when he was pounding me, in the hope that it would make them leave off. This just made them laugh more and kick harder. Nothing pacified them. I was learning that the best option in every area of life was to keep out of other people's way as much as possible, to disappear.

The school was a big brick building, maybe built in the 1930s, when the tenement flats between it and our terrace of houses were put up. It was still a fairly old-fashioned set-up when I was there. On one side was a yard where the girls went out to play with the infants, and on the other a bigger yard, where the boys played once they went into the junior classes. By the time I was old enough to go into this yard the bullying had become so bad that I risked complaining to a teacher about it.

'Stand there in the playground,' he said, pointing to a part of it that could be seen clearly from the staffroom window. 'If anyone bullies you, wave at the window. We'll see what's going on.'

I spent a lot of time looking at that staffroom window

after that. It was comical, really. When the bullies came near me I put my hand up and pretended to wave at the teacher. Of course, there usually wasn't anyone looking out and the bullies would just pull me away from the window and lay into me in a place where they couldn't be seen.

School was not a place where I found help. It was where I got a lot more things to worry about. It seemed to me that a lot of the teachers were as bad as the children. One day I went to school looking particularly filthy. I'd been sleeping in all my clothes for days, obviously, because they'd have been stolen by my brothers if I'd taken them off, and anyway I'd been sleeping rough for a few nights in a den I'd made on the wasteland at the back of our house, a place where I could just escape the madness of home. My teacher looked at me when I arrived and started telling me off for the state I was in.

'Look at the state of you, Roche, you're disgusting,' she said.

There was a big white stone sink in the corner of the classroom.

'Get those filthy clothes off and get in the sink,' she ordered. 'There's soap there. Use it.'

She said this as if I'd come to school dirty because it was the naughtiest thing I could think of to do. I had to wash in front of the whole class. I was already putting up with the bullying in the playground and all the stuff at home and I'll never forget having to wash in that sink in front of everyone as long as I live, with all the kids smiling and laughing.

'Don't you have a bath, Roche, don't you wash?' some kid asked me at playtime.

There was no answer to this except, no, I don't have a bath and I don't wash. I could recall a time when Mum had made some effort to clean us up regularly. For a while, when I was younger, Sunday was bath day. The only sink was in the kitchen, and she would put pans full of water on the gas stove and line us boys up in front of the sink. As ever it was biggest first, smallest last. I would be lifted up and put in the sink after all the others had been washed, sitting in the scummy dirty water, which had gone cold by then. It was disgusting and so filthy that you couldn't get a lather on the bar of Lifebuoy soap. There was only one towel and it would be wet through by the time I got to it, so I'd walk around the kitchen flapping my arms to get dry. This routine must have stopped quite soon after I started school, because it always seemed to me that there was never a time when I went to school feeling clean. I was permanently hungry, tired, dirty and lonely.

I hated one particular male teacher. In my eyes he was just another bully and the only difference was that he was bigger than all the other bullies at school and he should have known better. One day, a few weeks after I'd started at the school, our class teacher didn't turn up and we were split into two groups and sent to join two of the older classes. My group was sent into the horrible teacher's class and he took one look at me and straight away said: 'Not another Roche. Sit down and face the wall.' He left me like that for the rest of the day. I hadn't said or done anything and hadn't been given a second to prove myself. The only thing he taught me was that no adult could be trusted.

Unfortunately for me, this bully also took the older boys for football. On the day I was sent to school wearing my mother's coat and the furry grandma boots, it happened to be football day. I was standing in a corner of the playground hoping to keep well out of it and not be noticed, but he walked over to me, smirking, and said: 'Roche, where's your football kit?'

'I haven't got a football kit, sir.'

'Well, you really need to get one,' he said, and walked off, still smiling. He obviously enjoyed ridiculing me.

I'm sure we Roches were a wild lot but no-one seemed interested in asking why, and we were lumped together as if it was easier to assume that we were all the same, all a big headache. We were a problem family but no-one wanted to know what the problem was. We became the problem. I don't know what the adults around us thought. Maybe they thought that being poor was our problem, or that there were too many children for our parents to control. But I knew there were other big families in the area and they didn't look like we did or behave like we did, because they had parents who made an effort with them.

There was the Rogers family across the road in the council flats, ten children in five rooms, but always clean and properly dressed when they came to school. We knew the Craigs round the corner quite well because Mum and Mrs Craig, both Irishwomen, seemed to get on quite well.

Like us, they had nine children, who were not that much older than us, to look after, but they might as well have been living on a different planet. How Mrs Craig did it, I don't know, but whenever I went into their house I was always amazed by the flowery, sweet smell of the hall, and how white the paintwork was. They had very little furniture and no carpets, only lino, but everything was clean and shiny.

It was obvious to me that there was something wrong with us. We just couldn't live like other people did. We had no self-control because our parents didn't have any around us. Life at school, just as it was at home, was a wild free-for-all, a competition to find out who could batter the hardest or run the fastest.

Discipline at primary school usually involved being sent out of class to stand in the corridor. I seemed to spend hours of my childhood in that corridor and I used to while away the time by picking threads of cotton out of my old crusty clothes and holding them above the huge old-fashioned cast-iron radiators that lined the walls, watching as the threads rose and floated towards the ceiling on the warm air currents.

School holidays were a relief. Even though being off school left me with the problem of filling the days and finding food, for the first few days of a holiday at least it felt good not to have to worry about finding clothes to wear or dodging the bullies. Unfortunately we did have to eat, and Mum wasn't going to pass up the chance of getting free food into us, so when she heard about a thing called holiday school dinners she made sure we went.

These dinners were done for the poor children from all over the area, one day at one school and the next at another. The older boys were told to make sure that the youngers ones got there, so that guaranteed that I'd get a kicking going there and coming back. When we got there, we found ourselves in the middle of the biggest group of little thugs you can imagine. Some we already knew and some we didn't, but we might as well have had big blue, red and white targets painted on us. Even those boys who didn't know us could see us coming a mile off. We looked poorer and dirtier and rougher than anyone else and they knew they had their victims ready-made. This was when I would really see my big brothers, so handy with their fists on me when we were on our own patch, showing their true colours. They ran at the slightest sign of trouble. For once, being small seemed to keep me out of trouble. These lads didn't think I was worth bothering with, and if I could just hang around long enough to get some food in my pockets and get away to find somewhere to eat it in peace, I was reasonably happy.

One of these school dinner events was held in a place that had an adventure playground in it, quite a new thing with a climbing frame and monkey bars that I really wanted to have a go on. There were always women supervising the children at these things, and I think they must have been volunteers because they seemed kinder than most of the teachers I knew, and after the meal they took us out to the playground. A swing smashed into me and split my head open, and one of these women fussed over me, saying that I had to go to hospital. She was alarmed by how calmly I took the injury, not screaming, not even crying, and flatly refusing to go anywhere near a doctor. By now I had a healthy fear of any kind of institution, even one with doctors and nurses in it. They wore uniforms, and my parents didn't like uniforms. This woman insisted. I had a gash an inch long in my forehead spouting blood and, if nothing else, it had to be stitched. Then she insisted on seeing me home.

'I do have to come with you to make sure you get there safely. I must speak to your mother,' she said.

'You don't. I'll tell her. It'll be all right.' Now I was afraid, now I was crying, begging her to let me go home on my own.

'You have a head injury, I can't let you go alone.'

At home, it was almost as bad as I had feared it would be. The door was locked, and when the woman knocked, my father and Harry came to the door together. They were pissed. I leaped through the door to get my side of the story in first, and to get through the two of them so that I could bolt for the back door if things got nasty. I was sure Dad would think I had done something wrong and would belt me long before I had a chance to explain. The woman stepped into the hall too, holding out her hand to shake Dad's.

'Your son has had an accident, Mr Roche.'

She sounded quite normal, very polite, but standing behind Dad and Harry now, I had a clear view of her face. Her expression was unforgettable. I knew that she was looking at the state of the place, the filth on the floor and the crumbling walls, and I could see that the smell, of the house, of the two shambling men in front of her, had hit her. Shame and fear. That was what my life boiled down to. Shame and fear.

7. The Brothers

I had sisters but I barely noticed them as I was growing up. Kathleen, the sister in Australia who was over twenty years older than me, was long gone from our lives. Christine was seven or eight years older and within a few years of our move she had married very young and gone off with her husband to the north of England. Alison, six years older, was probably just starting senior school by the time I started at primary school. Strangely, although Rosemary was only eighteen months younger than me and would have been two years below me at school, I wasn't aware of her being there at all. Seen through my eyes, my sisters existed like ghosts exist. Because they didn't physically attack me, and because my parents and brothers always did, I wiped them out of the picture. I was in a state of constant alertness and anxiety, always on the watch for potential violence. The girls weren't a threat, so I didn't see them.

There was one evening when Alison was in her early teens and she came into the front room with her hair back-combed and piled on top of her head, beautifully styled. I would never have noticed this if one of the older boys hadn't suddenly looked at her very closely.

'Mum!' he shouted. 'Mum, Alison's hair is moving, look!'

We all looked. The part that was back-combed so that it stood up above her forehead seemed to be twitching. Mum grabbed her and pulled the hairdo apart while Alison howled with outrage at all the work she'd put into her hairstyle being ruined.

'You're jumping with nits, girl. Get down into the kitchen,' Mum barked. We could hear Alison's wails coming up the stairs as Mum took scissors to her head and cut almost all her hair off.

Alison was busy getting out and meeting boys, her own way of making the best escape she could from home. Rosemary was half her age and rather different. On the whole I think she was kept away from us boys because Mum didn't want her picking up our ways. She certainly wasn't allowed to roam the streets as I was. There were only two things she did that I ever noticed.

The first happened in the kitchen when there were just the two of us there. A pot of tea had been made – I forget who had made it – and we both wanted some. She went for the handle.

'Oi, I wanted some of that,' I said.

In the struggle to reach for the teapot, the lid came straight off and a tidal wave of boiling tea hit my chest.

'For Christ's sake,' I screamed, dancing round the kitchen, trying to hold the scalding front of my shirt away from my skin.

I spent the next hour doing the same trick with a needle that I'd had to do after Mum scalded my feet. In fact, it dawned on me that Mum would probably have loved seeing me in so much pain – she certainly wouldn't have helped me had she been around. My chest was covered in blisters and I was picking the dead skin off for days, walking around hunched over to stop my clothes rubbing on the raw patches.

With five brothers in between her and the next oldest girl, Alison, she was in danger of becoming as wild as we were. My other memory of her is the day a year or two after this that she climbed onto the roof of one of the toilets at the back of the terrace. The house it belonged to was empty, the tenants gone and the house waiting for the council to renovate it. This toilet happened to have a glass roof but I think it was so dirty Rosemary didn't realize what she was standing on. The next we knew, she'd crashed through it into the toilet below and the side of her face and neck had been gashed open by the broken glass. She spent a while in hospital and came out with terrible scars on her left cheek. It wasn't long after this that she was sent up north to live with Christine and her family, probably because everyone agreed that she couldn't be left to spend her time around all those crazy brothers.

I wouldn't have minded being sent north myself, and for much the same reason. If I didn't take much notice of my sisters it was because all my wits were constantly on the alert for what my brothers might do to me next. You'd have thought that once Dad was out of the house and Mum was off wherever it was she used to go – I never had any idea what she did with her days – there'd be some peace. Instead, it was non-stop dog-eat-dog.

There was often no sense to it. A friend of my

brother's, for instance, came round to the house now and again and decided I was an easy target. One day he pointed at me and said: 'I am going to nut you to see how hard your head is.' I can't have been much more than six or seven, and this lad would head-butt me over and over again. It was agreed that it was a very hard head indeed. I'd be dizzy with it, my head thudding. It felt like I was under water as everything swirled around me, but I'd try to laugh and put up with it. There was no point showing any emotion – it would only mean the ordeal would last even longer. I think I felt a certain pride in being able to take it and having a head that everyone thought was impressively hard. But it hurt like hell. Another household game, one that Dad particularly liked to play with an audience, was to order me to stand against a wall while he threw darts at me. I learned to stand as still as a statue and hold my breath with my eyes squeezed tightly shut. I still can't decide why I didn't ever feel one pierce my skin, why he didn't ever deliberately hit me. I can only assume Dad had more fun watching me sweat.

Dad also fancied himself as a martial arts expert. 'I could rip your nose, break your jaw, and make you bleed to death in a single punch,' he once said to me, his face pushed right into mine. 'It's all about self-control, discipline. Things you know nothing about, you little fucker.'

Sometimes any weapon would do. Once Dad told me to stand up in front of the others as we sat in the front room. He seemed quite friendly. Then he picked up a vase and brought it down on top of my head in one smooth move. There was blood everywhere, and that was one of the many times I had to be taken to have my wounds stitched up at the local hospital. I knew the tiled walls of the entrance hall as well as I knew our own front hall.

I wasn't the only Roche boy getting a rough deal and more often than not, we turned on each other. Until the day I die I will always be amazed that no-one was killed in that house. We regularly flew at each other and had full-scale punch-ups in the front room, while those not involved sat there and watched. None of us really got on, but Terry and Paul in particular had a difficult relationship. Terry tended to think that Paul was a bit of a pushover. Paul was not the sharpest tool in the shed, but he was bright enough to know when Terry was taunting him. Paul was quite ashamed of the fact that, at that stage, he couldn't read or write very well, and the others found out that referring to it was a really good way of winding him up.

Everyone seemed to have a temper. Sometimes, as a few of us sat in the living room, someone would simply walk in without a word and punch the nearest person to hand smack in the head, sending him sprawling and dazed onto the floor. Sometimes one of us would be knocked out cold. It was madness.

We seemed to have this crazy desire to torment each other. Dad had a distinctive way of walking, flat on his heels, so you could always tell when he was in the house, walking along the landing or down the stairs. One of the Roche boys' favourite games was to mimic him, walking around flat-footed, and it was usually the older ones trying to terrify the younger ones. If it worked we would all run and hide or belt down the stairs into the basement and out through the kitchen window if necessary, if the back door of the house was locked. Then you'd hear the mocking laughter behind you. This kind of thing obviously never happened when Dad was around, but Mum was often there to see it. She never tried to stop us hurting and brutalizing each other. I don't know whether she thought it was normal for boys to behave like this or whether she didn't think she was strong enough to get involved. Maybe it just saved her a job. When Laurence picked a fight with me in the kitchen one day my mother did yell at him, but only to tell him to take me out into the back yard and finish it there.

Laurence wasn't usually so keen to fight outside the house, but he never minded having a go at me because he knew it wasn't much of a contest. He obeyed Mum and dragged me outside and carried on while the others watched. This was one of the times when Raymond stepped in and said in his cold, calm way: 'I think he's had enough now.' Raymond was the only one who could have stopped Laurence.

By this time I was so accustomed to the violence that the pain didn't matter, I accepted that I was going to feel pain every day anyway. My injuries were neither here nor there to me.

When we were younger, Laurence liked to put his hands in his pockets and lean against a wall as I came towards him, so that he looked as if he was thinking about something else. If I didn't notice him or I couldn't get past him fast enough, he'd suddenly swing his leg out and kick me.

'Gotcha,' he'd say. 'Didn't see it coming that time, did you?'

It was like living with wild animals.

Our parents were very good at just one thing, and that was making sure none of us did anything outside the house that would bring the kind of people to our door who would have asked too many questions about the way we were being treated. Neither of them had ever had any control over themselves or ever tried to hold themselves back. They felt angry, they hit us, they hit us beyond any reasonable level of punishment and they didn't see anything wrong in it. But their cruelty had more method than it seemed to. As I got older it dawned on me that whenever we were beaten, whether Dad was whipping us or Mum was beating us with the sweeping brush, we were always beaten on the body and sometimes on the head, but never on the face or arms or legs, on any part of our body that might be on show when we went out. They had enough control to be calculating about where they hit us and they really considered what they could get away with, real thought went into the logistics of it all: what would be seen at school – in the classroom, in PE lessons, even in the playground. Always they could count on it that we would never tell for fear of more violence.

They did such a good job on me that all through my childhood, when mistakes were made and there was no choice but to get me to a hospital, I lied about my bruises and injuries. At the hospital I would always say that I'd fallen down or tripped up. Neither of them ever took us to the hospital themselves. It never occurred to me that they should. One of my brothers always took me. I assumed it was because they didn't care. It was only when I was much older that I suspected it was just as much because they didn't want to be asked awkward questions.

Just once I was taken to the hospital by the lodger, Harry, with blood pumping from a deep gash in the sole of my foot. It was the one moment when even Harry's simple mind decided that enough was enough. If he hadn't acted, I know I would have bled to death before Mum and Dad realized that this time their scorn for the pain and damage they inflicted on us had carried them over the edge.

He was a small man but a strong one. He wrapped his scarf tightly round the bleeding foot and put me on his shoulders, and walked up to the children's hospital with me. It usually took about fifteen minutes and he got us both there in half that time.

'Don't let them take my foot away,' I sobbed all the way there.

'They're not going to, lad, you'll be fine,' panted Harry, almost running.

'How did on earth did you do this?' they asked as they stitched me up yet again.

'I stepped on a tin can,' I said. Harry said nothing.

Neither of us mentioned that Mum had thrown the corned beef can at me as hard as she could because I'd been running away from her at the time. I was running away because she was hitting me over the head again and again. As I ran, the open, razor-sharp edge of the can and my foot met each other on the hard kitchen floor. It almost cut my foot in half. Seeing that she'd brought me down, she came after me so that she could carry on hitting me, and I had to use my hands to drag myself away from her because the can was stuck in my foot.

It was the excitement that had done it. Seeing her opening a whole tin of corned beef at the kitchen table had been too much for me. I wanted to know what it was, so, like an idiot, I had run round the table to get next to her, to get next to it. She shouted at me, and I suppose she gave me fair warning, but I couldn't bring myself to get away from the table. I just wanted to watch her cut it up, I wanted to smell it.

Harry had been sitting at the table waiting for his sandwich and had seen it all. The corned beef was for him, probably for Dad and Mum too. He watched as I pulled the can out of my foot, as my father sneered and Mum, realizing that she'd done enough damage to me to satisfy even her, left off thumping me and went back to making the sandwiches. They stared at him as he said nothing, but stood up and left the table and knelt down in front of me.

'Leave the little bleeder, Harry. He's got to fucking learn. They all have,' said Dad, but he didn't sound as angry as he would usually have done if he'd seen one of us being offered sympathy he thought we didn't deserve. Perhaps even he was a bit worried.

In the hospital, both Harry and I kept our family's secret to ourselves. We knew that making a fuss here about what had happened would only make things worse back there.

When the nurse told me I could have a toy to take home from the children's corner, I chose a red plastic telephone.

'I don't know, lad,' said Harry, shaking his head very gently. 'Maybe you should take the soldier. Your dad might like that better.'

We both knew what he meant. It wasn't about what he liked, it was about appeasing him, not giving him any more excuse than he needed to give me a hiding. It was the only hint Harry ever gave me that he thought Dad went too far, beyond anything that was reasonable.

If Mum had been scared by what had happened to me, or realized that the family had had its closest escape yet from having the police in the house asking how a child had come to bleed to death on the kitchen floor, she didn't show it.

'That'll teach you a fucking lesson,' she said, as I limped past her the next day with stitches right across the sole of my foot and up both sides of it, and a bandage the size of a clown's joke shoe. 'When I tell you to move, you fucking move.'

Whether it was neglect or cunning, our parents kept well out of the way of any awkward questions. Mum didn't even sit with us at church, which, like school, our mother insisted was not to be missed unless we wanted to feel her Sally. She had been brought up a Catholic, and if she had respect for nothing else, she respected the priest. The priest didn't think much of us. It always seemed to me that we Roche boys were segregated from the other people, made to sit together in another part of the church well away from everyone else.

Church was hard too. I could never understand for the life of me why we were given a penny that had to go in the collection plate when there never seemed to be any money in the house to buy food. I also couldn't understand how one of my brothers always seemed to have money to spend on the way to school on a Monday morning. I was obviously a bit stupid, because it took me a while to work out that he was palming his penny and probably taking a few more from the plate.

Now and again the older ones wouldn't be able to control themselves and would start fighting during the service, or f-ing and blinding at each other. It has to be said that our language wasn't nice. Cursing was part of Dad and Mum's everyday language; we just picked it up from them. Once, we behaved so badly that my four big brothers – Raymond was allowed not to go to church once he started working – were all hauled out by the ushers, still swinging at each other, and put on the steps outside. Then they came back for me and put me out with them. This was a result, because although I knew we'd get it from Mum if she heard about it – she wasn't there that day either – I also knew that it would be spread around a bit with all five of us in trouble. Better still, the plate hadn't been passed round at that point and we got to keep the penny. With a penny you could buy a couple of chews or a gobstopper. This was more than a treat. It was something that could stop the hunger for a couple of hours. Sometimes I would feel so hungry that I'd take a big risk and pretend I'd put the penny in, and hope and pray – that's what prayer's really for, I thought – that none of my brothers would tell on me. One very bad Sunday was the day when it snowed and I had no shoes to go to church in, only a pair of wellingtons. I had no socks, and it was a twenty-minute walk down the road to the church. My feet were so cold they hurt as if someone had stamped on them and then we had to walk all the way back again. It seemed my feet weren't warm again for days after that.

The worst church days of all came round every year without fail. If it hadn't been for Mass on Christmas Eve and Christmas Day we would never have known the difference. As it was, we had to go to church, and after that it was like any other day of the year except that Dad was around the house a bit more because the pubs weren't open for quite so long. So it would have been a good day to stay out of the house, except that the smell of food, good food, lots of turkey and gravy, coming from every street, every house, drove me mad with hunger. Even I understood that this was the one day of the year when there was no angle I could pull that would get me into those houses and into a share of what they had.

Just like every other day of the year, there was no food in our house, none that I ever got my hands on anyway. There was a Christmas cake one year, but what was left after Dad, Mum, Harry and Raymond – because he was working – had their big slices out of it didn't last long between eight of us. We went at it with our hands, grabbing fistfuls of crumbs. The smaller your hand, the less you got. The worst of it was that there were no people out on the streets either, so no chance of finding someone you could get money out of by begging and no shops open to buy food in anyway.

When I was bit older and we had the rented telly, we would be allowed into the living room for a few hours before we were expected to take ourselves off to the bedroom. The rules were exactly the same. Dad would have a supply of beer in bottles beside his chair and he'd work his way through them steadily, so it was one eye on the telly but never getting so caught up in anything that was on that you wriggled or spoke, or even laughed much if there was something funny on, and always keeping the other eye on Dad to work out whether he was getting himself into the mood for whipping one of us.

'What are you fucking laughing about, you little fucker?' Dad would suddenly shout, his face a dull red with beer and anger and the fire – which he was sitting right on top of, of course. Everyone would jump a mile and all the younger ones would be out of the room like rabbits. The official end of Christmas Day for us.

So when people talked at school about Christmas television programmes they'd watched, I had very little idea of what they were on about. What I could have talked about for hours was the adverts for Christmas food. These were much worse than the smell in the streets of Christmas dinner cooking. Shiny gravy on plates of meat, steaming Christmas puddings and iced cakes with cherries on them. It was all in black and white but I saw it in colour, as if the food was there in front of me, and I even thought I could smell it. I would sit there with my stomach echoing with emptiness and have wild, mad fantasies about reaching into the picture and pulling out all the food I could eat. It was torture.

There were obviously no presents, no decorations. We never asked for them, never expected them. We weren't stupid and we knew what a beating we'd get while Mum or Dad yelled – and both of them said it often enough when they were laying into us – 'You ungrateful little fucker. You'll be grateful for what you're given. You're lucky to have been born, and I wish to God you never had been, you shit.'

The only person who mentioned that it was Christmas Day was off-the-wall Paul, who would wake up in the morning and grin at me and say: 'It was Christmas Day in the workhouse, and Dangerous Dan McGrew . . .' Maybe he'd heard these two poems at school or from some other kids, and I had no idea what he was talking about, but it seemed funny. If I'd had any idea what a workhouse was, I would have gone out looking for one, because even there, it seems, they got a Christmas dinner and a present. I never heard anyone else in the house say the words 'Christmas Day'.

If my parents didn't care much about our bodies, they did feel a duty to pay some attention to our souls. I was confirmed – my mother saw to that – and for the occasion I was put into one of the older boys' school uniform of shirt and trousers with the hems folded up inside to fit my short legs, and one of my dad's ties. I looked reasonable, I think, even if the clothes were much too big for me. When I got back from church my father took me out, the only time in my life I went anywhere with him. He took me across the road to his local, and I sat outside for an hour or so with the glass of lemonade he'd brought out for me. Then we got on the bus to the pub that he drank in after he'd cleaned the toilets, and on the way he held my hand, the first and last time he did it as a father rather than during a beating he was giving me.

I sat outside the pub for another hour and he came out with one of his friends and both of them looked quite drunk by this time. His friend had a piece of cheese in his hand. As he held it out, saliva dripped from his mouth onto it. I took it and I wanted to drop it on the floor, but Dad was watching and I didn't like the look on his face so put it in my mouth and ate it, trying not to gag. When it started to get dark Dad came out again and said I could go home. I didn't have any money and he didn't offer me any, so I walked the two miles home alone.

That not one of us died in that house was incredible. But we were all left with mental scars.

Francis stopped talking when he was about seven and there was a lot of fuss about it. Specialists came to see him at school, and I even heard Mum and Dad talking to each other about it. As you might guess, they shouted at him until they were hoarse to get him to speak to them.

Dad would roar at him: 'Why? Why? Talk, you little bastard. Answer me!'

That seems just silly now, because it was obvious why. Francis had had enough of his parents, his brothers, the kids at school. Dad would shout at him until he was red in the face, but he didn't seem to hit Francis after he fell silent. Perhaps it was the superstitious bit of him that held back from something so strange as a silent child. Francis stuck to his silence and eventually went off to his special school. He made a good decision there, probably the best survival decision of any of us. When he started talking again he still seemed a bit strange, but it was a gentle strangeness and he seemed happier than anyone else in the family.

Despite all the things my brothers did to me when we were children, I often wanted to help them. I always feared them and sometimes I hated them, and I nearly always wanted to keep out of their way. But still I felt a sense of responsibility for them. I don't know where it came from because, after all, they were older and should have been looking out for me. It was as if I wanted to try to help other people even if I couldn't help myself. I was already losing my own mind, in a way. The constant alertness I had to maintain against the physical attacks that came from every direction, the never-ending hunger, the lack of sleep – all of this was grinding me down, as if I was a soldier on constant sentry duty, only there was never any leave, not so much as a moment when I could let my guard down. By the time I was about eight years old I had a new horrible feeling that seemed to go everywhere with me. I didn't understand what it was then, but I know now that it was anxiety. Yet in spite of everything, I always felt a certain loyalty to the family, and that was a kind of madness in itself.

One day I was knocked down by a car. At the time I was helping the local milkman in the hope of getting a pint of milk for myself and maybe a few bob that I could take home to Mum to buy her approval and attention for a little while, and I stepped out into the road without looking. People said that I flew through the air right over the car that hit me before coming down, splat, on the tarmac behind it. I was lying there, stunned but somehow not seriously injured, and I began to get my wits back at the moment that a policeman arrived and bent down to find out how I was. I was so desperate to get up and carry on that I swore at him.

'Fuck off, get off me, I've got to get home.'

I stood up and immediately fell over. Still protesting, I was put into an ambulance and taken to hospital. I had this crazy idea that they were depending on me back at the house. I had concussion, but I was with it enough to realize that hospital wasn't so bad after all. I had a clean bed with sheets on it, clean pyjamas, plenty of food and a lot of attention. It was brilliant.

Then Mum arrived. She'd had no choice but to come. The police had gone to the house to tell her about the accident and she obviously couldn't say: 'I hope the little shit dies,' and shut the door on them.

Doctors and nurses also belonged to the part of the world she thought of as authority, and if authority was taking an interest in us, this was the one thing that could make her or Dad do what they didn't want to do for their children. Naturally, she was not happy.

She sat down for a few minutes by my bed and left as

soon as she could, and she never said a word about what had happened to me or asked if I was feeling all right, nothing like that.

She hissed at me: 'You've cost me a fucking shilling for the bus fare and I want that money back.'

That was where loyalty got you.

8. Survival

I looked up and down the street, just round the corner from our house, and I was aching with hunger. I was five years old and I was planning to ask a stranger for money for the first time in my life. I had seen my brothers doing it and I knew I had to learn how to do it myself if I was going to survive. The old man coming towards me was wearing a long, shapeless old raincoat and he was stooped over, shuffling along. I suppose I chose him because he didn't look too frightening. I didn't think he'd be up to shouting at me or chasing me. So I walked up to him and, as cocky as I could manage because I was shaking inside with fear and shame, asked him for some money. He put his hand in his coat pocket and pulled it out again. When he opened his hand all there was in it was this pile of crumbs, and in the middle of the crumbs I could just about see that there was a penny. I looked into the crumbs and thought: 'That's the one I want.' But I couldn't take it. I reached out and took a couple of the crumbs between my thumb and finger, said: 'Thanks,' and walked away. I felt sorry for him. I looked like Charlie Chaplin myself and I ached with hunger, but I knew there was something not quite right about this man. I knew that he wasn't quite right in the head and I knew it wouldn't be right to take anything off him, not even a penny covered in crumbs.

I had uncomfortable feelings, which I couldn't understand, about that incident with the old man. I was embarrassed for him, of course, because he seemed so pathetic and vulnerable. But I was ashamed for myself too, because I didn't want to go about the streets asking people for their money. Never mind the shame, it was frightening – asking at home got you in bad trouble and I worried a lot about how some strangers might react, but by this point in my life it had become a question of survival for me. I had realized that all my older brothers seemed to find ways of getting hold of money so that they could buy food, because I would sometimes see them out around the streets where we lived eating whatever they'd been able to get. Not that they would share it with me, because we weren't the kind of family that shared. Sometimes hunger made me daring enough to ask for a bite, but I always got a 'Get lost, you little toe-rag, fuck off home.'

I was a bit mouthy with them when I was out of the house and sometimes I would try the classic 'You can't tell me what to do. Give me some of that.' And I would get a kicking. If I'd really annoyed them and, ignoring the kicking, still followed them, Dad would sort me out when I got home. I would be punched to the ground and kicked in the stomach and the head as I lay there. When I curled up into a ball, that was the signal that I'd given up and Dad would walk off, leaving me without a backwards glance.

Sometimes a kicking in front of the others wasn't enough.

'Yeah,' Dad might say with a sneer in his voice.

'Why don't you have some?' He'd hold a Mars Bar up to his mouth and spit on it, then hold it out to me. 'There you are, Dwarf, have a bite.' For all the squalor we lived in and for all the hunger I carried around with me day and night, I never could feel desperate enough to take a bite anyway.

It was obvious that strangers were the only chance I had left of getting more to eat. But how was I going to do it? I could have pretended to be pathetic and on my last legs – although it wouldn't have needed much acting – but that wasn't my style. Something, some fight, some spirit, survived. I began to develop a cheery, cheeky little chappie way of talking to people, because I discovered that sometimes it made them see past the clothes I was wearing, past the grubbiness and the perpetual smell that hung around me. For the sake of what passed for company, for a bit of attention from other human beings, I had always been willing to talk to anyone at all, postmen, milkmen, dustmen, strangers buying papers at the news-stands, and even the woman in the corner shop. She knew us well because our parents generally had a slate running with her, and we were always being sent round there to get Mum or Dad a packet of fags or tea and milk and sometimes biscuits, and now and then we'd take a chance and get ourselves some sweets or bread on the slate, but that wasn't a risk you could take too often. I probably only did it half a dozen times and I don't think I was ever caught out, which was just as well because it would have meant a brutal beating. Stealing from them, which is what they would have called it, deserved as much punishment as they were physically capable of inflicting on us. They didn't spare any thought for why we needed to steal.

By the age of seven my life had become a matter of staying out of the house as much as possible and about getting through school without the other children or the teachers hurting me too much. But most of all it was about always being on the lookout for an angle, for the main chance, for any way at all of getting a penny here or a sixpence there.

There was, for instance, a man called John who lived in one room in a house across the road from us and who put Mum's bets on for her. I don't know how she got to know him, but he was the only means she had of putting money on the horses, because women didn't go into betting shops in those days, it just wasn't done. She couldn't send us, because although the woman at the corner shop might have been happy to give us cigarettes and sometimes beer for Dad, betting shop staff wouldn't have let a child through the door at any price, and there was no chance Dad would have done it for her. She probably wouldn't have wanted to give him the money anyway, because he'd have only gone down the pub with it. I presume any money she had was from the Family Allowance book.

Mum liked to get the paper on a Saturday morning, look at the racing and decide on her bets. One of us would run round to John with the horses she'd marked up and the money she wanted to put on them. When I started doing this, I also started going down to the corner shop for John to get his week's paraffin for him, for the old stove he had in the corner of his bedsit room. He'd give me sixpence for that, which seemed a fortune. This was fantastic as far as I was concerned, because it felt like money I'd earned, something honestly come by. Sixpence was a lot of money. A hungry child with a bit of money doesn't go looking for a pound of apples. A Wagon Wheel was a good meal for me, and I could have two of them for sixpence. Sometimes, when I was very hungry, I'd decide on a bag of chips with scraps, but mostly it was sweets or sometimes a packet of biscuits so that I could eat half the packet and have some hidden away for later. My favourite place, a safer place, for hiding food was not in the house. Having spent all my short life looking for other people's hidden food there, I knew where most of the hiding places were and I guessed that everyone else did too. Even if I was caught getting out my own food I'd get a beating, so I needed to be more clever. I preferred to find somewhere out at the back of the house, in the mud and rubble of the back garden and, more and more often, in the derelict factory yard and boarded-up houses behind it. There was always the risk that the rats would find my food before I came back, and often I would return and find that there was nothing left of my biscuits or sweets except the wrapper, or that they had been nibbled. I just knocked the nibbled bits off and ate the rest anyway.

For a few years after we moved there was also sometimes treasure to be found at the back of our house. In the triangle between our terrace were scores of Victorian terraced houses that were boarded up, condemned and earmarked for demolition by the council. The local kids, of course, found ways past the sheets of galvanized metal that the council had put in the windows and doors and played in them after school and at weekends. There was even an abandoned pub that still had all its counters and shelves and a big old till that rang when you pressed the keys to open the cash drawer. We played there for hours sometimes. I didn't have any friends, but for a few hours I could sometimes make a loose kind of alliance with other kids who had turned up to play there. It was as close as I could get to a social life. I never tried to make friends. I didn't know how to talk normally to other kids, and my experiences with my family meant that I didn't trust anyone, child or adult.

There were a few houses that we didn't go into because we knew tramps lived in them. They weren't tramps in the old sense, of course, the kind of men who spent their lives walking all round the country. These were men who were homeless and who were usually drinkers, and they were scary, even to kids who had a drunken father. If you made a mistake and went into a house they thought was theirs, they'd come at you yelling and waving sticks and bars and anything they could get their hands on, so we all kept away from those houses.

But many of them were full of stuff that the last people who'd lived there had left behind. To most of the other kids these things were rubbish but to me and even some of my more grown-up brothers they were a treasure trove. There were old bits of carpet, rags really, but we could take them home and put them on the boards beside our mattresses. Sometimes I even found things I could sell for a few pennies, old boxes or chairs missing a leg that the second-hand furniture shop might take, or an old bit of clothing that even I couldn't wear but which the local ragman might give me a penny for. Shoes were the best find of all. I could just about stand being seen in the clothes I had to wear, but going out without shoes was more shame than I could bear. Finding an old pair of shoes, no matter what size they were, was a happy day. Mostly, though, I liked the feeling of finding something that didn't belong to anyone else. It's amazing how much pleasure I could get from 'owning' an old biscuit tin, even if it was only for an afternoon until one of my brothers saw me with it and took it off me. Sometimes they really did want it for themselves. Often they took things off me just because they could.

The old-fashioned milkman who delivered to doorsteps was a godsend to me. Sometimes I would get up very early, maybe five or six in the morning, and sneak out of the house to steal a bottle of milk from a doorstep so that I could drink it and not have to go to school hungry. Once I saw a pot of double cream. I had no idea what it was, but it looked fantastic, like it would really fill my stomach up for a good long while. I had a good look round to make sure I wasn't being watched and swiped it. I found a quiet place and tried to drink it. It was terrible, far too rich for a kid who wasn't used to eating much, and it made me feel so sick that, hungry as I was, I couldn't take more than a couple of gulps of it.

Once I'd got the hang of the idea that money certainly helped to fill some of the gaps in my life, it didn't take long for me to start wanting other things than food. I became possessed by a ferocious desire to be able to do the kinds of things other kids did, things you could only do if you had a bit of pocket money or parents who would take you out and treat you, and one of the things I wanted to do more than anything else was go to the fair. A huge funfair with rides and stalls and candy floss came to town two or three times a year. It was only a ten-minute walk up the road, and when it was there I often used to go and hang around in the crowds, watching other children being taken on the waltzers by their parents or being given threepence to have a go on the rifle range. Sometimes, if I looked hard, I might get lucky and find a sixpence that someone had dropped on the ground, although it was a good idea to be careful about how you picked it up. If one of the fairground lads saw you and it was near their ride, they'd knock you over and get it off you, saying it was theirs.

I had reached the stage where I would steal anything if I thought I could get away with it. I would even steal from my older brothers, though I knew they would give me a beating if they found out. Raymond was working and we all knew he was careful with his money. He had to give some to Mum, but even so he was the only person in the house who always had cash. He also had his own room. It was at the top of the house and there was no other room in the house like it. It had furniture and rugs and even curtains, I think – he'd made quite a nest for himself. He had no trouble hanging on to these things because he was as hard as nails. He had to be, otherwise the rest of us would have run all over him, like we did with the next brother down, Paul, the one everyone called Dunce. Raymond never had a nickname, but we wouldn't have dared use it even if he had. Raymond wasn't a particularly big boy, but he was wiry and strong.

Even so, one day the temptation was too much to resist for me. The fair was in town and I wanted to go more than anything. While he was out I went into his bedroom and found where he'd hidden some cash and took a £10 note. That was a hell of a lot of money. I decided the clever thing to do was to hide it and wait and see whether he noticed, so I hid it right there in his room under a bit of carpet. All those years of hunting for bits of bread the others had hidden were at last paying off, and I thought I was being very cunning. There was still a way out if he noticed the money was missing and all I had to do was be patient.

I went back for it the next day. Then my bad luck caught up with me. Paul, the Dunce, was already in there looking under the carpet and he'd found it. 'That's mine,' I shouted.

I wasn't exactly on solid ground with this argument, but both of us knew that each of us had something on the other. Just being in the room would have been enough to earn either of us a hell of a beating if one of us had decided to tell Raymond. We agreed instead to split the tenner. So far, so good. Paul came with me to the corner shop and we asked the woman there to split it for us.

Paul was just as keen as I was to blow our unaccustomed wealth at the fair and we went off together. We went on every ride, ate candy floss and doughnuts, and, because we felt so flush, when we met a few boys we knew we offered to pay for them to come on some of the rides too. It was our generosity with our brother's money that did for us.

Our luck finally ran out when one of these boys was seen by someone who knew his family. When his parents heard about it, they demanded to know where he'd got the money, more concerned about their boy's honesty than ours ever were. Most of the kids round that way would only have had enough pocket money for one or maybe two rides. Their dads wouldn't have been earning much more than eight pounds a week. A kid of eight with a fiver was likely to be a kid who was a thief. That's how it would have been seen in those days. The boy told his parents that it was the Roche boys who had been flashing the cash, and his mother came round to our house to tell Mum that two of her boys had been at the fair with more money than they could have come by honestly.

There was hell to pay. I blamed Paul, he blamed me. Paul got his beating from Mum upstairs and he told her the whole story, and then I got mine, fists, feet, the lot, in the kitchen and, as ever, back and back until I was curled up in a corner of the basement room, curled among the stinking rubbish down there while she kicked and kicked me.

'You keep your thieving little hands off what isn't yours,' she screamed at me over and over again. Then, pausing for breath, something else occurred to her. 'And if you have so much as a fart in your pocket, you selfish little shit, it doesn't belong to you. You give it to the family. You think you can go out and have a fine old time while the rest of us sit here with nothing? Laughing at us, were you? I'll give you something to fucking laugh about.'

This was one beating Dad didn't get involved in. He didn't need to. It was the morning after our night out and he hadn't yet been drinking, so he was in that cold, calculating mood he often took on when he was sober, his skin a pasty grey instead of its usual dull red. He looked at me with a vicious pleasure. 'You'll wait until the boy gets back,' he said, meaning Raymond, who was out at work and still didn't know about his ten pounds.

Strangely, although Paul had spilt the beans about where the money had come from, Raymond did not come after us. I was expecting him to. So was Dad, obviously, and I can't believe he wasn't told, but he didn't ever mention it. For a while after this Paul and I hung about together a bit, even though he was so much older than I was. I suppose I was a bit braver and brighter than he was, and being the youngest I was probably the only one he could hope to keep up with. Raymond and Terence, the brothers nearest to him in age, gave him a hard time and didn't want much to do with him. Like me he was generally left to hang about on his own and so for a while he attached himself to me. He came with me one day when I was exploring one of the derelict houses behind our house, and under the roof of one porch we found a wasps' nest. It was a knobbly brown lump stuck to the wall, a bit like a brain made out of mud, and I didn't know exactly what it was, but I did know that it didn't look good. There were hundreds of wasps buzzing round it. There was just a moment when neither of us moved, but I knew straight away what was going to happen because Paul was always likely to do something a bit mad. Even as I shouted: 'Don't touch it. Bad. Wasps,' I felt the panic rising and I turned to get out of there fast.

I heard him say: 'I ain't afraid of that,' and I glanced over my shoulder to see him going for it with his fists. Although Paul was five or six years older, I knew at that moment that I was the most sensible of the two of us by a long way. That was a feeling I had about all my brothers in one way or another over the years, but particularly when I was with Paul, because he just didn't seem to have any sense of self-preservation.

He ran one way, towards the nest, punching and batting it like an absolute moron, and I ran the other way. Of course, the wasps swarmed out and attacked him and I heard him running down the street behind me, screaming like a maniac. I was gone like greased lightning.

Paul was the brother who had a pee out of the bedroom window one day when Harry the lodger happened to be at the front door. Harry came inside saying to my mother that it was raining. She looked out of the door, past him, a bit puzzled and said: 'It's not raining, what makes you think that?' Then she saw the sprinkling of wet on the path in front of the door and guessed. I suppose he must have done it before, because she was up the stairs to the bedroom like the wind with her Sally in her hand. I winced, hearing her feet go up the stairs as fast as if she was still a teenager, waiting for the screams and wails that were only seconds away. When it began I did what I always did. I put my hands in my pockets and left by the back door to get away from the sound, and didn't come back for hours.

Still, even though Paul was a bit more out to lunch than the rest of us, he was useful to me because I sometimes found I could interest him in some of my madder schemes to get money.

I heard some boys talking on the street one day about a milk depot where you could help the milkmen load up their floats with bottles before they went out on their early-morning rounds and get a fiver for doing it. It seemed to be somewhere round the Elephant and Castle, which was quite a distance from our house. I was accustomed to walking about at all hours of the night but even for me this seemed quite a long way off my patch and a bit unnerving, so I persuaded Paul to come with me. I woke him up about three in the morning and we climbed out of the kitchen window into the back garden and out into the street.

We walked all the way to the Elephant and Castle, a young teenager and a primary school kid who was small for his age, not a coat between us and both of us wearing damp smelly trousers because we were the bed-wetters. We were smart enough to keep to the backstreets, but even at that hour of the morning someone must have seen us from one of the houses we passed, maybe a night-shift worker just home or an early-morning worker getting ready to go out. We must have looked like two

Victorian kids on their way to sweep chimneys. Of course, we never found this wonderful place where they handed out fivers to starving kids willing to stack a few crates. We walked round the whole area for a couple of hours and then set off back home when it was getting light. A wild goose chase, Paul called it, with a lot of f-ing and blinding thrown in to hammer his point home. He was well pissed off, but at least he didn't give me a slap for it. I think he was too tired.

I always wanted to get what I needed honestly if I could. I don't know that I was any more honest than anyone else in the family, but my favourite way of coping with my life was to try to be unnoticed, to make myself invisible. I found that stealing made me feel as if the whole world was watching me and I didn't like it. Nothing frightened the pants off me more than the thought of being caught and hauled in front of authority to explain myself, whether it was to my parents, teachers or the police. It wasn't them I was afraid of, but what came after, when the authorities were gone and the front door closed. Dad or Mum walking off towards the back of the house, towards the steps that led down to the basement room, barking those words that we all dreaded.

'Get down here. Now. I mean fucking now.'

So I developed another technique for getting stuff, which I liked to think of as 'befriending'. I was discovering that, with my new cheeky-chappie hat on, I could sometimes make people forget about my clothes and the smell and the generally dirty look of me, and get them laughing and thinking that maybe they liked me. This was how I got to know a girl who lived a few streets away and who was about thirteen or fourteen years old.

She was pretty – at the grand old age of eight I thought she was a goddess – a skinny girl with shiny brown hair that was usually tied back in a ponytail, and she was nice to me, even though to my eyes she seemed impossibly clean and well-dressed. She would let me talk to her as she walked home, all sorts of rubbish about anything I could think of to natter on about. Eventually, one day she invited me into her house and took me upstairs to her room. She had an ulterior motive, I discovered. She had a record player in her bedroom which had a soft green, fake-leather clip-down lid, and next to it was her collection of Donny Osmond and David Cassidy records. She would play them to me, one after the other, while she danced around the room like she was at a disco. She wanted an audience, and anyone would do.

'Did you like that one?' she would ask.

'Yeah, that was a great record,' I'd say.

She'd put another one on.

'Did you like that?'

'Yeah, that was terrific.'

'Let's go and get a piece of cake.'

'Yes, please.'

So we'd go down to the kitchen and she'd help herself to cake. The kitchen was clean, all the tops were shiny, and it had an electric kettle that you could see your face in. There was food in all the cupboards. When she opened a cupboard door to get out the cake, it looked to me like they had a whole supermarket in there, boxes and tins and packets of every kind of food I could think of, beans and tomatoes and peas and – an unimaginable luxury – sausages in tins. I thought it was like something out of a magazine. She was allowed to help herself to whatever she wanted, even if her mother was still out at work. Even if she'd stood there for a fortnight and eaten, and that was what I wanted to do, there would still be plenty left. The idea of more food in one house than the people in it could eat in half an hour made me feel dizzy, unreal.

We'd go back upstairs with our cake and she'd play some more records.

'What did you think of that?'

'Oh, that was a great song. Can I have another piece of cake?'

I would stay as long as I possibly could, and sometimes I'd even get to stay for tea. I'd stay until her mother got fed up with me.

'Tell that boy to go home,' she'd finally say at nine o'clock at night.

It was nice while it lasted, but she naturally wanted to hang about with kids of her own age and she started to get a bit embarrassed about this dirty little kid who was always hanging about, waiting for her to come home, and I'd been her audience long enough. She dropped me and I drifted off in search of someone else who might be willing to take me on.

A little while later I made a friend of a lad called Bernie. He wasn't at my school, but his gran, also an Irish lady, knew my mum. He was an only child who lived with his mum. Perhaps because he wasn't from my neighbourhood or school, he didn't feel the need to give me a wide berth like the other kids did. We got on okay and one day he asked if I wanted to come to the pictures with him. This was a more normal friendship, because he was my age. If he noticed how I was dressed and how dirty and smelly I was, he didn't mention it. He was one of only two boys I was able to call my friend. He would even call round to our house for me, although I never let him in. I'd just walk straight out of the door and set off with him wherever we were planning to go.

We got into the habit of going to the pictures on a Saturday morning at the old cinema in Lambeth. Obviously I came up with some dodge or other to get the money for my ticket, but he never knew that. It did amaze him, however, that I never had to ask my mother or father if it was okay if I went out. He'd suggest going to the pictures and I'd just say: 'Okay' if I had the money, and off we'd go.

He started to ask his mother if I could come round to his house on the Friday night before we went to the pictures, and then to ask her if I could stay the night.

'Just tell your mum that you were there when I asked my mum if it was okay,' I said to him.

'What will happen if you don't come back and she doesn't know where you are?' he asked.

'Nothing. She won't notice. Honest.' And, of course, no-one ever did notice. He accepted it after I'd stayed at his place a couple of times and it became quite a regular thing.

He knew our house wasn't exactly a palace, but he

never knew quite how bad it was. So he also didn't know just how good it was for me if I could get an invitation to stay over. There was a spare bed on the other side of the room from him and it was so good to sleep in it, a whole bed to myself and it had sheets and blankets. By this time I was coping a bit better with clothes, getting pants and trousers from second-hand shops and jumble sales when I could and generally managing to hang on to them, but I was still wetting the bed now and again. I'd lie there after everyone had gone to sleep thinking hard about whether I wanted a wee or not, and I'd get up to go to the toilet every half-hour until I finally dropped off.

What really got to me more than that when I was staying there was when we'd just got into bed and Bernie's mum would come in to tuck him in and kiss him goodnight. I didn't know how to deal with it.

Bernie would always say to her: 'Will you kiss Peter goodnight as well, Mum?'

He didn't really know what was going on in my life, but he knew that I wasn't having a great time at home and I think he just wanted to share a bit of what he had. It was funny, really, because his dad was serving a sentence in Brixton Prison just down the road, so Bernie couldn't have been having such a great time himself and his mum couldn't have been that well off, but his house was always clean and his mum was lovely.

Even so, when Bernie told her to give me a kiss I'd find myself thinking: 'Oh, dear, no, please, no. This isn't normal behaviour.' I'd clutch the blankets to me as tight as I could as she came across the room, praying that she wouldn't try to give me a cuddle. Physical contact of any kind was unbearable to me. The only kind I'd ever had was violent, and physical kindness was something I didn't understand and didn't want. It made me feel panicky. But it was a small price to pay for the bed and for the great cooked breakfast that was on the table on Saturday mornings, with a bowl of cereal to start off with and then a fried egg and sometimes a bit of bacon with fried bread.

One Friday night Bernie told me his dad was getting out of prison the next day and, sure enough, at about half past eight in the morning his dad walked in. It was the first time I'd ever seen him and I don't think he took too kindly to Bernie having a friend who looked like me. I think Bernie guessed what his dad's reaction would be and had made a point of letting me have one last night in the spare bed. We stayed friends for a while longer, until my family moved out of the area, but I didn't stay at his house again after that.

9. The Refuge

The light was on in the kitchen, which was a bit strange. I wasn't sure whether to climb in through the window as I'd been planning to do, or whether to spend another night outside in my secret den. But it was a bitterly cold night and I decided that for the sake of a few hours in the bedroom before school it might be worth whatever might happen to me in the thirty minutes after I got into the house. It wasn't that much warmer in there, but at least I would be out of the freezing wind.

As I clambered through the kitchen window, I heard footsteps coming down to our basement kitchen from the ground floor. I was relieved to see my sister Alison appear in the doorway. She was in her early teens and quite pretty, with masses of curly dark hair that she tried hard to keep clean and brushed so that she'd look reasonable at school. Although she was never kind to me, she left me alone most of the time, and even when she lost her temper she was never as brutal as my brothers were.

Still, I was on my guard. There weren't usually people up and about in the house at this time of the night. I knew, because I often was, coming and going as I wanted to through the kitchen window. The back door was usually bolted at night but the window didn't lock.

'Where the hell have you been?' Alison hissed.

'What's it to you?'

'They're out looking for you, you stupid – get upstairs and pretend to be asleep before they come back.'

I was surprised, and that was putting it mildly. I had roamed all over London for years, and no-one had ever looked for me. But I knew better than to waste time asking questions about this sudden concern for where I was and what I was doing. I shot upstairs and curled up on one of the mattresses next to my brothers. Mum left me alone that night, maybe because she was too tired and just wanted her bed, but I was woken up in the morning by one of the worst kickings she had ever given me. She just walked in and started attacking me as I lay there, asleep and defenceless.

'I was out all fucking night walking the streets, looking for you, you little bastard. The day you were born was the worst fucking day of my life. You'll never do that to me again, I'll kick your fucking brains out first . . .'

She was so beside herself with rage that, for once, she hadn't got me backed into a corner. I had enough wit to work it so that I crawled and scrambled away from her feet while getting my back towards the door. Eventually there was just enough of a pause in the kicking for me to get to my feet and literally leap down the two flights of stairs to the ground floor and get out of the front door. I could still hear her screams at the end of the terrace as I turned the corner, running like an Alsatian was after me, even though I knew she'd never be bothered to follow me that far. As usual, the only solution was to run away and stay away, only returning when it seemed likely that someone else had become the focus of her temper, even if that took days.

Alison was right. I had been stupid. Coming back at two in the morning was nothing. By this time I often didn't come back into the house for days on end and no-one ever asked me where I'd been. I'm not sure whether anyone even noticed. Our parents hardly tucked us up at night or checked on us before they went to bed. The house could have been completely empty of boys at midnight and I doubt whether they would have given it a moment's thought. The mistake I had made was the same one I had made when I was four and ended up at the police station. I had gone wandering the streets of London, mostly up at the West End, where the bright lights stayed on every night until the early hours and the streets were always full of people, but I had taken a boy with me who had parents who cared. He wasn't a friend, because I had none. He was just a kid that I'd met out in the dump yard at the back of the house and who had tagged along when I suggested we could go into the centre of the city for a couple of hours. Like John-John's parents, his parents had noticed when their son hadn't come home and they had gone out looking for him. They'd been told he'd been seen with me and had come round to our house. Our mother had felt obliged to go out looking with them. It was the only time I can recall after the day at the police station when anyone ever noticed I was missing.

Although I officially had a home, I was really a street kid. I had only just moved out of the babies' playground, as we called it, and into the youngest class in the junior school. There were still kids in my class who were brought to school and picked up by their parents, and I was leaving school and going straight to my den.

This den had been some years in the making. I'd started it within a few months of us moving without any idea of how useful it would become as a second home. What made it possible was the waste land behind our house, which was boarded off from the streets around it on all sides, where there had once been some kind of factory. Before the whole area and all the houses behind it had been condemned by the council, just before we moved in, it had been used as a garage mechanic's business and was still strewn with old bits of cars and drums of filthy black oil, but it was empty and no-one was working there when I first climbed over our back wall to have a look around it. People from the surrounding houses and flats had begun to use it as a dump yard, throwing mattresses and broken furniture over the walls, and there were loads of old wrecked cars, just shells with seats in, standing about the place.

It was a no man's land, a place no-one cared about and where adults never went. So, of course, it became a play area for the local kids. And it became my one and only refuge.

It was interesting because you could sit in the cars or climb on them and lie on their warm roofs when the sun was shining, or explore the old factory buildings, fiddle with the rusting bits of machinery that had been left there, even get some wood together from the abandoned houses behind it and light fires, and no-one ever came to see what you were doing. To me it was a place, the one place, where I could relax. I loved it.

The point was that it didn't just give me a temporary bolt-hole. When something really, really bad happened in the house, I could exist out there for many days.

I did it after stealing Raymond's ten-pound note, and after the worst thing I ever did – setting fire to the house. One day Laurence called me down into the basement room so that he could show me how to smoke. The house was empty, and if the room was a good place for Mum and Dad to do the dirty work that they wanted no-one else to know about, it was good enough for our secret goings-on too.

Strewn all around it were the piles of rags and mattresses that had become too filthy and flea-ridden even for us. Laurence lit the fag he'd stolen from Mum's packet, took a drag, and then handed it to me so that I could have a go. Like any small child trying his first cigarette, I thought it was terrible and I threw it down on the ground. Laurence can't have been that bothered either, because he didn't try to pick it up and carry on smoking it. We both lost interest and went off to do something else.

About an hour later I heard screaming from downstairs.

'What in God's name?' Mum's screech of fear and alarm cut through the house. Clouds of thick smoke were billowing up from the basement and I could hear my mother swearing and screaming as she tried to beat out the flames. There were a few of us in the house at the time and we all ran down to see what was going on. We yelled, cheering her on as she dealt with the burning rags as if one of us was inside them. That fire wouldn't have dared burn a moment longer, if it knew what was good for it. Mum, panting and ready for another fight, turned round to look at us.

'Which of you bastards did this?' she yelled.

I looked at her and she looked straight back at me, and she knew. I was off. I legged it and I didn't dare attempt to get round the treacherous bend in the stairs to the back door in case one of my brothers decided to get hold of my shirt and deliver me to her. I went straight out through the open kitchen window like a high-jumper, across the back garden and over the wall into the dump yard. I slept there that night and for several nights afterwards. There was no way I was going back in that house, not for a while anyway.

After a while I started getting together all sorts of bits and pieces to make my den more of a home. At first it was just a place to play, a space between a car and a mattress that was already there when I first arrived, and somewhere to hang around after school or at weekends, and most importantly the place to go when Dad came in drunk. But then I began to take the idea of a den more seriously. I got hold of sheets of galvanized metal that had been ripped off the condemned houses by other kids and dumped in the yard, and made walls and a roof, and stuffed rags and cardboard into the gaps to keep the wind out. Old bits of carpet made a half-decent floor. With an old kitchen knife and a couple of spanners I'd found lying around the old workshops I managed to get one of the seats out of the wrecked cars to put in it. At first the seat was upright, like an armchair. Later I broke the hinge so that I could lay the back of it flat on the ground and make a kind of bed. It wasn't bad. It wasn't as bad as my bed in the house. Other kids used to come into the yard, of course, but they would only stay for a few hours at most and they always went home for their tea. It began to feel like my own private world, a place I had all to myself, where I could get the peace that I wanted so badly.

I could escape from home in this way, but there was no escape from school. Whatever else happened, no matter how many nights I didn't come home, I knew that I had to go to school to make sure that the truancy man didn't come to our house. When I spent the night in the yard I found that, even if I'd had a good night's sleep, it was hard to stay asleep for long after the sun came up, so waking in time before school started wasn't a problem. That was when the cold really seemed to get to me.

But timing it right was important. I didn't want to be hanging about in the streets leading up to school too long, because I had the bullies to think about as well. I'd get up, wander about my yard for a bit, and then, when I felt it was getting near school-time, I'd stand at the galvanized metal fence covered in fly posters that separated the yard from the road at the end of our terrace. I'd watch carefully, dodging behind the fence when necessary. I didn't want to be seen by anyone I knew. I didn't want my secret to be discovered.

Fortunately the most direct way to school from our house was through the flats opposite the dump yard, so, keeping a careful lookout for kids, walking that way guaranteed that I wouldn't be late. Sometimes, if I wanted to sneak back into the house to use the toilet or try to clean up a bit before school, I'd call to someone passing by and ask the time. In the summer this could often be as early as half past five or six o'clock. There were usually quite a few people in the area setting off for work at that time in the morning, but goodness knows what they thought of an infant school kid popping up from behind a dump-yard wall at dawn. It had to be done, though, because I wanted to be sure of being able to get in and out of the house before anyone else was up and about. On the whole our parents left us alone in the mornings, because they were usually still in bed and it wasn't as if they made sure we had breakfast, but I had to make sure I didn't wake them and I had to watch out for the brothers.

At the other end of the yard was another wall, with a boarded-up gateway in it, and from there I could look out onto the street. Our terrace was split in the middle by this small dead-end street. Behind our terrace was the dump yard. Behind that, on the other side of the street, was a lorry park. This added a bit of extra interest to the yard for me, because when I got bored with whatever I'd found to do there, I could sit up on the wall and watch the lorries come and go at all hours of the day and night. I could hardly read, but I did manage to make out the names of two of the lorry companies that were painted on the cabs and the sides of the trailers, Valley Carriers and Jerome Transport.

It wasn't a loading depot, just a safe lock-up yard where the drivers could park their lorries at night. It was exciting, particularly in the early hours of the cold morning when I couldn't get to sleep in my den, to sit there and watch the drivers walking down the street at four and five in the morning, carrying their bags with flasks of tea and sandwiches for the day, and knocking up the nightwatchman to let them in. Then they'd climb into their cabs, fire up the big roaring diesel engines and switch the headlights on, before pulling out of the gates to head off who knew where. Most of them were probably going no further than Streatham, but I liked to think of them driving out of London and just keeping on going until they got as far away as possible from Lambeth. If it had been me, I would never have stopped.

It was only a lorry park, just like a hundred others dotted around various run-down parts of London at that time, yet it was the place where I met the only two adults I learned to trust when I was a child.

Vincent had a limp. That, and the fact that he was black, made him a target for the rude, vile little kids who lived all round the area. Sometimes, as he shuffled along the road towards his nightwatchman's hut in the lorry park, they would run along behind him throwing stones at his bad leg. They always called him names, usually nasty and pathetic racist insults. I have to confess that for a while I did my fair share of name-calling from my wall on the other side of the road. Eventually, though, I got curious about this old black bloke who never seemed to lose his temper or his dignity when he was being tormented.

He never got confrontational with us kids. The most aggressive thing I ever saw him do was to stand still, turn round and look at the boys who had thrown a stone at him and hit him in the back. He opened his arms and raised his hands, almost as if he was shrugging. All he said was: 'Look, there's no need to do this.' I'd never seen an adult be so reasonable and tolerant.

At night, when there was no-one about and I could see the light on in his little cabin, I started to climb down from my wall, cross the street and climb over his wall. The gates were always locked unless there was a lorry going in or out. I used to sneak up to the window of his hut and try to look in. Sometimes he'd leave the door open and from inside I could hear a radio playing. It wasn't playing music; it was just people talking all the time in posh voices. It sounded boring and I couldn't understand why anyone would want to listen to it.

The first time he caught me there he was just as calm as he was with the kids who threw stones, but he was cautious, and who could blame him? I must have looked like a kid who was up to no good. I immediately swung into my cheeky, cheery little-kid routine. Sometimes it worked, sometimes it didn't, but I had learned that it could be a good way of stopping a grown-up from shouting at me, except of course for any of the grown-ups in my own family. I don't think Vince would ever have shouted at anyone under any circumstances, but he did keep me at arm's length for a long time. That was fine by me. I was desperate enough to keep going either until he gave me something I wouldn't have been able to get otherwise, or until he turned nasty. For the moment, he hadn't shouted at me when he first found me in his yard, and that was encouragement enough. I started hopping over the wall and going to the door of his cabin several nights a week. He was another human being awake at all hours of the night, like me, and although I was sure that grown-ups weren't to be trusted, at home or school, I was happy enough to stand at his door asking a whole load of stupid questions, because I knew he wasn't going to give me an earful. I was getting a different, unusual feeling about this man. It wasn't just about his company, any food I might be able to persuade him to give me or the warmth of his shed any more. I was slowly learning to trust him. I told him my name and demanded to know what his was. He was a polite man, so he told me, and after that it was 'Hey, Vincent,' every time I saw him. He told me often that I should go home, and always I said that it was okay, no-one was looking for me. I never went into any detail about it, but it must have become obvious to him that it was true that no-one was ever worried about where I was. I kept pestering him to let me come in his hut. He must have thought it just wasn't right to encourage such a young child to be with him alone at night, but I thought it was that attitude I'd come across in the strangers on the street I tried to beg from, when they told me to get lost and pushed me aside like they were batting away a fly that was buzzing round them.

Still, until Vincent told me in no uncertain terms to go away, I wasn't going to stop trying. I'd had to grow a very thick skin.

Bit by bit, over the months, he let me come in now and again and have a look around and maybe even sit down for five minutes and get warm before he told me to get myself back home. Eventually he got used to me appearing out of the night, and when the nights were very cold he began to let me sit with him for a couple of hours. He'd give me coffee from his flask and share his sandwich with me. I think he probably began to bring extra sandwiches just in case I turned up, because after a while there always seemed to be plenty of food in his bag, enough for me to feel that I wasn't leaving him hungry.

He never asked any personal questions about my family. He was very tactful. He never asked me why I was wandering around in the winter nights without a coat, or mentioned the holes in my shoes or the fact that I didn't seem to have any socks.

Now and again he would still say: 'You should be at home, Peter.'

My answer was always: 'I like it here, Vincent, this is all right.' I never told him why home wasn't all right, and he never asked. I was grateful for that. I didn't want to talk about what happened at home. I felt ashamed about it, it felt like my own fault, and when I was out of the house I just wanted to forget about it.

At various points through the night he would have to go out and unlock the gates and I'd jump up and offer to do it for him. I wanted to help out a bit, to thank him for the food and hot drinks, and for his company and his kindness to me. Some nights he would make a bit of a bed for me on the floor of the hut, probably because there were some nights when I really did look in bad need of a good sleep.

We didn't talk a lot. I'd sit there in the warm with him and the two of us would listen to his radio. I had discovered that the station with the posh people talking that he liked so much was called Radio 4, and late at night it would turn into the World Service.

'The BBC is a wonderful thing, Peter,' he would say. 'You can learn all sorts of interesting things about the world by listening to the BBC.'

He was a good, good man. And because he was a good man, I met another one just like him.

Johnny Kingman, one of the drivers, got on well with Vincent. He was one of the regulars at the yard who drove a Jerome Transport lorry, often coming in late at night after finishing his run and coming back to go out again early the next morning. He was a stocky man, not very tall but very strong and fit-looking. I discovered later that he came from a well-known south London family and quite a few of them had been successful in the boxing ring. I was probably about eight years old by the time I found the nerve to speak to him myself. I was running out to the gates every time a lorry came in by now, saying to Vincent: 'I'll do it.'

He was very patient. He never shouted at me to get out of the way. All he ever said was: 'Okay, but you're not doing it on your own. I'm coming with you.'

I'd stand there at the back of the lorries, doing all the guiding-in signals that I'd seen Vincent doing. The drivers were watching Vincent, of course, but it made me feel grown-up and responsible. I had seen Johnny coming in and out of the yard a lot and I decided that I liked the look of him. Since he got on so well with Vincent, I thought there was a chance I might be able to work my charms on him too.

Eventually, one night after he'd parked his lorry, I went up to him as he was getting down from his cab and asked if I could come out with him sometime.

'Can I come out in the lorry with you? Go on, let us come out with you.'

'No, son, you're too young.'

This went on for a while until he began to say: 'I'll have to speak to your parents first.'

That I couldn't risk, but at least I knew I was wearing him down.

'You don't need to ask my parents. I'll ask them. It'll be all right.'

Finally came the night when he looked at me hard. He thought for a moment. He gave in.

'Be at the top of the road at six tomorrow morning. I'll have to go if you're not there.'

'I'll be there, I'll be there,' I said, hopping about the yard like I'd won the pools.

I knew that he was banking on me not being able to get up that early. He didn't know that this was probably the most exciting thing that had ever happened to me. He didn't know that I had the kind of bed that I was glad to get out of. It was the middle of a week of school holidays in February, otherwise I wouldn't have risked missing school even for an adventure like this, and I'm sure he wouldn't have offered to take me.

Vincent sent me home that night, telling me that I couldn't sit up with him if I wanted to be out there in time to meet Johnny. I went back to the bedroom and I was so excited I couldn't sleep. At the time, I had been kicked off the mattress by my brothers because of my bed-wetting, so I lay down on the floorboards. I was quite good at getting to sleep even there, but on this night I was terrified I wouldn't wake up. This was a chance I couldn't miss. I must have fallen asleep, though, because the next thing I knew was that I'd wet myself and I was soaked right through. It must have been about five o'clock, still very dark outside, and I felt my way down to the basement in the hope of finding some other clothes that I could wear. There was nothing there, of course. I went back up to the bedroom hoping to find a pair of trousers that one of my brothers had taken off before going to sleep. As luck would have it, they'd all kept their trousers on to make sure no-one could swipe them.

Then I had a bright idea. I would walk round the streets for the next hour or so, walk very fast, and maybe by the time Johnny arrived I'd have dried out. That was what I did, with a cold, early-morning wind whipping round my wet clothes and making my legs sore, but I did manage to get myself to the stage where I was more damp than wet. I saw Johnny's lorry up ahead, waiting at the junction, and I suddenly remembered that, although I wasn't wet through, I was probably very smelly. 'He'll smell it,' I thought. I was frightened. I thought that as soon as I got in the cab he would tell me to get out.

There is no way that he didn't notice how bad I smelled that morning. Yet he never said a word, not once during the whole day, and it must have been really bad in that small, warm cab. So I spent the whole day sitting in the passenger seat of his cab, watching the world go by as he collected his load for the day, drove out of London and up a motorway to wherever it had to go, and then drove us back again.

Shortly after he'd loaded the lorry he said it was time to stop for breakfast. He found a roadside café that he obviously knew well and parked up. He started to get out and as casually as I could I said: 'I'll wait here for you. I won't touch anything.'

'You'll come in with me. Get out.'

Inside, the place was busy with lorry drivers like him all taking their first break of the day, and he found an empty table and sat me down.

'What are you having?' he asked.

'I'm all right.'

'You're having some breakfast with me.'

'Yeah, okay then.'

He came back with two huge plates, both with an enormous working man's breakfast on them. I had no trouble eating the lot. It was heaven. At lunchtime he shared his flask and sandwiches with me. On the home run, he even stopped off for dinner and it was the same routine, me pretending that I didn't need to eat and him having none of it. Two huge meals in one day. It was amazing. I have no idea where we went that day, or any of the other many days when he took me out with him after that first time. My understanding of the geography of England was hazy to say the least. I didn't even understand that there were other countries in the world. Where we were didn't matter to me because everything about being out with Johnny was fantastic.

A whole day would go by without one moment of hunger. We were always moving and I loved that feeling of being on my way somewhere, getting out of London, getting a long way from everything. I had never even been to a park with a grown-up, let alone on a holiday. These days with Johnny were like the holidays I never had. I don't believe any child was ever more happy about going to the seaside than I was when I knew I had a day in his cab to look forward to.

I liked all these things about our trips together, but what I liked best was the way Johnny made me feel about myself. I never felt bad or ashamed when I was with him. I don't think I can ever have looked like a normal kid any time I went out with him, but he never made any mention of how dirty I looked or what I was wearing. He treated me with respect.

One evening during the summer holidays, when I was going out with him almost every day, he dropped me off at the top of a street near our house. The only gaffe he ever made in all the time I knew him was when he called after me as I walked back home.

'We might be going to the Isle of Wight tomorrow,

and if we do, we'll have to stop over. So make sure you bring your pyjamas,' he said.

Pyjamas. He must have known. I bet he kicked himself all the way home. I knew what pyjamas were but I'd never had any. Even Dad slept in his underwear. I just thought it was a really odd idea, but I knew him well enough by now to know that he wouldn't say anything if I turned up without any pyjamas. We didn't go to the Isle of Wight that next day and never did do a run where we had to sleep the night on the road. Maybe he decided that it would be too hard for us both to ignore my embarrassment if I wet myself in my sleep or had to admit that I didn't own a pair of pyjamas.

There was nothing bad about that man. Nothing at all. At the end of a week when I'd spent every day with him, he would give me 50p, sometimes even a pound, and tell me that was my wage for helping him out, although he must have spent that much and more already on feeding me. Sometimes he'd tell me to meet him very early in the morning at his house before we went off on a run, and when I got there his wife would have a cooked breakfast waiting for me.

He had a son who was a few years younger than me, a really nice kid, and it was obvious that his mum and dad thought the world of him. I didn't feel jealous of him, funnily enough. By this time I just accepted that this was what other kids had, not me. Years later, I heard that Johnny's son had become a high-ranking officer in the Royal Navy, and I thought that was some achievement, growing up in the area where we did with a lorry driver for a dad, and then making that kind of career for himself. A lot of it must have been down to his parents, kind, decent people who brought him up well, never made him feel useless and always encouraged him. I know that's how Johnny treated me, and I bet he was a fantastic dad.

Those years, between the ages of eight and ten, when I had Vincent and Johnny on my side, were a golden time in my childhood. Just for a short time there were, thanks to them, enough good times to make me forget the bad stuff. Johnny and Vincent gave me their bit of goodness for no reason except that they were good people. If I hadn't met them, I would never have known that there were people out there who could be nice to you even when there was nothing in it for them.

10. Friendship

Vincent and Johnny were good for me, without a doubt, but there was only so much they could do and their presence in my life gave me no more than short moments of relief from the cruelty that always threatened whenever I was in the house, and from the hunger that went with me everywhere. I was lonely too, because even with all those children in our house there was no friendship there and none of my classmates would accept me. In fact, I felt hated by everyone.

Again it was my dump-yard refuge, the one place where good things happened, that filled the gap. It had helped me find Vincent and Johnny and now I found there, for a while at least, the kind of friendship that most children take for granted in their early childhood.

Just outside my shanty town den I had made myself a fireplace out of a circle of old bricks, and I was poking at a few bits of wood and rubbish in it one day, trying to get a fire going, when a head popped up over the Vassal Street side of the dump-yard wall.

The head had loads of tight, dark, messy curls plastered around a small, sharp-looking face. This boy had a look that I recognized straight away, a pinched look about his mouth and dark circles round his eyes, and although he had quite dark skin, like the Italian priests we sometimes saw at church, his face was almost grey. I knew right off that he was hungry a lot of the time, like me and my brothers and sisters were.

But two or three years of bullying at school had battered into me the rules about how to deal with other kids, especially any kid you'd never seen before. Don't look them in the eye, don't ask any questions and, if at all possible, pretend that they aren't even there.

'All right?' he said. I was to find out later that this was always his first greeting to everyone, friend or enemy or stranger. I said nothing.

'You ain't doing that right.'

After my first swift glance up to see who was looking over my wall, I'd gone back to staring at my fire, poking it with a stick. I ignored him.

'That's not how to light fire.'

I ignored him again.

'You don't do it like that. I can make a better fire than that.'

Even though I didn't look up, I was aware that he was now climbing down into the yard. I knew that if I turned and walked off, I'd be giving up my territory to him. This place was my private slice of peace and I decided I wasn't going to give it up without a fight, so I carried on poking my fire and ignoring him, but silently I was getting myself ready for a confrontation. He sauntered across the yard and came up to the fire with his hands in his pockets. It seemed that he didn't want to fight after all and that at least was a relief, but I was still uncomfortable and anxious. We both stood there for quite a while on either side of the fire, watching it slowly go out. We didn't look at each other. I could get a good look at his legs, though, and I could see that he had an old pair of wellingtons on his feet and a stripy pair of trousers tucked into them.

'Hold on,' he said when the last flame flickered and died. He went scrambling off over the rubble and rubbish in the yard and a few minutes later came back with some bits of rag and a few sticks of wood.

'You got matches?'

I looked straight at him for the first time since he'd looked over the wall. He might be all right, I thought to myself, so I took the box from my pocket and handed it over. He built a fantastic fire while I weighed him up. I realized that the stripy trousers were pyjama bottoms. I could see the cord hanging down from under his jumper. He had nothing on under his jumper. I guessed he didn't have any socks and that there was no underwear under the pyjama bottoms. This, I thought, is a kid like me. It turned out to be absolutely true. Dave was the only boy I ever met who had a life like mine.

'This is how you get a fire going properly,' he said, but it was friendly information he was offering, not a put-down or a challenge. 'Now watch this,' he said, and he chucked a small piece of something that looked a bit like cardboard onto the flames. Whoosh, bang! The thing cracked and popped for what seemed like ages, like he'd thrown a jumping jack on the fire. I was impressed. 'That's alibasters,' he said confidentially. 'It pops like hell if you get a really good fire going. There's loads of it in the houses round here.'

There was, and in the time we knew each other we banged and popped a hell of a lot of it, just for the fun of it. (A long, long time later I discovered that most people call it asbestos.) Dave and I clicked right away, even during that first wary meeting over the fire. I suppose it helped that even before we knew anything about each other, we could see that neither of us came from homes where anyone cared what we looked like or how we felt. For once this was something neither of us had to apologize for. We both knew the score. That made it easier for us to forget all that stuff and decide that we were just two people who liked each other, never mind what was happening to us anywhere else in our lives. It was the first time this had ever happened to me. It wasn't like the befriending I did, when I was well aware that the other person was only putting up with me and wasn't really interested in having me around. Dave and I liked each other's company, and it was a good, comfortable feeling that I couldn't remember ever having had before. At long last I had a proper friend. In his own way he was a nice kid. He didn't want to do anyone any harm or get involved in the really bad kind of stealing, like trying to get into other people's houses and taking their stuff. But he did want to have a good time if he could, and when it came to having fun he was the most inventive and resourceful person I had ever met, even if he was a bit crazy with it. Dave taught me a lot, and one of his most wonderful revelations was that Marks and Spencer stocked a certain kind of metal button that worked a treat in the London Underground's ticket machines. We were the haberdashery shoplifters of Lambeth. The stock-takers and store detectives there must have been mystified.

The first time Dave ever took me into Marks and Spencer to get them, I thought he was mad. Why would anyone risk getting caught stealing from a shop for the sake of half a dozen cards with five big lead-coloured raincoat buttons stitched onto them?

But I was fascinated by him. He was different from me because he swaggered about the place with his hands in his pyjama bottom pockets, saying a loud 'All right?' to anyone he passed. My way of coping with knowing that I didn't look right was to ignore everyone and pretend that I was invisible. His was the opposite, to make sure everyone knew he was there, letting them know he didn't care a bit what they thought of him. I always avoided people's stares; he looked right at them. And so, having pocketed several cards of buttons, he swaggered out of the shop and I did my best to swagger along behind him as if we'd done nothing wrong. We got away with it and our next stop was Brixton Tube station, where Dave now demonstrated the magic they could work for us.

A button went in the machine and out came a ticket to ride, for nothing. The little that Vincent and Johnny were able to do to broaden my horizons was nothing compared to the thrill of suddenly discovering that I could travel miles and miles across London without having to ask a favour from anyone. You could get on those trains and just keep going. And in central London, with Dave as my guide, I discovered the wonders of Leicester Square and Soho, the sympathetic tourists and prostitutes willing to give us a few bob, and the fabulous bright-coloured lights everywhere that seemed to stay on all day and all night. In time Dave taught me how to dodge the hostile drunks who seemed to be all over the West End and how to weigh up the older street kids who were everywhere, kids like us who had no-one to care about them, and to work out whether they were going to be friendly or if they were about to turn on us and take the little we had in our pockets.

Sometimes we would simply get on a train just to see where it went. We ended up in Chelsea, in Victoria, even in Highbury once, near the Arsenal ground, and sometimes in the City. These were places that were okay in the daytime, when there were plenty of people about, but, like Lambeth, even Victoria was dead at night, and nowhere was as good for begging as the West End. But it wasn't just the money we were after. Dave, like me, wanted to fill the afternoons and evenings and the night-times because neither of us wanted to go home.

It was a while before Dave let me come round to his home, just as it was a while before I was willing to let him see where I lived. I suppose it was a question of both of us taking our time to decide how much we were willing to trust each other. We'd both had to take a lot of stick from other kids because of the way our families lived, but we must have reached a moment when we knew we were in the same boat and neither of us would judge the other. Eventually I did know where he lived, and I started to go round and call for him.

The first time he ever invited me into his flat, I went into the living room and his mum was lying on the settee naked. My family wasn't your usual kind of family but I'd never seen my mum or my sisters without their clothes on.

'Come in, come in,' Dave had said. He was excited.

'Do you fancy some Toast Toppers? Come in and have some, it's fantastic. Mum's been shopping.'

Not like that, I hoped. I had no idea what Toast Toppers were, but Dave and I thought alike where food was concerned, so I knew it was worth having. But here I was in this sitting room with a naked woman who was smoking one cigarette after another and every now and again drinking something from a bottle that was standing next to the settee, while Dave was in the kitchen making this feast for us. I didn't know what to do. Fortunately she was very drunk, I knew the signs of that well enough, and I don't think she really registered that I was there. It was obviously all quite normal to Dave, so I sat there politely and pretended nothing unusual was going on, just occasionally sneaking a look at this amazing sight. It was disgusting and fascinating all at the same time. I have to say that the Toast Toppers, a kind of cheesy spread mixture out of a tin that you put on toast, was good. I could put up with any amount of weirdness for a decent bit of food.

His mum never did anything to clean and I suppose she had less excuse than my mum, because there were less of them. His dad, he told me, was in prison. Dave was allowed to roam around at all hours of the day and night without his mum ever coming to look for him. He began to spend a lot of nights sleeping with me in the dump-yard den.

He helped me improve it a bit so that it didn't leak – with two of us it was easier to get some bigger sheets of metal on the roof and make it watertight – and we found another abandoned car to rip a second seat out of so that we each had a bed. The one difference between his home and mine was that there'd be more times when his mum had got her act together enough to buy some food, and with fewer of them in the house to eat it, he had a better chance of getting his hands on a treat that he could bring down to the dump yard to share with me. It was like a partnership, almost like a marriage, and he was the breadwinner. Loads of times I'd be sitting in the yard wondering what to do with myself and he'd suddenly appear on top of the wall with a loaf of bread and half a pound of butter, or a packet of bacon or some sausages. We'd get a fire going and sit in the den toasting bread and eating well for a change, chatting and having a laugh. We'd sit in front of the fire looking at the dark sky until we felt like going to bed, and then we'd lie in the dark in our den talking about what we wanted to do when we won the pools, or just about what we might do tomorrow, where we could go, where the best begging was to be had. Those were great nights and we slept well, because we weren't hungry and – as we weren't alone – because we weren't afraid of the dark.

I have to say that I usually wasn't afraid in the dump yard at night even when Dave wasn't there. In those days people just didn't seem to be about at all hours of the night like they are now and no-one ever came into the dump yard after dark except me and later, after we'd teamed up, Dave. The only thing I ever saw that gave me a bit of a fright one night turned out to be nothing more than a fox having a late-night look around, and he was more worried about me than I was about him.

Dave was a lot more switched on than I was, more streetwise, even though we were much the same age, probably about eight, when we first met. He hadn't had the fear of God beaten into him like I had about going to school, so he'd been out on the streets fending for himself for a lot longer. He did go to school, but not in our area. He was picked up by a little minibus in the mornings. It wasn't polite between two kids like us to ask those kinds of questions, but I thought he had probably been put into some kind of school for difficult kids after playing truant a lot. There was certainly nothing backward about Dave. He was so wise to all the ways that a small kid could get money that he would change tactics depending on what time of year it was.

After Easter and all the way into summer, the West End was great for begging from the tourists, who were always a soft touch for a cute, dirty kid asking for a few pennies. In October and November it was penny for the Guy at Kennington Tube station. I was so naïve that when a couple of bigger kids came up to me after I'd been there all morning with my Guy – our basement could have been a Guy factory – and asked for some change, I got out my bag of pennies and opened it. They snatched it off me and ran away screaming and laughing. Dave would never have been that soft.

Carol-singing was one of his big money earners when December came round. He was as cheeky as anything. Quite often people would come to the door and ask: 'Which church are you from?'

Dave always had an answer.

'St Margaret's in Clapham Road.'

'St Mary's up Tulse Hill.'

'That big church on the green at Kennington.'

Or, when we were a long way from our own patch, it would be simply: 'From the local church.' He always had an answer.

We didn't often get the door slammed in our faces. Sometimes I think they gave us money just to stop us wailing the way we did, at the tops of our voices, me as ever taking my cue from him. It was fantastic fun, but I don't think it was music.

We didn't have it all our own way. One night he'd used the buttons to get us up to Highbury to go carol-singing.

'Why go up there?' I asked him.

'Because it's better than round here, and no-one knows us up there,' Dave explained patiently. So off we went. At one house we were singing away just inside the front gate when this teenager opened the door.

'My mum can't hear you. She's in a wheelchair.'

Dave pumped the volume up a bit.

'Come closer, to the door, she can't hear you. You won't get any money if she can't hear you.'

We moved onto the path in front of the door and the

next thing we knew we were wet through. We spluttered and staggered back onto the pavement. There was another kid at the open window upstairs with a bucket in his hand, laughing his head off.

The time that was lean even for Dave was the first two or three months of the year, especially January, just after everyone had had their fun and spent their money. That was when Dave's gift for shoplifting came into its own. He showed me how to get all sorts of things, from food and fruit in the local shops to clothes from Woolworth's. I got myself some decent underwear for the first time in my life. I didn't bother with socks, because wearing them at home would have been too risky. They would have been taken off me and I would have got a beating at the same time, because Dad and Mum would have known that I couldn't possibly have bought them. At least I could wear underwear without anyone noticing if I was careful.

In small shops Dave's technique was to follow a woman in, as if he was with her. He would stand quietly behind her for a while, until he was sure she and the shopkeeper were concentrating on each other, then wander casually about to have a good look around at what was worth having. He'd keep his hands in his pyjama pockets, except for the all-important moment when he pocketed what he wanted. That was where the pyjamas came in really handy, because they were very baggy on his thin legs and the pockets had no bottoms. He could hold things there, next to his left leg, until he was out and away. It would have been tricky, maybe, to get out without being rumbled if the counter was on his left as he walked out, but I wouldn't have put it past Dave to choose only shops that had the counter on the left when you went in, so that it would be on his right on the way out. He would always try to leave at about the same time as the woman he'd come in with, not too close behind but close enough so that he wouldn't be asked any questions by the shop staff.

I don't know how he got away with it so often, because he hardly melted into the background in his pyjama bottoms and wellingtons. He was a walking target even by my standards. Yet he always seemed to get away with it. He was kind to me. He knew I was much more afraid of authority than he was and he never gave me a hard time about how difficult I found it to go into a shop and take something. It wasn't that I didn't want to, and sometimes I did it just because I felt bad about leaving him to take all the risks. But he was brilliant at it and more often than not we'd be walking along the road and he'd suddenly say to me: 'Wait here.'

That would be it. He'd be gone, and I'd look round me to work out where we were and realize that we were outside Woolworth's in the centre of Lambeth and he'd be in there in a flash and out again just a few minutes later. A bit further down the road he'd produce a couple of bars of chocolate he'd nicked and give one to me.

'Bloody hell, thanks, mate. How'd you do that?' I'd ask, mouth full of delicious chocolate, awed by his daring and his speed.

'Simple, Pete, when you know how.'

He'd wink at me over his chocolate wrapper, and I'd

know this wasn't going to be like a conversation with one of my brothers, where that was all I got, with a kick into the bargain for asking too many questions.

'Thing is, see, you got to look like you mean business. I go and ask one of the security guards what the time is.'

'You *speak* to them?'

'Yeah. Puts them off their guard. You got a reason to be there. Then I say something like "My sister sent me to get cotton wool, where is it, mate?" and they take me there. I clock where the chocolate is, and usually they leave you when they've pointed to what you've asked for. On the way back I lift the chocolate and as I go out I say something like "They ain't got the ones she wants, like little balls, it's no good" and off I go through the door before they have chance to think.'

'Bloody hell. You've got nerve, Dave.'

'You will too, Pete, don't worry. We got a few buttons left and I'm hungry. Let's go up West.'

Then it was into the Tube station with the buttons and off to wherever Dave decided we should go, down into the other world of the tunnels and the trains that I loved. The old Underground, as it was then before it was modernized, had a special smell. The wooden escalators, the red and blue trains with little bits of red leather on the arms of the seats, the smoking carriages, they all had this dusty, foggy, oily smell to them. It wasn't a dirty smell, just the smell of a place that was well-used and had been there for hundreds of years, as it seemed to me. Whenever I caught a whiff of it I thought of freedom and escape and adventure.

For Dave the biggest adventure was his favourite Tube train game. I tried to be cool about this game of his, but sometimes I just had to cover my eyes because what he did was so scary. The old London Underground carriages had handles on the back of them for the train workers to hold on to when they were coupling one carriage to another. A train would pull into a platform and Dave would head for the back of it, saying: 'Let's not get on this one, let's ride it.'

There was usually a guard at the back of the train, checking the platform to make sure everyone was on before he closed the doors and gave the signal for the driver to set off. When the guard's door closed, Dave would reach out for the handle on the back of the last carriage and swing his feet down onto the rail nearest the platform and then surf along behind the train as it headed into the tunnel. Just before it disappeared, he'd swing himself up again and throw himself back onto the platform, laughing his head off. He'd dust himself off and then say: 'That wasn't right. Let's try again.' So he'd cross over to the opposite platform to catch up with the next train in and do it again. Maybe he did it partly to impress me because I was often too frightened to try it myself. I did do it from time to time, because I copied almost everything that Dave did. But mostly he did it just because it was a thrill. He reckoned his wellingtons were perfect for the job, slipping nicely along the rails with just a bit of drag to keep him in control. They were old wellingtons, of course, worn smooth on the soles, and they were so good for this game that I don't think he would have thanked anyone who had tried to give him a new pair. How it was that he never fell off and got himself fried on the electric rail, I will never know.

Another of his favourite places when we were both bored of the West End was the river. He generally seemed to know when the tide was out and he'd say: 'Let's go to the seaside, Pete.'

Often we wouldn't bother wasting a precious button on a Tube ride. We'd walk up to Vauxhall Bridge or straight up through Kennington to Blackfriars and go down the river stairs onto the mud next to the Thames. It was a dirty old river then and sometimes the smell was so bad that it was like standing in a sewer, but on sunny days, with a good fresh wind blowing, it could be very good down there by the water, with a great big wide sky above your head, a very nice change from always feeling closed in by buildings and traffic. We'd spend hours digging about in the mud. Dave would say people were always dropping stuff in the river from the boats or the bridge and if we poked about long enough we might find something good, something we could sell up West. We never found anything like that, just rusty bits of metal and plastic rubbish, but it always felt like we'd had a day out after a morning or an afternoon by the river, before the tide started coming back in again.

The river made a nice change now and again, but nothing much happened there and it had nothing on Dave's West End, the one he introduced me to. I had done a lot of wandering of my own, of course, before I met him, but the furthest from Lambeth I had ever been was to the place my dad's toilets were. Money came too hard to me from begging round the streets where we lived to waste on a bus when I could get more instant pleasure from a bag of sweets or chips, and until I met Dave I didn't understand how the Underground worked. I knew Raymond went on it to get to the central London hotel where he worked, but going down there on my own was too big a step for me.

Although I could chat up strangers round our way in the hope they might offer me something, I was very hesitant with these well-dressed tourists when I knew I wanted to ask them directly for money. 'Um, could you . . . have you got . . . excuse me, can you help?' and to start off with, when I first went to Soho with Dave, it was all in a whisper.

'Blimey. Watch, I'll show you how,' said Dave.

'Hey mister, all right?' he would say, walking right up to some rich-looking man or woman who was walking through Leicester Square or down Charing Cross Road. He'd always have his hands in his pockets and he'd look them right in the eye. 'I'm a bit hungry. Can you spare a few bob?'

It didn't matter how often he was ignored or told to get lost or go home, his approach was always the same. He never seemed to lose confidence. He had an eye for people who were foreigners, tourists, even before he heard them speak, and slowly I learned to see odd little things about the way they were dressed or the look of their skin that told you they weren't British. Shoes were a big give-away. Foreigners' shoes were always a little bit smarter-looking, better kept, somehow a bit more stylish, and they didn't look cheap. Their clothes seemed to fit better and, of course, they usually had bigger bags, or an extra bag to carry their cameras in. The funny thing was that I didn't really understand about other countries. I was barely aware of what people meant when they said we lived in England. The idea that there were other big chunks of land where people spoke and behaved and ate differently went straight by me. I wasn't even curious about it. All I cared about was that these people were kinder and a much softer touch than any of the adults who lived round my bit of London.

Dave knew, and I learned, that for every two hours you might spend in a place like Lambeth asking for money, you'd spend maybe only ten minutes in Soho, especially during the high tourist season, to get the same amount of cash. If you picked your punter carefully, you'd get money from maybe six out of every ten people you asked. It was fantastic. Getting hold of five shillings in an hour was almost guaranteed. In today's money, that's 25p, which doesn't sound much now, but there were plenty of places around the area to get a snack, a hotdog or a burger, for a shilling at most, and often after a whole day and most of the night out there you'd still be going home feeling full and with money left over in your pocket.

The West End was a strange and wonderful new world and Dave introduced me to every corner of it, from the bright lights to the tough, dangerous community of street kids that seemed to be invisible to all these comfortably off people who had come there to have fun, but which existed in a kind of parallel universe alongside them, feeding off them, even sleeping at their feet. In that respect, at least, we were better off than the other boys we got to know up there. We had the dump yard and our den, so we had, as we thought of it, a home to go to that was a lot better than a cardboard box. We always went back to Lambeth at night feeling as good as any millionaire with a swimming pool.

11. Funerals and Perverts

Living like this, always out on the streets and always looking for friendship and company, it was inevitable that somewhere along the way I'd come across perverts who wanted to take advantage of a vulnerable boy. Jim was one of them, a bloke who lived on his own nearby, and I got to hear from the talk among the kids at school that he was always giving away sweets and bottles of pop. Of course, I wanted some of that, so I followed a few of the others to find out where he lived and started knocking on his door myself. He seemed a nice bloke, very friendly and always happy to give me a couple of sweets and have a chat. He had a walking stick with a sword in it that he used to show to kids who came round.

I went round there for a while. He would give kids like me sixpence or a shilling and tell you to go off to the local shop to get sweets and lemonade. He never told you to come back, but I did because it seemed such an easy way to get the things I wanted, money and attention. Then the day came when I found out what the deal was. He said I could have my shilling, as usual, but this time we would have to play a game first. To say thank you.

'You are grateful, aren't you?' he asked.

'Yeah, Jim.'

'I've been good to you, haven't I? Here's another

shilling. It's yours, son. Come and sit on my knee and say thank you to me properly.'

I wanted to tell him to get lost. I had no idea what was coming, so it wasn't that I was afraid of what he might do. My fear of all physical contact, even if it was meant kindly, made me want to run a mile from him. But I felt confused, a bit guilty, that maybe he was right. I was grateful for the money he gave me. Maybe I should say thank you.

I didn't really know what to do. I went close to him and he pulled me onto his lap and put his arms around me.

'There, that's not so bad, is it, son?' he asked, and there was a strange, happy sound in his voice that confused me even more. I thought: 'This will be over soon. I just have to hang on until he's happy that I've said thank you properly.' Then, very slowly, he pushed his hand into the top of my trousers and started moving it downwards. Alarm and fear, although I didn't know what I was afraid of, shot through me. I still didn't speak, I just pulled his hand out and moved right away across the room. I sat down on a chair over there, struck completely dumb by what he'd tried to do and, at the same time, feeling really guilty because by now I knew I just hadn't been grateful enough and never would be. There must have been something about the way I did all this or the way I looked that told him there was no point wasting any more time on me. He literally threw the shilling across the room at me.

'You weren't even worth it,' he sneered. I took his shilling because I wanted it so badly, but I never went back there again. Even for a shilling it wasn't worth it to me.

There must have been plenty of boys in that area who weren't as bothered as I was by what men like Jim wanted to do to them.

It wasn't just the shock and bewilderment I felt at why grown men would want to do such things to young boys that kept me quiet. Even if I'd wanted to find someone to confide in, it was too hard to trust anyone enough to talk about anything that was happening to me. I liked a quiet life and the best way to get it seemed to be to keep quiet.

That was why I behaved the way I did on the day Dad died, walking away from the hysteria that spread through the whole house when he was dragged out semi-conscious from his bedroom, and away into the peace of the dump yard and the streets beyond, becoming a spectator to my own father's last moments. I never could stand commotion. It had always been that way with me, I knew, right from the earliest memories I had of myself being desperate to get out of the flat.

It could just have been the way I was made, but even if it hadn't come naturally I had learned early that commotion was dangerous, out of commotion nine times out of ten came violence, and the most sensible thing you could do was get away from it as fast as you could. In my world, lots of things were dangerous. Every kind of situation and even the most straightforward event was dangerous in our house, so it wasn't as if I had any way of understanding that something momentous was happening on the day he died.

All I knew was that if I'd been a bit more with it when

I got up that Sunday morning and went down to the kitchen in the hope of finding a slice of bread and found Mum there, I would have got right out of the way before she turned round. I would have realized that she had just finished filling the kettle and was about to put it on the gas. As it was, I was the one in the firing line when she barked at me: 'Go ask your dad for the lighter.'

She could have asked him herself. She could have gone into the bedroom my parents shared, the one directly above the basement kitchen at the back of the house that might have been a dining room a long time before we moved there, and got the lighter herself without asking him at all. She knew as well as we did that no child in their right mind wanted to be the one who asked my dad for anything, especially when he was still in bed, like he was that morning. If someone came to the door bothering him, no matter what reason they had for it, that was excuse enough for him to come out onto the little landing just above the steps that led down to the kitchen and thrash the living daylights out of you with his belt until you were flat out on the floor, bleeding, making as little noise as possible as each blow connected, and praying silently that he would soon decide he'd been kept from his bed long enough. Mum knew all this, and I never saw any sign that she cared one way or the other how hard the beatings were or how long they went on. More than that, there'd be a beating as bad from her if I didn't do what she said. I couldn't win. It was either a certain beating from Mum or the faint possibility that Dad might be too hungover from his usual Saturday night binge to put himself to the trouble of getting out of bed and finding his belt. I went up the stairs from the basement to the ground-floor landing and knocked on the bedroom door.

I didn't get a reply. Terry heard what was going on and came down the stairs from the first-floor bedroom. He reached past me and knocked again, probably because he knew that this would really wind Dad up and he'd be able to nip back up the stairs and watch me take the beating that was coming. Terry's favourite form of self-defence was to get someone else into trouble. Quickly I asked through the door for the lighter for Mum in the faint hope that Dad would leave me alone if he knew she'd sent me. We heard a low mumbling, a murmuring, nothing you could make sense of. Terry, smug, said: 'He's pissed.' All the more of a beating on its way, then. Terry got the beating instead. From the kitchen below Mum heard him and suddenly found that after all she did have the energy to get herself up the short flight of stairs. She flew up them, screaming: 'Don't you say that about your father, you little bastard,' and she really went for him, thumping him over and over again in the head and whacking him into the wall.

Then we heard a sort of thump behind the door. Mum paused in mid-attack, tried the doorknob and couldn't get the door open. Things started getting really strange. Raymond and Paul were sent out to shin up the drainpipe from the basement yard below Mum and Dad's bedroom window. They looked in carefully first, I bet, ready to get away fast if Dad looked like he was up and about and fit enough to give them a hiding. Then they climbed in because they couldn't see him anywhere, but they knew he had to be in there. Once inside they found him lying in front of the door, not moving.

Mum was hysterical by the time they'd pulled him away from the door and opened it. Raymond and Paul picked him up and carried him into the front room. I didn't go in to see, but there had never been anything in there except for a couple of tatty old chairs for Mum and Dad and a few wooden orange boxes for us kids to sit on, not even a rug, so I suppose they must have put him on the floor. Terry was told to go to the phone box down the street to call an ambulance and everyone in the house started going mad. As the noise level rose, that was when I decided to leave, walking out through the back door, climbing over the wall into the dump yard behind the terrace, past my secret den, and over a wall and out into the street to get away from it all.

After I'd bought the old bloke his loaf of bread, and the kid watching the drama outside our house had recognized me, and I'd turned my back on the ambulance that was taking Dad away, I went back to the dump yard and hung around there, just waiting. I never expected anything except that he'd be back and everything would be the same as it always had been. Eventually, after sitting for hours and hours out there, towards evening I decided it might be safe to go back into the house. Mum was sitting in the front room crying and one of the neighbours had come in to sit with her. In the back garden, if you could call it that, with all the mud and weeds and charred patches where there'd been occasional bonfires of flea-infested mattresses and other rubbish, I saw Francis and Paul dancing and laughing. They were hard-bitten young teenagers and didn't generally do much dancing or laughing. Something special had happened; something really good had happened.

'What's going on?' I asked.

'He's dead,' they said, grinning like maniacs. 'You know what, he's died, and guess what, even better – there's no school for a week.'

It was a strange time in every way I can think of.

Mum, who I'd never seen show any kind of affection for anyone or anything, wailed and cried for days. She screamed the place down at the funeral parlour when we all had to go and look at him in his coffin. I took a good long look at him and thought: 'He really is dead, then.' Then I had a moment when I felt pure cold fear, as if he might be able to read my thoughts and know that I wanted to be sure he was dead. I thought he might suddenly sit up in his coffin and whack me for it. He didn't. I was glad to get out of there.

It was all new, all exciting in a way, because until then every day had been much like every other day. Birthdays, Christmas, nothing made any difference in our house. Suddenly relatives started to turn up, something that had never happened before. We never had visitors and it was amazing to discover that my mother, for instance, had two sisters, who came over from where they lived in west London, near Shepherd's Bush. They brought cousins with them that we'd never met before. Before the day was out, two of my five brothers had predictably found some reason to have a full-scale punch-up with one of them. One evening quite a crowd of people who were related to us turned up, but to this day I have no idea who they were. What I did know was that with all these strangers around I was crawling with embarrassment at the state of our house. One visitor, a grown-up cousin from some unknown branch of the family, stood up and looked like he might be heading for the kitchen. I jumped up too and said to him: 'I'll get you a drink of water.' All the rooms upstairs were absolutely horrible, but I didn't even want anyone from outside the family to go into the kitchen. Even at my age, and never having known anything else, I knew thanks to the school bully's teatime visit that no kitchen should look like ours did. The place was thick with grime: the floor, the cupboards, the table, even the walls. I didn't want strangers going in there to try to make a cup of tea.

Someone went out to get some black ribbon to make mourning bands and we wore them on our arms for days. The funeral itself was a blur to me. The only one of us ten children who wasn't there was Kathleen, the oldest, who had emigrated to Australia with her husband and children. Christine was pregnant and came with the husband she'd run off with the year before. Raymond had a decent jacket to wear because he was working. The rest of us had been dressed as well as we could be in borrowed and second-hand clothes and old school shirts. My two other sisters, Alison and the baby of the family, Rosemary, had dresses that looked fairly new. Mum, who couldn't have cared less whether we boys had underwear or not, did at least seem to feel that she had some responsibility for making sure the girls looked okay when they left the house.

Two moments stuck in my mind. One was getting to the funeral and the churchyard in big luxurious black cars, although I have no idea who could have paid for them. Maybe Mum and Dad had some kind of funeral insurance policy, but it seems a bit unlikely given that their priorities for any money they had were fags, drink, the betting shop and tea, milk and sugar, in that order.

My other memory is of looking down into the grave after my father's coffin had been lowered into it, standing next to a woman who I think must have been my mother's sister. She spoke to me a few times during the service, but for some odd reason the only thing I heard her say was 'Don't get too close, you'll be down there with him.' That gave me a bit of a shock and was the only time when I didn't feel numb. I didn't feel like crying. I didn't seem to feel any emotion at all. I felt guilty for a long time afterwards for not feeling like a son should have felt at his father's funeral.

My father had been killed by a brain haemorrhage brought on by years and years of smoking, heavy drinking and fighting with other drunken blokes on the streets. My mother said some years later that just a few days before he died someone had hit him over the head with a brick. Perhaps that was true, or perhaps it was just one of her stories. She always remembered the past as it suited her.

I used to imagine that the nickname Harry called him by, Jacksaw, had something to do with the way he fought, that maybe he had a way of ripping open the flesh of the men who angered him like the teeth of a saw rip wood. That was what it felt like when he took his belt to my back. I'm sure it had a less sinister meaning and was just a childhood nickname he'd brought with him from his native Ireland, something to do with a timber yard he'd lived near when he was young. But when I was a child my explanation of it fitted well with the father I knew.

He was only fifty-two when he died. On the other hand, it was amazing that he lasted as long as he did, given the kind of life he'd lived, amazing that he had the strength and energy to be as brutal as he was with us right to the end. What I do know now is that although it wasn't a long or a happy life, or a nice death, my father was lucky. And at least one of his sons, although we'll never be sure which one, was even luckier. His six sons were all getting older and bigger, even me, the youngest boy and definitely the runt of the litter, the one he never called Peter. If he called me anything other than 'bastard' or 'you little fucker', I was 'the Dwarf' to him until the day he died. And I decided that if he hadn't died then, one of us would eventually have killed him. It could even have been me.

After Dad died, although it was a huge relief to know that he would never again be calling me down to the basement, it did change something in me. I had no way of understanding these strange, difficult emotions I was feeling, because it would never have been possible for me to grieve for him in the normal way that a child might grieve for his dead father. But I did miss him in some strange way, and not long after he died I found myself heading again and again towards the toilets where he had worked. I would never have gone there while he was alive. Fear of him and the shame of having a father who did such a job had always made me avoid the area where he had spent his days.

But I was trying to work it all out in my head, how I had felt about him when he was alive and how I felt about him now that he was dead. I wanted to be close to the place where he'd spent a lot of his time, as if this would make me understand him better. It was here that I got to know Leo.

He seemed friendly enough, and was sympathetic when I told him about Dad working there, and how he'd died very suddenly. He seemed to be there a lot pottering around, so I started heading down to see him more and more – after school, at weekends. There was no money in it for me. Leo seemed to like me, that was all. It was a bit of fantasy for me, almost pretending he was my father and here I was, making a friendship with him, a great father and son relationship, which I had never had when my dad was alive.

He wasn't like Dad, of course, but that was important too. He obviously wasn't a drinker, or at least not the kind of regular drinker that Dad had been. He was kind and wanted to tell me things about life, talk to me. He seemed like the dads who sometimes came to the school gates to pick up their sons, caring and interested. We would chat about everything from bikes to the bullying that I had to put up with at school. He seemed to know that things weren't right at home, but he didn't pry. Sometimes he worked away in silence while I sat, watching.

'Hello, son,' he would always say when he saw me coming.

Eventually, after a few weeks, he asked me if I'd like to come to his flat one day.

'Yeah, I'd really like that,' I said. I felt warm, wanted, almost as if I'd found the father I'd never had.

When I got to his flat he took me into the living room and gave me kids' comics and some sweets that he'd obviously bought for me.

'Oh, thanks, Leo, these are great,' I said, sitting down on a sofa that was old but comfortable and clean, starting to look at one of the comics and feeling as if I'd come home at last.

Then he sat down next to me on the settee. I looked up, expecting him to offer me a sweet or ask me what I'd been up to that week, and he grabbed me, holding me round the waist, and wouldn't let go. I was too small and slight to get away from him.

Every alarm bell I had inside my head started ringing like hell. It wasn't just the physical contact that was scaring me this time. By now I knew what some men thought young boys were for.

'You are a lovely boy and we are special friends, aren't we?'

I nodded frantically, struggling and trying to back off

from his face, because it was far too close to mine for my comfort. Until this moment he had been like the father I never had. A battering from him, or from my mum or my brothers, would have been better. I would have known how to endure that.

'Come on, son, show me how much you like me,' he said, smiling, but through teeth that were clenched together with the effort of clamping his left arm round my body and grabbing one of my hands with his free hand so that he could pull it towards his crotch. He didn't try to do anything to me, he was just intent on getting me to give him the sexual satisfaction he wanted. My arm and hand froze solid as a broomstick as he rubbed it on the front of his trousers. Then he got hold of my wrist and twisted my arm, letting go of my body so that he could spin me round until I was helplessly kneeling on the carpet in front of him. He held my imprisoned arm high in the air so that I couldn't move while he undid his fly, and then he forced my head down towards his groin.

I'd had some pain inflicted on me in my time, but this kind of torture was more than I could begin to understand. The moment came when he collapsed back against the cushions of the sofa satisfied, letting go of my wrist. I threw myself backwards, got to my feet and was out of that flat like a bat out of hell.

I never went looking for a father-figure again. Something I had thought wasn't possible happened inside me. A new anger was born to go with all the other anger and grief I was already carrying around with me. It was sheer fury that he could have found a way to make me feel more humiliated, more filthy, than I already felt. The person who had done it to me was someone I had dared to trust, and he had turned out to be just like all the rest. Of one thing I was certain: of all the ways there were for a streetwise kid to get money, this was one that I was never going to get drawn into.

12. Soho

Piccadilly Circus's famous Coca-Cola sign was now as familiar to me as the dump yard. This was the place that Dave, my dump-yard buddy, took me to on our very first Underground train ride together paid for with Marks and Spencer buttons. From there it was a short walk to Leicester Square and Soho, the centre of London's tourist trade – and, of course, its sex trade. That side of the daily life of this part of London passed me by at first. What amazed me, as a boy who had known only the most run-down parts of south London, was the grandness of the streets and the masses of people walking around them who looked so rich, well-fed and well-dressed that, to my eyes at least, they might have been aliens from another planet.

On those first few trips to the West End with Dave I trailed along behind him, sticking to him like glue, with my eyes out on stalks and my mouth permanently open. Although he was much the same age as me, he already knew his way around this fantastic new world. Not only did he know all the tricks of the begging trade, but he also knew when trouble was brewing and how to avoid it. He seemed to have eyes in the back of his head, especially when it came to police officers on the Soho beat who might be taking too much interest in us and what we were doing.

'Let's scarper, quick,' he'd suddenly say to me. Usually I had no idea what was wrong, but this was his patch and I did what he said without any questions asked. The favourite escape route, I quickly learned, was down the series of narrow streets that led away from Soho and down the side of the National Gallery to the north side of Trafalgar Square. There we could sit on the sides of the fountains among all the tourists, watching them feed the pigeons and eat their ice creams, until it seemed safe to go back again and work the theatre district for a few more bob.

I have no idea why Trafalgar Square was thought of as a safe haven, but I soon discovered it was where all the street kids who hung around the West End went to regroup if there was any trouble, like one of them getting arrested for pick-pocketing or if the Vice Squad were out picking up men who were picking up boys. This was probably the first part of the West End sex trade that I got to know about, although exactly what being a rent boy involved remained a mystery to me for the time being.

Dave knew some of the street kids already and introduced me to a few of them, all of them quite a bit older than us, maybe ten years old and upwards, and I noticed that grown men would come up to them now and again and, after a bit of talk, some of these kids would go off alone with them. Sometimes I'd see them later and they'd have money, pound notes instead of the coppers and silver that Dave and I had got from begging. Naïve as I was, I was suspicious from the start about what you might have to do to get that kind of money. My experience with Leo had given me some idea of what might be involved. I had promised myself that nobody would ever touch me like that again – and I meant it.

Once Dave had shown me the ropes and I started to pick up a little of his skill at begging, I would sometimes go to the West End on my own if he wasn't around. I went up there one day and teamed up with a street kid who was quite a bit older than me, perhaps thirteen or fourteen.

'Let's go to the pictures,' he said.

This sounded good to me. He took me to a place somewhere near one of the big railway stations, King's Cross or maybe Waterloo, where they showed cartoons all through the day. Pictures of cartoon characters were on display along with old publicity shots of the Marx Brothers just outside the cinema doors and it looked a fantastic place. I was really keen about going in to watch. It's disappeared now, but for years it was a magnet for West End street kids, although not, as I half realized that day, because of the cartoons. Of course, I wanted to sit right at the front.

'No, no, we need to sit in the middle rows,' said this kid. 'Here's some money, go and get some sweets for us.'

Off I went, happy enough, and looking forward to a good couple of hours eating sweets and watching cartoons and old Marx Brothers films. When I came back I couldn't find him. Then I saw him, right in the very back row, sitting next to a man who had his arm round him. Suddenly this didn't seem such a great place after all.

I sat down on the end of an aisle in the middle of the cinema so that I could get out fast if I needed to, even though I still wasn't quite sure what kind of trouble I might need to get away from. I kept glancing back at the boy I'd come in with and a few minutes later I saw him get up with this bloke and go with him into the gents' toilets at the back of the cinema. Right there and then I got up and walked out, thinking: 'This isn't for me.' I still had powerful, disturbing memories of that encounter with Leo. I didn't want to wait around to hear what the kid might tell me about what he'd had to do in there. I didn't want any more of those pictures inside my head.

When I'd been around the West End a while and felt surer of myself, the cinema became a place that I did go to from time to time, because, if nothing else, it was a warm, dry and comfortable refuge in the winter, somewhere you could sit down in comfort for a few hours without anyone telling you to get out, and there was always a chance of meeting up with other kids and finding a bit of company for an afternoon or an evening. But I was always very careful about where I sat and wary of any men who got too near. Poor and hungry as I always was, and even before I'd had my own encounters with paedophiles, I became quite certain that I didn't want to try whatever it was they were doing with these men to get that kind of cash.

Maybe Vincent and Johnny had given me a bit of self-respect and Leo had given me a healthy fear of that kind of exploitation, but I think it was as much that my father and brothers between them had made me very suspicious of all men and what they could do to you if they turned nasty. One of the things I did notice was that the older boys tried to dress like they were grown-ups. It was the era of the hippies and I was used to seeing blokes with long hair and flared jeans, even in Lambeth. Then there were the much older men, who like my dad wore suits and ties whether they were on their way to work or the pub. But these boys, I eventually realized, were trying to dress like most of the men who came to the West End looking for boys to go with. They wore straight three-quarter-length jackets like a mod's Crombie, a shirt and tie underneath it, and straight trousers and brogues. They looked very strange, these twelve- and thirteen-year-old kids in what was almost a middle-aged man's uniform.

I didn't get to know these kids in any real sense, but a lot of them became familiar faces who might be all right to hang out with for a few hours. I couldn't always find Dave when I needed to be out of the house and wanted to fill the time, so once he had shown me the ropes I would get on the Tube and go there on my own, knowing that I'd be certain to come across someone I knew.

The rules about getting along with these kids were less certain. I didn't know about drugs and I didn't understand at first why some kid who had been friendly one day would be someone you should avoid the next day, either because he was high or because he was badly in need of a fix. Weighing up the mood of the other kids was something Dave was pretty good at, but it took me a while to learn. I might have had a good run begging one morning, perhaps, and a couple of the older lads would suddenly be by my side. They might be genuinely friendly or they might be after whatever I'd managed to get, and ready to take it from me with as much force as they needed to use. If they were on drugs and looking for their next fix, targeting the younger kids like me was the easiest way to get some cash.

They had all kinds of dodges for getting cash, these boys. Some of them had mobile stoves made out of oil drums that they could cook burgers on to sell, and which they could wheel off at a moment's notice if any police officers came along. I think the police ignored them as much as they could as long as they weren't blocking the pavement or putting passers-by in any obvious danger. Some had strange little vending machines, on trolleys, something I've never seen since, that had sweets in them. They'd park them up on a pavement and shout out: 'Gobstoppers a penny,' or whatever it was that the machine had in it. Some of them sold lighters and others sold gold Parker pens. At least, they said that's what they were, but I assume that these must have been cheap copies from Hong Kong. Some did the old shoe-shine thing, carrying a box with polish and brushes round the streets and setting up wherever there were no police in sight, kneeling down in front of customers. I thought that was extraordinary, a well-dressed man with his feet up and someone polishing his shoes while they were still on his feet. I couldn't believe anyone could do a job like that and be happy about it, but I also understood that it was a question of survival. They had to survive, these kids. I still hoped I would never have to do anything like that.

A lot of what I saw amazed me. It took me ages to get to the point where the drag queens walking round Soho didn't make me stare. Dave told me they were men dressed up as women, but I couldn't get my head round why anyone would want to do that. The funny thing was that while I was staring at them, they were staring back at me. I am sure I looked like a tramp. One of them walked up to Dave and me once, after I'd been staring for five minutes or more at this woman who looked like a movie star who'd stepped straight off the screen, and trying to work out what it was about her that wasn't quite right.

'Have you got a light, kid?' she asked, in a deep man's voice that made me stand there gawping at her with my mouth open. Both she and Dave laughed their heads off at the expression on my face.

Nutters' Corner, as we called it, was another place that made my head spin. The rest of the world knows it as Speakers' Corner, at the Marble Arch end of Hyde Park, where anyone can spout off about the end of the world or vegetarian diets or, as I recall a lot of speakers doing at that time, the Vietnam War. Obviously I had no idea what that was about, and I thought that altogether it was the craziest collection of adults I'd ever seen, particularly since there didn't seem to be any money in it for them, but it was good entertainment that filled an hour or so and it was a laugh to go up there and heckle them a bit. I did admire them in a way even though I thought they were crackers. I decided it must take some courage to make speeches like that when no-one was listening.

For similar reasons I was impressed by the entertainers

who were just starting to appear on the streets around Charing Cross Road. At that time Covent Garden was still a fruit and vegetable market, not the tourist centre it is now, and these entertainers weren't the kind you see there these days. They were one-man-band men with drums on their backs, and there was a bloke who dressed up in a waistcoat, top hat and a coat that had feathers stuck to it and played the harmonica for the theatre queues. We called him Chicken Man. We used to follow him around, clucking. Another man wore a dress and a fez like Tommy Cooper. They seemed to get a fair amount of money and I toyed with the idea of dreaming up something like it that I could do myself, but I also used to think: 'God, they've got some nerve to do that,' and I doubted if I could carry it off. I never thought about the nerve we had to have to do some of the things we did.

Fencing the things we'd stolen was something we took in our stride, for instance. In the run-down buildings in the side streets of Soho there were doors you could knock on that would be opened by a man you knew by sight, who would look at anything you brought to him and give you money for it if he wanted it. There was one man in particular I began to recognize. All the kids knew him. If it sounds like the plot of *Oliver Twist*, that's because it was. I hadn't seen the film, let alone read the book, but when I went to the West End from Lambeth it was like stepping out of the Tube station into the middle of some fantastic, glamorous, tacky film. It was another life, another world, and only four miles and a fifteen-minute train ride from the crap I lived in.

We knew that if someone had managed to steal a handbag or pick a pocket, you could ask this bloke if he was interested in what you'd got. When I saw him I knew it was always worth asking for a few bob even if I hadn't got anything to offer, because now and again he would be feeling generous. So he should have been, given the prices he paid for the stuff that came his way. His profits must have been huge.

He took the most spectacular haul I ever saw off Ken, one of the kids I hung around with quite a lot. He was much older than me and he'd been on the streets for years if what he said was to be believed. I would usually find him in the arcade near the Odeon in Leicester Square. A lot of the rent boys gathered there, and like the Eros statue in Piccadilly Circus it was a well-known pick-up haunt for the men who wanted boys for sex. I don't think that was Ken's thing at all, but there was always company to be found at the arcade, and it was dry and a bit warmer in the winter than the Square. One day Ken turned up with this bag he'd managed to take while the owner's back was turned in a Soho café and he showed me what was in it. It was full of jewellery, gems and rings and gold chains, the works. I walked up to Piccadilly Circus with him to look for this bloke. We had to go back there a couple of times before we found him. He knew how old we were, so he didn't give Ken much, maybe a pound or two. We weren't in a position to argue with him.

When I was hanging around with some of these kids and I realized they were heading for some unsuspecting, well-dressed people who might be sitting on a bench or standing in the street with all their attention somewhere else, I was often a coward. I hung back and tried to stay out of sight. I knew they were angling for a bag they could steal, some of them creating some kind of diversion while one snatched and ran. I'm not trying to excuse myself and suggest I wasn't involved in this kind of stealing in any way. I wanted some of whatever was coming, whatever they managed to get, but what bothered me was that I was small and just couldn't run as fast as the others. I wanted the money but not as much as I wanted not to get caught and have the police knocking on Mum and Dad's door.

I only realized very slowly that there was more to what they were doing than just getting cash and finding a way to survive on the streets. Some of them, the ones that looked quite well-dressed to me, told me that they lived in children's homes further out in various parts of Greater London. I wondered why they would want to spend all day and all night out here when, as they told me, they had three good meals a day waiting for them and a clean warm bed to sleep in at night. Of course, they weren't in Soho just for the excitement and to fill the gaps in a starvation diet like I was. Some were there for the excitement, but a lot of them had serious drug habits and that was expensive. Mostly they were into heroin, but they would take anything they could get their hands on. If they found tablets in a handbag they'd stolen, they'd try them to see what they did. One kid turned up one day with a little blue tin with brown powder in it.

'This is great, try it,' he said, shoving the tin at me. 'I

nicked it off my granddad. You do it like this.' He took a pinch and sniffed it up his nose. 'Not as good as coke, but it's okay.'

I did try it. I sneezed like mad for half an hour. It was horrible. A long time later I realized it must have been snuff, the old men's version of cigarettes.

I will never be able to explain how I didn't become a junkie myself. Cigarettes, of course, I had no problem with. Both my parents smoked like chimneys and at the age of eight or nine, sitting round in Trafalgar Square with the others, I was puffing away like an old man, and certainly by the time I was ten I could get through a packet a day if I had the money. Drink too, if someone had any, wasn't something I wanted to stay away from. But drugs, and especially injecting yourself with needles, I just didn't fancy at all. It was like the rent boy game. I was prepared to go only so far into this world and I worked out quite fast which bits of it I didn't want any part of. There was a boy called Bob, who was about fourteen and who I knew quite well. I think I actually first met him at Kennington, but he was a regular on the West End streets, and he found me one day on my own up there and asked out of the blue whether I'd ever been to a football match. I hadn't.

'Come on then,' he said, and we set off for the bottom end of Fulham, where the Chelsea football ground was.

'Leave it to me,' he said as we walked into a café near the ground. It was match day and the place was heaving, but there was a bloke who might have been about forty sitting at a small table in a corner on his own.

'That's our man,' said Bob, and he went over to talk to him, pointing at me. I was waved over and the man bought us both tea and cake. That would have been enough of a result for me on any day of the week, but then he got up and Bob signalled that I was to come with them. We walked up to the turnstiles and this man paid for all three of us to get into the ground. We went onto the terraces and he pushed his way through to get us to the front, and then he went off to get hotdogs for us both.

Even at that age I had some idea of what loneliness was. This man struck me as genuine, even decent. I didn't quite believe that his only motive for doing all this for us was just that he was interested in young boys. I saw him as a lonely old man. Of course, once we had the hotdogs in our hands Bob decided that we'd had all we could usefully get out of him.

He turned to me and said: 'Come on, let's go. Just push your way into the crowd.'

It was packed and we would vanish in moments, and this man wouldn't have a chance of finding us again.

'What about him?' I asked Bob as I followed him up the terraces. 'It's bad, he's just paid for us to get in and have something to eat before the game.'

'Don't worry about him. He's a fucking nonce' was Bob's dismissive answer. It took the novelty out of the day for me. It was okay, but I didn't register much about what was going on on the pitch. I couldn't get that man's sadness out of my mind.

Kids like Bob were being used and exploited every day,

and it was no surprise that a lot of them thought only about how they might be able to use and exploit everyone they met. Even so, there were quite a few older kids who hung around me a lot when I turned up, and who I slowly realized were chasing a genuine friendship. There wasn't anything they wanted from me. It was even more surprising when I realized they were doing it because they thought I was too young and small, even by their standards, to be out on these streets and living this life. They were trying to do what they could to keep me out of the worst of it. Some of them would buy me a hotdog just because I looked hungry, and look out for me if they saw the police or nastier kids heading our way. They were living horrible lives, but they still felt some compassion, still had some empathy.

Still, these weren't friendships like the one I had with Dave. At the end of a day hanging around with them I knew I would be on my own again. They seemed to disappear in the evening. I don't know whether they had serious rent boy business to do once darkness fell or were off to look for a fix, or maybe some of them were heading back to their children's homes. I think some probably had to report back to an even older boy or a man who controlled them in some way, to hand over cash and stuff they'd stolen in the day.

Some did have real homes, quite nice ones. I know this because now and again one of them would ask if I wanted to stop at their place for the night if we'd been out together until early in the morning. The Tubes and buses stopped at midnight and it was a four-mile walk back home for me. These were boys who lived maybe only a mile or so away, around Marylebone or King's Cross. They'd take me home with them and put me on the sofa and in the morning their mothers would turn out to be really pleasant, quite normal.

'Oh, my mate stayed over last night, he couldn't get home,' they'd say, and the only reply would be: 'All right, love, that's fine.' They didn't know who I was and I was usually a lot younger than their sons were, but they didn't seem to think anything of it.

There were plenty of boys who had nowhere to go, of course. I saw them, along with all the down-and-outs, sleeping under cardboard boxes on the streets, usually down the back alleys behind the shops among all the rubbish that had been put out in the evening. I tried it myself once when I'd begun to get pissed off with walking three or four miles home in the early hours, but I couldn't hack it.

I didn't like being around people at the best of times and I just didn't like having so many people around when I was trying to sleep. I wanted to be awake and alert, to know what was coming. I never did it again, and if I really couldn't face the walk home I would walk out of the centre a bit to find a quiet stairwell in a block of flats, where I could get some shelter and sleep for a few hours before the buses and Tubes started running again.

There were some strange people around the place, the glamorous women who had men's voices, the barmy tramps, with their pushchairs full of bags of stuff, who talked to themselves, but it was usually other boys like me that bothered me. Some of them were just nasty, especially the ones who did have homes outside central London and had come in from the same area together for a day of hanging around. Once there was a day when Dave had gone off on some scheme of his own and I struck up a friendship with three boys who were from Acton. It seemed to be going well until one of them just turned round without any warning and spat in my face. He was the one who reckoned he was the leader and he wanted to make the other two laugh. So there was spit running down my face and I knew I had to just turn round and walk away, and that was the end of that very close friendship. These alliances were nearly always about convenience in the end. It was handy to have someone with you if you wanted to look through the street waste bins, for instance, because that was one thing the police really didn't like. I suppose it looked bad to the tourists. I used to do it, just like the others. I often didn't know why I was doing it, what I was looking for. The others did it, so I did too. I never found anything someone had thrown away that was worth selling, and I was getting enough from begging not to need half a hotdog. It was a different story for the dossers.

That was what we called the down-and-out tramps, grown men who didn't have a home to go to, and seeing them out looking in the bins always made me feel sad. I thought it was one thing to be living the way I was when I was a child and didn't have a choice, but I still hoped things would be different once I was grown up and could get a job and get away from my family. You'd see a few of them around during the day, but loads of them seemed to appear everywhere from the river to King's Cross late at night, looking for a place to sleep. They could be quite aggressive, so I had to be very careful around them. But if they didn't feel threatened even they could be kind. I was very nearly freezing to death in the early hours of one morning near Waterloo station as I tried to get back to Lambeth. The Tube was closed and I'd missed the last bus, and I was walking along hitting myself with my arms to try to get a bit of warmth into my body.

'Here, son!'

There was a tramp sitting on a bench by the side of the road.

'Here you are, son, put some of this down your shirt,' he said, waving a newspaper at me. I was a bit suspicious of him, and even as a young kid, without a coat to his name, I had my dignity and didn't fancy walking round looking like a packet of fish and chips. Then I decided I was too cold to worry about dignity and took a chance that this bloke wasn't planning to do anything awful to me.

It was miraculous stuff, newspaper, I discovered. I wrapped it right round my body, back and front, and it certainly broke the cutting edge of an icy wind. I thanked him and walked off and made it back to Lambeth feeling pretty good, considering. It was amazing what a little kid should have had to do to keep warm.

It was amazing that no real harm ever came to me. I got beaten up a few times by bigger boys who wanted the money I'd begged, but they never did anything that hadn't been done ten times more painfully to me by my dad. It got a bit scarier when you were dealing with the really old boys – I mean boys who were sixteen or seventeen – because they tended to carry knives. Mostly, though, they just wanted to show the knives off and tell you what they'd done with them, how they'd cut someone who refused to hand over their wallet, or what they were planning to do down some dark alley if they found a homosexual on his own. They were the hardcore muggers, and I kept as far away from them as I could.

Somehow I never got picked up by the police, even though once I sat with a group of boys on a bench chatting to two others who were busy breaking into the car parked next to it so that they could steal it – the whole car, not just something in it. I was always walking past fruit shops and helping myself to something from the display out on the pavement. For a couple of years, between the ages of eight and ten, I was in the West End maybe three or four nights a week, yet I managed to avoid most of the terrible things that could easily have happened to me.

I was very young and I didn't know much, but I did understand somehow that the West End I knew, the world of the street kids and the dossers, the drag queens and the prostitutes, was full of sadness, as sad as anything I'd had in my life. Maybe sadder. Sometimes I'd see a kid I knew sitting down, on a bench or even on the pavement, a couple of years older than me but tearful, perhaps even crying. I couldn't go up to him and ask: 'How are you doing? What's up?' because it wasn't on to do that kind of thing. You couldn't show any emotion in that world.

But I knew I could only half imagine what they were going through, what their stories were, and the sort of filth they had to put up with to survive. I had to pass them by, pretend I hadn't noticed. I knew instinctively that to offer any sympathy would somehow only make it worse for them.

13. Moving On

When it came down to it there was no escaping the fact that Vincent and Johnny, Dave and the West End, were just very brief diversions from the horrible life I had with my family. It was strange how I felt compelled to go back, even though I knew that a lot of the boys I'd met in the West End had run away from homes a lot like mine. Although I don't suppose either of them had consciously planned it, there was something about Dad and Mum's regime of brutality that tied us to them and to each other in a way that was impossible to break free from. The biggest part of it, I think, was this business of always having to turn up at school and never bringing trouble to the door. Even running away seemed too risky. The thought of being brought back to them and what would happen the moment the door closed and I was alone with them again was terrifying. Running away, and perhaps trying to explain to someone outside the family what I was running away from, would have been seen as disloyal. The beatings were bad enough when Mum or Dad decided I was ungrateful. So although I never wanted to, I always went back eventually. I had, in any case, no sense of there being anyone out there who would care or who could help. No-one had ever tried to help me.

After the massive relief of a whole week off school

after Dad collapsed and died that Sunday morning in 1971, absolutely nothing changed.

In 1973, a couple of years after Dad's death, we moved out of the Lambeth area for good. We'd been there for almost seven years in a house that even when we arrived wasn't considered fit to live in, and the council had finally given us notice that we had to leave. My older brothers, particularly Raymond, had become the breadwinners of the family – not that this meant there was any more food in the house than there ever had been – and Mum had begun some kind of part-time job around this time. It was hard for me to be sure, because I was hardly ever there and no-one ever told me what was going on when I did turn up.

The most stupid attempt any of us ever made to get money was on the day the removal van came to take what little we had to Wandsworth, where Mum had been offered a four-bedroom house. It was one of three or four the council had bought in quite a nice Edwardian terraced street. Most of the other houses were rented out by private landlords and a few were actually owned by the people who lived in them. They looked okay and it seemed we were moving up in the world. But we were still the Roches.

After the removal van had set off for Wandsworth, Raymond and Paul decided that before we left they'd get into the electric meter and take the cash. They were standing there, hammering away at it, when the man from the electricity board arrived. They knew he was on his way, because the meter man always did come on the dot in those days when someone was moving out. They knew the score. But this meter man was about half an hour later than the electricity board had said he would be, and Raymond and Paul thought they'd chance their arm. They took hammers, chisels, screwdrivers, everything they could get their hands on, and attacked the cash box on the side of the meter. By the time the meter man knocked on the door it was in a terrible state, hardly square any more, all misshapen and dented, but still locked, still with the money in it.

All of us stood in the hall, looking at it.

'What happened here?' asked the man. He sounded tired, really, not angry or official. Just weary.

Someone said: 'Well, we're moving.'

'And?' asked the electric man.

'We didn't want to leave the money in there because . . . well, we didn't think it would be safe. You know what people are like.'

I've never forgotten the look on his face. It said: 'For God's sake, is that the best excuse you can come up with?' but he didn't say a word. He just sighed and we left him to do what he could to unlock the battered cash box.

I realize that it was about this time when I began to consciously tell myself that I'd had a bellyful of my life and my family. I'd had enough. In Soho I was begging for money and being told by sneering toffs to get a job, even though I was an undernourished ten-year-old in rags. I was starting to give people like that a real mouthful of bad language back, something I hadn't done when

I was younger. Then when I got to Wandsworth with the family, it was clear from the first that, although there were four bedrooms in the new house, and it had the unimaginable luxury of a bathroom upstairs and a separate toilet, I had no place there.

By this time there were only Mum and us six boys at home. My older sisters were all married and gone and Rosemary, the youngest, had been sent off to the safety and relative sanity of Alison's young family in the north of England. So it should have been possible for us all to have beds, even if we had to share rooms, but it quickly became apparent that I wasn't going to get a bed to call my own. Mum and Raymond got the two biggest rooms and that left one bedroom and a tiny box room for the other five of us. More often than not I had to sleep in the living room on the sofa. If my older brothers were sitting up watching the television, as they often were, and I wanted to go to sleep, there wasn't much I could do about it.

Lying down on the floor at the back of the room until they all went to bed might have been possible if they had been a more reasonable bunch of brothers, but making myself that defenceless so close to them wouldn't have been sensible. They would have tormented me just for the fun of it, even if they hadn't had any particular reason to pick a fight with me. All I could do was sit on the floor with my back to the wall, trying not to let my eyes close, waiting for them to decide their bedtime had come.

Despite my age the general assumption was that I would fend for myself. Food was still the problem it had always been, even though there was probably more money in the family than there had ever been. All the younger ones, including me, were out doing Saturday jobs or paper rounds or any other bit of work we could find to get a few bob for ourselves, and even we were expected to hand most of what we got over to Mum or to Raymond, who was paying the rent. At the same time, the conflict that Dad and Mum had beaten into us was raging as viciously as ever. It was particularly bad between Raymond and Paul.

I think the chaos of our upbringing really tormented Raymond. By nature he was someone who liked order and calm and he'd had no more of that than the rest of us. Paul, by contrast, was even more of a wild card than ever, impulsive and always a little bit crazy. It is easy to see why they could hardly stand being in the same room together. Paul lasted less than two years in the Wandsworth house and then, when he was seventeen or eighteen, walked out and never came back. It was years before any of us heard from him again. From the moment we got to Wandsworth, Raymond was in charge and Mum relied on him totally. He took Dad's place, this was his house and his rules, and none of us doubted it. I suppose he was at least more rational than Dad had ever been. You could say that I was beginning to be a bit rebellious. I don't like the word, because it suggests I was rejecting a way of life that was good for me and was choosing to be bad. I would rather call it a kind of fighting back. If there really was to be no escape for me, I would go down causing as much aggravation as I could.

It was a bit like living with total strangers. The ones who had enough money to buy the food they wanted had their own cupboards in the kitchen and there was hell to pay for anyone who tried to take what wasn't theirs.

I knew that Dad's death had changed nothing in the Roche family and that nothing now ever would. Those of us who were too young to bring in regular money had no place at the table. Mum now had a meal waiting for Raymond, for Paul until he left and often for Terence, the one who got as close to being a favourite as it was possible to be with Mum, although even he still found himself on the receiving end of her punching and kicking when he pushed his luck too far. Francis, Laurence and I were still at school and would be for a while yet, and as ever we had to make do with bread and marg or milk and cereal when there was any in the cupboards, and maybe a share of a meal that Mum might make on a Sunday for everyone.

I soon stopped going up West once we'd moved. It was a more complicated journey from Wandsworth, and it was much too far away to walk there and back. Dave, the only real friend I'd ever had, was long gone. A good year or so before the move to Wandsworth, he had simply vanished. He hadn't come to the dump yard to meet up with me for a couple of weeks and that was odd, so I had gone round to his flat and knocked on the door. His mum answered, and before I had a chance to say a word she went ballistic, f-ing and blinding, a blast of rage that knocked me right back on my heels.

'Don't you fucking come here ever again, you little

shit,' she screamed and then she slammed the door on me.

I didn't dare go back there again, not ever. I heard some kids saying that Dave had been killed under a Tube train, and I knew only too well how likely that was. But then I heard other kids saying that he'd been taken away in an ambulance from his flat, blue from a drug overdose. Yet another kid, one who had come with Dave and me on a couple of our West End adventures, said it was all rubbish, Dave wasn't dead, it was just that the social workers had come and taken him away to a home a long way from London. I didn't know what the truth was. I never saw him again and never heard what had become of him. I missed him badly. Whenever I was in Soho after that I would always be half looking for him, hoping that he'd turn up. His disappearance left a big hole in my life.

Wandsworth should have been a fresh start, but for me it was the very opposite. For all the squalor of the house in Lambeth, leaving it meant that I lost every last bit of the little happiness I had. I had already lost Dave, and now I lost Vincent and Johnny too. No more nights in Vincent's shed, no more trips out in Johnny's lorry. Worst was losing the dump yard and the den, my only refuge. I couldn't check out of the family any more when things got rough. I couldn't even go back there from Wandsworth, because the bulldozers had moved in. It was the front room in Wandsworth or the streets, and I had seen enough of what street life did to kids like me to know I wasn't strong enough to stand it for very long. I had tried the cardboard box and given up after one night, and I had found that quiet concrete stairwells in the flats further out of the centre were too cold even for a dump-yard-hardened boy like me.

There was a moment when I thought I might have fallen on my feet. I was half asleep in one of these stairwells in the early hours one morning when a woman came up the stairs and stopped in front of me.

'You all right, love?'

She was a prostitute coming home after a night's work, I knew that right away as soon as I looked at her – the short skirt, high heels and a certain kind of heavy make-up that was as much a uniform as the Crombies the rent boys wore. That was good. We kids knew that the working girls were sympathetic to us. This one was no exception.

'Get up off that floor and come with me,' she ordered, and I followed her clicking stiletto heels up another couple of flights of stairs. We walked along the fourth-floor balcony until we came to her front door. Inside it was actually warm – she had central heating – and although it wasn't posh, it was very cosy. She had a flat-mate, another working girl, and for three or four days they let me stay with them. I slept on the sofa and they fed me, let me have a bath – that was fantastic, in a bath-room with hot water that came out of the taps – and found some clothes for me that were second-hand but loads better than the ones I had. They mothered me, I suppose, and for a few glorious days I thought they might let me stay for ever. But they had clients coming to the flat too, they had money to earn, and in any case I think they wanted their own space back. They didn't ask me to leave but the feeling that I was in the way grew on me, until I felt I had to say that it was time to go. They were nice about it – they didn't try to stop me, but they asked if I would be okay and gave me a bit of money to help me on my way. That was as close as I ever got to running away from home.

After Dave had disappeared I had got to know quite a lot of the kids on the Soho streets on my own terms, so I wasn't short of people to hang around with if I went there, but by now everyone I knew was getting into really heavy stuff, lots of drugs and lots of rent boy work to pay for it. They weren't dabbling to get by any more. This was their life. I had enough sense of self-preservation to realize that I was getting to an age where it would be harder and harder to avoid doing the same, and even if I had no idea what I wanted from life, I knew it wasn't what they had.

When I was fifteen or sixteen and occasionally going into the West End with a few mates for an evening out, I would still sometimes see faces I knew, but by then they really were completely messed up. One kid recognized me.

'How you doing?' Errol asked me, slapping me on the arm and looking genuinely pleased to see an old street companion from the past. 'I'm not doing so good,' he added, but he didn't need to say it. He looked worn out, skinny, ill, and I knew straight away that he had a very bad drug habit. There was an older guy with him and it seemed as if they were together. He was asking how I knew Errol and I was vague, saying that I'd known him a few years before, when we were kids. I think Errol was just glad to have someone familiar to talk to, but his conversation was all about the problems he was having finding a vein he could inject heroin into. He showed me his arms where the veins had blackened and collapsed from years of shooting up, and the guy he was with said: 'Yeah, he's injecting into his feet now.'

It was horrific. I didn't have much cash on me but I gave him some money, even though I knew Errol was only looking for his next fix, and I got away from the two of them fast. I felt really sorry for him, and I thought: 'Christ, why didn't I end up like that? Why wasn't that me?'

I saw quite a few kids like Errol during my teenage years, the ones I'd first known when they still looked reasonably healthy and young, and they all looked like the life had been kicked out of them. I can't believe many of them lived long enough to see their twentieth birthdays. Why I hadn't taken that road myself, I don't know. Maybe it was down to the little bit of kindness and the glimpse of a better kind of life that Vincent and Johnny had given me. Every time I saw one of those kids a few years down the line from where I'd first met them, I was always horrified and sad for them, and always as grateful as hell that it wasn't me.

Moments like this could trigger the anxiety attacks that were starting to become a real problem for me. I still wonder what a ten-year-old boy thinks. I wonder about the ability I'd had, before I hit eleven and it seemed that my mind began to change and become less controllable, to cope with all the experiences that were forced on me. For a long time I was able to blot out as much as I needed to of all the terrible things that were happening to me, because I knew that to try to make sense of it all brought on terrible feelings of anger and fear. That ability was beginning to fail me, I think, and the anxiety would come out of the clear blue sky and make me shake uncontrollably. When these attacks came I felt as if I was going to die any moment. Keeping away from Soho seemed one way to stop them happening. The only part of my secret Soho life I hung on to as I moved into my teens was the ritual Dave had introduced me to of spending New Year's Eve in Trafalgar Square. It was a great time, because anyone could join in with the hundreds of people who gathered there every year at about eleven o'clock on 31 December, waiting to hear midnight strike on Big Ben just down the road, and everyone cheered and hugged and kissed. Even for me it seemed like a hopeful moment. I was surrounded by happy people, a new year was starting, and it was as though I had loads of friends and everyone wanted to be friends with me. There'd be people with guitars singing songs and everyone joining in, people sharing their drinks and even food. There was always a sense that something wonderful was about to happen, that a new year had potential and possibilities. Out of those two minutes before midnight came some kind of hope, and even I could imagine for a few hours that things might change and a better time was coming. Anything seemed possible.

Mind you, on the day we had moved something very

odd had happened, and when I remembered it in the low, anxious moments that were becoming more frequent, it convinced me yet again that escape would never be possible.

I was the last to leave the house with Mum that day. The others had already gone on with what furniture and belongings we had to the new house, and I was told to stay to help Mum do whatever she needed to do before she locked up and left. As we walked away, southwards down the road, we both heard someone shout my mother's name.

'Bridget!'

We stopped dead and looked at each other. We both looked back towards the house. There was no-one on the street behind us and the house looked just as dead and near-derelict as it always had during the years we'd been living there. The owner of that voice certainly wasn't there and yet it had made all the hairs on the back of my neck stand up, and I had felt the old, familiar cold stab of fear at the sound of it.

'That was your father,' Mum said, almost whispering. It was the only time I ever saw her looking frightened.

I didn't speak. I didn't know what to say, because she was right. A voice from the grave, dead two years, demanding to know why she was leaving without him. It was an omen. No matter what we did or how far away we got, the past would never let go of us.

14. School: Part 2

Any time I tried to do something positive, something good, the kind of thing that would have earned me approval in another kind of family, my efforts were always sabotaged. A few years after we moved, I came into the house one afternoon and saw that Mum, Raymond and Terence were all sitting round the table in the kitchen. On the table was a pile of notes, mostly pounds and a few fivers. I knew instantly that this must be the money I had been secretly saving and that one of them had found its hiding place. I would put my money on Terence, the one who enjoyed getting everyone else into trouble.

'What's this?' my mother demanded within seconds of me walking through the door, stabbing her finger aggressively at the pile.

'Is that my money – what's it doing there?' I shouted back, already frightened but not so frightened that I couldn't still be a bit angry. I was outraged, in fact, and yet I could feel my stomach hitting the floor. The money was lost, I knew that straight away, and there was probably a kicking coming too. I could almost have cried with the way the fear and anger were swirling around together inside me. I didn't know whether to run or lay into the lot of them.

'Your money? How is it your bloody money, then?

How do *you*' – said with a sneer – 'come to have forty quid, you selfish little shit?'

This was Raymond. Terence had the usual smirk on his face that said someone else was in trouble and he wasn't, and he liked it that way. I had a girlfriend, my first real girlfriend, and every other girlfriend in our neighbourhood got nice presents from their boyfriends. I wanted to get Clara something really impressive, like a gold chain or bracelet, and for about three or four months I'd been saving what I could keep back from the family from the various odd jobs I was doing at the time.

'You, buying presents for girlfriends,' my mother screamed at the top of her voice, getting to her feet. 'Who do you think you are, you little –? Taking money out of this house to spend it on some slut . . .'

I was standing in the doorway of the kitchen. They had all forgotten that I'd begun to have a fairly spectacular growth spurt and now I was a good few inches taller than Mum. Still skinny, but big enough to put my hands out and get hold of her wrists and stop her going for me with her fists. Raymond and Terence suddenly looked alarmed. I heard Terence shout: 'He's going to hit you, Mum' – which wasn't true, of course, and I think they all knew it – and I could see them shifting, as if both of them were about to get up too. I knew I wouldn't have a chance against all three of them, so I made a conscious decision to collapse on the floor in front of Mum, in the old way, and let her do what she wanted until she'd kicked her temper out on me. When she'd finished, I got up and walked back out of the house. I never saw the money again. I don't know what happened to it, whether they split it between them or it went into Mum's purse. It was never mentioned again, and it's interesting that no-one accused me of pinching it from somewhere. I'm sure that's what they thought when it was first found, stashed under a loose floorboard in the back room where I had imagined it would be safe. But there must have been something about the way I'd said these were my savings that convinced them I was telling the truth. In their hearts, I think, they knew that kind of stealing, taking large amounts of cash off other people, wasn't yet one of my faults. I had stolen to eat and survive, like we all had, but I had never stolen to get money for the sake of it. I suspect Mum's outrage had a lot to do with her realizing that I could do something she had never been able to do, get money and put it by instead of blowing it the moment I had it in my hand.

But, of course, that incident and many others like it killed any motivation I might have had to break out of the mould.

Moving to Wandsworth and, at the same time, starting at senior school could have led to good things if I'd had anyone at home who cared about that kind of thing. But that would have taken affection and affection was an alien word and an alien kind of behaviour. All they cared about was that I didn't cost them anything and that, if possible, I brought in some money so that I could make some claim to a place in the family. I did try to tell myself that this was a new start and things were going to be different. This was a place, if nothing else, where no-one knew my brothers, so I didn't have to put up with having their reputation handed down to me.

As it was, with the daily struggle for enough to eat still rumbling along in the back of my mind and the fear of daily attacks from any one of the six people I was living with, my mind was a mess of worry. I worried about whether I could keep up with helping the local milkman on his round in return for maybe 50p a week and the odd bottle of milk, because this was what kept hunger at bay, and I worried about whether I would get a decent night's sleep. For a few short days I worried about getting up in time for a paper round I'd taken on. I gave that up very quickly because part of my round was a fourteen-floor block of flats where the lift never worked. I couldn't get to the top of those flats without feeling like I was on my last legs. I think I was so undernourished that I just didn't have the strength to do it. I could just about cope with walking on the flat with the milkman, because there were lots of stops and starts, moments when I could gather my strength.

I worried about whether I had clothes to go to school in, and this seemed even more important for an eleven-year-old who could see that all the kids around him seemed to have all the latest gear. It wasn't like North Lambeth, where no-one looked terrific because most families were short of money. There were a lot more middle-class people around in Wandsworth. That's what they looked like in my eyes at least, and I don't think anyone looked as poor as I did. I did get a uniform from an educational charity when I started at the Wandsworth comprehensive I was sent to, but there was only one shirt with it and that soon bit the dust. Within a couple of days of me first putting it on, an attack from Mum left it covered in blood and irretrievable. It wasn't as if she was going to come up with handy household hints about how to get blood out of cotton. Everyone else seemed to have their place in the house and seemed to get the clothes they needed, but I never had enough to wear. Sleeping on the sofa in the living room was a big drawback. I woke up one morning and my trousers had gone. It was just like being in the old house again, so it wasn't that unusual, except that by this time all my brothers were about twice the size of me. I sat there and wondered how the hell whoever had nicked them had got them on. Then it occurred to me that one of them had probably taken them as they were passing through, seeing me there spark out, because it was a funny thing to do.

I wouldn't say I was getting braver, but I was certainly getting more bloody-minded. I was going to get a beating at one end of my life or the other, so I began to think that I might as well get it while I was standing up in something decent. I started stealing my brothers' shirts quite often, going off to school, coming back forgetting that I had it on, and in the evening taking the kind of hiding that always left me bleeding once the shirt's owner laid eyes on me. Outwardly I don't suppose I seemed that different to the rest of my family for quite a while after the move, but I knew my mind was slowly falling apart. I found myself thinking that this way of life had to stop. I felt so alone all the time, I had no-one to support me, no-one to express myself to, because no-one was interested.

Shortly after starting senior school, I found myself standing next to a brick wall near the new house and punching it with my bare fists over and over again. Punch. I wanted, for the want of a better word, some dignity. Punch. I didn't want to be looked down on all the time, and at the new school it was already the same old story. Punch. You're a disgrace, Roche. Punch. You look like you've slept in your clothes. Well, I had. Punch. If you can't be bothered to concentrate, get out of my class. Punch. I'm putting a chalk line on the seat of your pants and now I'm going to cane you until I've beaten the mark off you. Punch. My hands were bloody from thumping the brickwork and pain was shooting up my arms. Punch. See, I can take pain, I can take it better than anyone. Punch. I need to be able to take it because there's no-one around to help, no-one to look after me. Punch. When does it end? When does it ever fucking end?

The cane was the only part of life at senior school that was new to me. Yes, it stung, but it didn't terrify me. How could it? I was being beaten to a pulp at home, so whatever the headmaster did to me at school because of my behaviour hardly mattered. It's actually hard for me to know what kind of a kid I was, because the inside of my head was such a mess at the time, but I know I must have been disruptive. I couldn't concentrate on anything for more than a couple of minutes and then I'd get fed up and angry, and I'd answer back when teachers tried to pull me back into line. I never did anything violent, but I had a complete lack of respect for anyone in authority – what adult had there been in my life, really, apart from Vincent and Johnny, who deserved respect? – and I must have been a tough kid to have around.

I was once caned for something that wasn't the usual scenario of cheeking a teacher. I saw some kid about my age being given a hard time by some bigger boys. That was another thing: at senior school the bullies were naturally much bigger than they had been at the junior school in North Lambeth and could do real damage when they picked on a victim. The school was huge, and this kid wasn't in my class, but I had heard that his dad had died. That touched something in me. I couldn't say that I knew what it was like to grieve for a father, but I knew about the confusion it made you feel. I went over to speak to him, to let the others know he wasn't alone.

'What's wrong?' I asked. The bullies hung back a little to weigh me up, see what I was going to do. Then it was: 'Who are you looking at, you little punk?'

'Leave him alone,' I told them. One of them went for me and I gave him what for, as well as I was able to given that this kid must have been at least six inches taller than me. I, of course, was the one who got sent to the headmaster's office. Another caning. Yet I was often doing things like this, seeing kids even weaker than me being picked on and trying to help. It was as if I was seeing reflections of myself everywhere and, even if I couldn't help myself, I wanted to help them if I could. One girl, quite a plain kid who wore specs, eventually begged me to leave her alone. She looked quite middle class to me, nicely dressed, and I don't know why she was being picked on. One day I saw one of the boys just smack her round the face and she was cowering, expecting more. I couldn't help myself – I attacked him and he wasn't expecting it, and I punched him over and over again until his face was bleeding. He backed off and went off to one of the toilets to clean himself up and – this was a weak mistake I regret – I followed him because I was still angry and still wanted to fight him. Fortunately one of his friends went with him and fought back as I tried to go for this kid again while he was washing his face over the sink.

A little later I saw the girl again and asked if she was okay.

'Go away,' she said. 'If you go away, they might leave me alone. It's you they're after.'

And I guess that was true. As ever, my clothes marked me out as a target. But it seemed to me that the people who had been picking on her left her alone a bit after that, so perhaps I got a result there.

I still couldn't eat properly, not in a way that other people wouldn't think was strange and disgusting, so it was into the dinner hall every lunchtime, grab a bread roll or anything that was portable, and get outside fast to eat it alone.

There were other things, quite little insignificant things to other kids, that set me apart. I was always being told off by teachers for not having pens and pencils. I was lucky if I had a pair of shoes to go to school in. I didn't have things like a pencil case and I couldn't have hung on to that kind of stuff for more than twenty-four hours if I had. One of my brothers would have taken them off me just for a laugh. The most violent thing I ever did – and I'm not proud of it – was to throw a pencil at a maths teacher. He'd given it to me, but only after making a whole load of snide remarks about the way I was dressed and how I never seemed to be able to get to school with the right equipment. His comments were horrible, just horrible, and without any doubt he was trying to make me look silly in front of the class. He succeeded, and I couldn't control my anger.

The teacher walked out of class. This was a dramatic thing for a teacher to do in those days and everyone went silent. He came back a few minutes later with the head of maths and I thought: 'I'm really for it this time.' The rumours were that in his office he had the biggest, thickest cane in the school and you couldn't walk when he'd finished with you.

I went off with him, following him through the school and up the stairs that led into the oldest part of the building where his office was.

'Why did you do that?' he asked when he'd closed the door.

No kid in that situation can tell it like it is. 'I don't know, sir,' I said.

'What do you think I'm going to do to you?'

'Cane me, sir,' I answered.

'No, Peter, I'm not going to do that. Sit down.'

He talked to me. He talked for maybe fifteen minutes. I didn't take in a word of what he said because my mind was such a scramble of fear and confusion I couldn't hear him. All I could think was: 'He's a teacher. He's head of maths. And he's being nice to me. What the hell is going on? What's the catch? When is he going to turn nasty?'

The bell went, he stood up, opened the door and told me to go off to wherever I had to be next. I still feel confused when I think about him. There is no doubt that within a couple of months of me starting there, I had a reputation. If my behaviour in class was poor, my behaviour in the playground was very nearly psychotic. I used to run round and round every break-time, round and round and round the whole playground, never stopping moving for a moment if I could help it. I think I had some idea that if I kept moving I'd be safe, but there was also a kind of jumpiness in my bones that made it hard for me to keep still, and running like this helped me to get rid of some of it. I was a bit like those animals you see in zoos that go nuts because they can't cope with being in a cage, and they end up walking incessantly backwards and forwards, wearing a groove in the ground, or even standing still and swaying from side to side. In fact there was one teacher who said something like this while he was telling me off before he gave me the stick. I have no idea why he caned me. 'I look out of my window and see you running around this playground like an animal, Roche,' he said. I think he had it about right.

On the way to and from school, and sometimes even in the playground in full sight of the school buildings, there were always the bullies to deal with. Sometimes when the older lads from school booted me, and I do mean that they really put the boot in, it did hurt so badly that it even got through my hard shell. I'd be in a lot of pain and desperately wanting to cry. I didn't. I began to laugh when this happened. I'd take a kicking and I'd get up and laugh at them. This may have helped me a little, because I think some of them began to think I was a bit odd, a bit weird, and that frightened even them just a little bit.

I couldn't trust adults, I couldn't trust other children and I certainly couldn't trust authority. At the same time I had worked out that I didn't want to be pushed around any more. I wanted some pride, and I wanted other people to like me for a change.

It wasn't just myself I was ashamed of. Laurence and Terence were still making the journey over to their secondary school in North Lambeth, and one evening I saw Terence getting off the bus on his way back home and then saw that three older boys from our school had spotted him. One of them had a bottle in his hand. I thought: 'Christ, they're going to give him such a beating.' I knew that one of the reasons why he would get a really terrible going-over was because there was no chance he would stand and fight. Me, I would have tried a bit of bravado if I was cornered, even though I was no match for even one fifteen-year-old. There was something about fighting back that got you off a bit more lightly, as if they had just a bit of respect for your nerve. I had also learned, thanks to my new-found bloody-mindedness, that refusing to take it lying down, even though I knew I would have to take it, seemed to make me less of a target. It was as if afterwards I was seen as being more trouble than I was worth. Not always, but maybe five or six times out of ten. But Laurence and Terence would always turn and run like hell and I hated to see that. Ever since the days of the holiday school dinners I had understood that if you made a victim of yourself, they wouldn't stop bullying you, and I just didn't want it.

Wandsworth was where I discovered a new and astonishing side to Mum. She could beat the hell out of us, we could beat the hell out of each other without her turning a hair. But when an outsider started on one of us, she wouldn't have it at any price, and there were several times after we moved to this new territory that she laid into anyone who tried it. She must have been in her late forties at this time, quite a stout middle-aged woman with hair that was now completely grey, but she still packed a lot of power in those broad shoulders of hers.

I ran home and told her that Terence was for it if she didn't help him. She picked up her Sally and moved along the street at surprising speed, meeting Terence belting round the corner the other way. The kids behind him were taken completely by surprise and she laid into them, slashing this way and that, connecting quite a few times with their legs and heads, and shouting: 'Try that again with one of my boys and I'll come after you till I find you, you filthy little bastards.'

My misdemeanours at school continued and I was getting into more and more trouble. I did a horrible thing, really. One day one of a group of older boys dragged me into the toilets and tried to push my head into the bowl and flush it. I managed to fight him off me a bit, and he eventually gave up when someone came in and saw us in a bit of a tussle. But I'd got to the stage where I just didn't want to accept this kind of thing any more. Things were going to change, I told myself. Later in the day I stole a compass – one of those things with a spike on the end for drawing circles in maths lessons, and of course I had to steal it because I never had one of my own – and as I left school that afternoon to walk home, sure enough I saw this kid coming towards me.

'Here we go,' I thought. When he got up to me with this sneery smile on his face, looking to finish what he'd started in the toilets, I pulled the compass out of my pocket and stuck the point in his belly. He looked at me, surprised as hell, and looked down at the compass, just sticking there, right through his shirt and into his stomach.

'Roche,' he gasped, 'you're a fucking nutter.'

I wasn't a nutter. I just wanted to be left alone. I seemed to be excluded from everything and it wasn't as if people left you to be excluded in peace. They had to keep doing things to you to make sure you knew you didn't belong. There was me and there was society. Other kids came back from the school holidays and talked about where they'd been, or what presents they'd got for Christmas or their birthday. For us these days were, as ever, a normal day. What came out of the incident with the compass was a mystery to me. At the time I turned and walked away fast, although I felt reasonably sure that he wasn't going to come after me. Not long after this, however, although I never seemed to be punished directly for what I'd done and no-one spoke to me about it, I was sent to a child psychologist, who asked me all sorts of questions about my problems at school. My mother was with me, one of the few times I'd had to go with her to see someone who fitted her idea of 'the authorities' and wasn't beaten senseless afterwards. I could tell this psychologist woman only half the truth, of course. I just kept on about the bullies at school and never mentioned the bullies at home. Then she announced that she wanted to do a physical examination of me, and I wouldn't let her.

'Your mother doesn't have to be in the room,' she said, and I thought: 'I couldn't care less. I already have more than enough people messing about with my body and I'm not going to let you add your name to the list at any price.'

Mum was unusually quiet. She hardly said a word, to her or to me. I wonder whether she was thinking about how she might explain the state my body would have been in at that time, what with all the kickings I was getting from her and the beatings from my brothers. My injuries were still mostly of the kind that could be covered up by a school uniform. Not that it mattered. I was so afraid of physical contact that there wasn't a chance I was going to take my clothes off for anyone.

I did a lot of tests and the psychologist decided that I had a good IQ and she couldn't understand why I didn't want to learn. Yet she must have seen some sign of the state I was in because within a week or two I was sent to a place in Battersea for the rest of that school year. It was called a Guidance Centre, a special school for disturbed children. It was a collection of huts in an old school yard where we mostly seemed to hang around doing nothing in particular. I don't suppose I was what you might call a normal child at the time, but there were kids there who made me feel as sane as a doctor. A girl who was caught smoking drugs in one of the huts was told she would have to be expelled.

'Please don't send me home, my dad'll kill me,' she screamed over and over again. When they wouldn't listen to her crying and begging, she went berserk and started throwing furniture at the teachers and the other kids. She was so wild they couldn't get near her to stop her, and in the end they had to send for the police and clear the rest of us out of the way. All of us were standing outside enjoying the drama while a policeman with a megaphone shouted: 'Come out without any trouble, or we'll have to send in the dogs.' It was mad. She came out in the end.

Floyd, a boy who became my best friend there, was told he would have to go home after he kicked the headmaster's door in.

'How are you going to get me home?' he asked, very cocky but very sullen with it. 'My dad's in a wheelchair. He can't get down here to get me. There ain't no-one else.'

In the end he was allowed to stay, just as I was a bit later when I broke the rules. I ended up in a fight with another lad and I was told that my mother would be on her way to take me home. I didn't want that, more shit, more grievance from her, but she was called down to take me home. That was another beating, then, but they did at least allow me to go back.

I haven't a clue what the idea was at this place. There were lessons but they were a lot easier than anything I'd been doing in Wandsworth. They used to bring cups of tea round – like it was a hospital – and dinners would be delivered to the main building, where we ate. It was a very strange place, it seemed to me. Sometimes you'd have to go and talk to one of the staff about how you felt and what you'd been doing. Once a week they'd give us a ticket that we could use on the train to go into central London to a museum. We had to take a form with us and get it signed by the museum staff to say what time we'd arrived and what time we'd left. Obviously I tried a few times to leave earlier than we were supposed to so that I could get into the West End and maybe do a bit of begging, just a quick trip and a bit of a change, nothing that would alarm me too much and bring on one of those panic attacks, but it was hard to get out without being spotted. If I did get out, there was the problem of getting back in again so that I could come out and get my signature at the proper time, so most of the time I decided it wasn't worth the effort.

As I say, it was a nice rest, but I never did really work out what the point of all this was. I was back at my old school for the beginning of my third year there and things, if anything, were worse. Now we were doing a subject called technical drawing that I'd never heard of before and for this you needed a lot of kit – pencils, rulers, geometry instruments, the works – and of course I had none of it. I had to go to the front of the class and borrow what we needed for that lesson, but it didn't solve anything. I was so far behind the other kids it was a joke.

'Are you stupid?' the teacher yelled when I put my hand up for the fifth time to ask him to explain what I was expected to do. I wasn't stupid. I'd think no, of course I'm not, I just can't think properly about anything. In another class I wasn't concentrating and the teacher came up in front of me and slammed a book down on the desk to make me jump. I jumped and then I shouted: 'Fuck off!' at him.

'Get out of my class,' he shouted back, so I did.

And I gave up. That was it. I'd had it with school.

It was about this time, after I'd got sent back to the senior school and I was getting into more trouble, particularly for being caught fighting the older boys yet again – although, God knows, they started it – that I had my first major panic attack. It wasn't a little anxious thing, like it had been, it was the full works. I was walking back home after school and suddenly it was as if my whole body was screaming: 'Don't make me go back there!' I couldn't stand the thought of all the confrontation I was going back to. I actually thought I was having a heart attack. I collapsed on the pavement on all fours with my heart beating so fast and so hard I thought it might burst out of my chest. I didn't see how it could keep going like that. I felt sick and weak, and it was hard to breathe. I didn't die, though, and I pulled myself towards the garden wall that was next to me and sat there with my back against it, trying to recover enough to get up and walk the last few yards home.

'Go to the doctor's,' said Mum, not much concerned

when I staggered in and announced that I had heart trouble. She lost interest within seconds so I took myself off to the doctor, and he gave me a bottle of green medicine. I think it was a tonic, some kind of vitamin potion.

I started my old trick again of staying out of the house at night if I could. I didn't have the dump yard this time, but there were a few lads in the area I was getting to know on what felt like an even footing. If I could persuade one of them to let me sleep on his mum's floor at night, I would choose that every time. The problem was that some of these lads were no better than they should have been. They were into all sorts of things, stealing cars, burglary, even bag-snatching. Again there was a limit to how far I was prepared to go along with them, but I was long past the point where I could see anything wrong with a bit of stealing if I couldn't see any real victim at the other end.

A letter came from school. I had been playing truant all over the place. Mum's threats about going to school were beginning to lose their power over me, not least because I was getting a beating every day anyway, whether I went to school or not. One more here or there hardly mattered, whereas a day not spent at school was a bonus. When I did turn up, I was fighting in the playground and making no effort at all in the classroom. Uncontrollable, the letter said. I was to be expelled indefinitely. I was a month or two short of my fourteenth birthday.

Although the letter got me a real kicking from Mum, it was worth it. It was such a relief to be told that I never had to go back there again. Ironically, I saw it as freedom. I didn't realize then that what I was now free to do was, inevitably, become what at the time they still called a teenage delinquent.

15. Teenage Kicks and Girls

Some time before I was expelled I had begun to do some serious stealing, although it didn't seem that bad to me at the time. It was just another kind of survival. I had not seen much of Francis while we'd been in North Lambeth, because he was being bussed out of the area to his special school, but after we moved he was put back into a mainstream school. I don't think this did him a lot of good. Although his two-year silence had ended a couple of years before the move, he remained a bit apart from the rest of us, always slightly out to lunch. If he spoke to anyone, it was usually to me. I think he felt I was the least threatening of all of us and I was the one he could count on to help him with any scheme he had in mind. He was hungry too, being one of the younger ones and still at school, and he came to me one evening and said that he'd found out where we could get a few loaves of bread completely free. The catch was that we had to get up very early in the morning. That was no problem for me, especially after all the training I'd put myself through to meet Johnny on time to go out in his lorry, so the next morning we were awake at 4.30 and sneaking out of the house.

Francis had discovered that the local bakery did its baking very early in the morning, and as loaves came out of the oven they were wheeled on tall trolleys out into the yard behind the shop to cool off while another batch was baked. The yeasty, mouth-watering smell filled the air, calling to our empty rumbling stomachs from streets away. We could climb the wall from the street behind and without even having to get into the yard we could nick three or four loaves from the top shelf of the trolley. This was a fantastic discovery, an almost risk-free way of getting some really substantial food and a lot of it. It didn't seem that much different from taking bottles of milk from doorsteps, something I'd been doing for years. I thought I'd never tasted anything as delicious as that warm bread. We'd run a few streets away with what we could carry and eat it just as it was, pulling chunks off and stuffing them in our mouths while we crouched in the half-light of dawn behind someone's garden wall.

From there it was a short step to Francis's next project, which was inspired, I think, by the fifteen-year-old local lad he'd got to know who had lived round that way for years. Off we went in the middle of the night, feeling like grown-up cat burglars, heading for the huge milk depot on an industrial estate on the outskirts of the district. It was where all the milk floats were parked at night in a warehouse behind big metal gates. This was a late-night job rather than an early-morning one, because the milkmen started work at about 4 a.m., and the lorries bringing the bottled milk for that day's deliveries began to arrive even earlier.

I couldn't understand Francis's interest in this place at first. The milk would all be gone, I pointed out, and anyway it was a lot easier to wait until it was on a doorstep.

'No, you don't know nothing,' he said. 'The floats have got food in them. Bread, eggs, orange juice, yoghurt, even butter, all that kind of stuff. That stuff stays on the floats all night. It's easy pickings.'

It did sound good, and it was. We were in and out of that yard quite a few times and for a while our stomachs were full of decent food for a change. We didn't just take what we could put in our pockets. We had to climb over the roof of the warehouse to get into it, and once we'd reached the milk floats we'd get a milk crate, fill it with whatever we could find, and head back over the roof carrying it between us. We felt bold and daring, strong and clever. Some of it we consumed on the spot, drinking orange juice and spooning yoghurt out of pots with our fingers, and some we took home. When we brought eggs and bread back, food that could be got rid of quickly, Mum never questioned us too closely. As it had always been with her and Dad, honesty wasn't the issue. Getting caught was what worried them. At one point Francis had come back to the Wandsworth house carrying a television that he claimed he'd helped himself to after spotting it just inside an open window a few streets away. Mum went berserk, screaming: 'Jesus, Mary and Joseph, get that bloody thing out of here, you thieving little bastard.' She had the self-control to wait until he'd put it down before she started to hit him and punch him. Food was different. In our house the evidence would be gone faster than even she could move towards her Sally when her temper was up. She'd see us coming in with the stuff and turn her back on us. Her silence, the absence of the few choice abusive words that usually greeted us when we made an appearance, was what passed for approval from her.

Then we did get caught. That night Francis, the crate and I had all made it up onto the roof. The other boy was still in the yard below. Francis and I heard some kind of commotion out in the street and from the roof we could see that there were maybe half a dozen police cars all round the yard. As we wondered what the hell to do all the lights came on. The nightwatchman had obviously arrived with the keys, and officers swarmed into the yard and grabbed the other kid as he tried to get to the railings on the other side. For a few minutes Francis and I thought we might be okay if we laid flat on the roof, well out of the lights, and kept quiet. We could hear that some of the officers were trying to get up on the roof. I heard one of them quite close to me saying loudly: 'They're not here.' I relaxed just a little. Seconds later, off guard, I was grabbed by the hair and hauled to my feet.

We were taken down to the police station, my mother was fetched out of bed to get us, and the minute we got home we were both punched to the floor and given a really vicious kicking. This was serious stuff, getting caught by the police in the middle of a burglary.

Raymond sneered: 'You think you're so fucking clever, don't you?', Mum backed me into a corner of the kitchen, her usual trick, and was kicking and punching me, using her fists when I tried to fend off her feet and switching back to her feet when I put my hands over my head to shield myself from the punches.

I was pissed off. I would never have tried to fight back, but I was fed up with this kind of beating.

'God knows, I wish you'd never been born,' she screeched.

'That's not my fault,' I yelled back. 'You shouldn't have bloody had me, then, should you?'

There was a pause, and then the blows and kicks came thick and fast.

'Who the fuck do you think you are, you cheeky little shit,' she yelled, so furious and beside herself that the spit was hanging from her mouth. Raymond came into the kitchen and put the kettle on.

'Fuck off out of here, and let Mum get a cup of tea,' he said, and only then did Mum stop, panting as if she'd run a couple of miles.

There was obviously no acknowledgement from either of them of the real problem, that here we were, two Roche brothers, out stealing food because we were hungry. For some reason I didn't understand, things had recently got so bad that one of the neighbours had brought food round for us. I had thought that both Mum and Raymond and even Paul were working from time to time, but maybe they weren't. I was never told anything. All I knew was that even bread and margarine weren't making an appearance in the house at that time.

I was lucky. I got a caution from the police for that offence, rather than being charged and taken to court, but there was nothing going on in my life that was likely to change the way I was thinking or the things I was doing. For a while after I was expelled from school I was sent to a tutor, who was supposed to be giving me the lessons that I would have had at school, or at least helping me to read and write better. Instead I ended up doing odd jobs for her and her husband, painting fences and clearing their garden. Maybe I just couldn't concentrate and they thought that if there was no way I could settle to learning, it was better that I was doing something constructive and feeling useful while I had to be there. At the time I saw what they were doing to me as more of the same old business of every adult I knew taking Peter Roche for a sucker. After a while I stopped going and no-one came looking for me. My education was over.

I was not at school, but I still wasn't old enough to have a proper job. I had tried quite a few ways of getting money honestly. For a while I hunted round the area for building sites, asking if I could do a bit of labouring. At one place I was told that I could help reclaim old bricks, chipping mortar off them so that they could be reused. I was paid perhaps £1 for a couple of days of this. After a third day of hard graft the boss flatly refused to give me any money at all and laughed when I argued with him. There wasn't much I could do about it. I shouldn't have been on a building site at my age and we both knew it.

I carried on helping with the milk round, and I also got some work with a hardware and grocery shop nearby that paid local boys 25p a day to do errands like delivering paraffin to customers, tidying the shelves, and fetching and carrying from the stock room. One of the jobs we had to do, even though we were really far too young for it, was to siphon paraffin from the big storage tank at the back of the shop into the smaller one inside, where the cans were filled for customers.

It was a long day in the shop, and if I wanted to keep my slot there I had to turn up when I'd said I would and jump to it when something needed to be done. So I knew that I was capable of working hard and being reliable, and that I really did want to work. I didn't want to be hanging around doing nothing. But I could only have the odd day's work there, and without money or support from home it was hard to find anything else to do to fill all the free time I now had.

So this is how it was. I needed food and clothes, and I was at an age when I wanted things too, things like other kids had. There was no legitimate way I could get these things. The hardware shop and the milk round didn't exactly pay well, and even when I tried to save from what little I was getting, the family would have it off me. As a result I was rapidly losing the uncomfortable feelings that begging and stealing had always given me. I couldn't learn, I couldn't do proper work, I couldn't save, and I couldn't look for a safe place to live.

I could steal, so I stole.

I started to steal anything, particularly what was lying around in other people's gardens. Toys, pushbikes, tools. I graduated to breaking into cars when I could see something inside that I wanted or that I might be able to sell to people coming out of the local pubs. Holdalls, clothes, radios. At the shop, once I was trusted enough to go on the till, I started to take a 10p here and a 10p there when I had the chance. I have to say that for a kid with no money and no happiness, seeing all that cash in the drawer was an irresistible temptation. Of course I knew it was wrong. But I let myself believe that there was so much of it there in one place that I couldn't possibly be hurting anyone by taking a bit of it. I also told myself that at 25p for a day's work, I was being ripped off. I was only topping up my wages, and I deserved it.

I was clever. I wasn't like one of the other lads who took money out of the till and kept it in his shoes. One evening the boss told him to stand where he was while he checked him over. He'd looked through all the kid's pockets and I thought he might have got away with it, when the boss suddenly said: 'Now take off your shoes.' That kid never came back again. What I used to do instead was pocket a few 10p pieces and then head for the toilet upstairs. Up there, just as I'd often done at home, I hid my takings under a carpet close to the toilet door. I'd leave it there for days sometimes, until I felt quite sure that this was a day when the boss wouldn't be around and it was safe to smuggle it out in the evening. I was often searched and was never found out.

The tension back in our house was so bad between all of us that we didn't even acknowledge each other if we happened to pass in the street. We would all put our heads down and keep our eyes on the pavement. But this strange loyalty I nevertheless felt for the family was still so strong that if I saw one of the brothers walking past the shop door when I was alone behind the counter, I'd call him in and give him a bagful of whatever we thought might be useful at home.

Because I was working there, I was getting to know more of the local kids. Away from school it seemed a lot easier to get on with other kids and I was beginning to hang around with groups of youngsters who lived on the high-rise estates nearby. Maybe they had been watched more closely than I had ever been by their families when they were younger, but by their teens, like me, they were getting wild and were out at all hours up to no good, and not that many questions were asked when they got home. For the first time in my life I was finding quite a lot of company among boys who were living my kind of life.

Through them I met kids from children's homes who were completely out of control, and older kids who were living in probation hostels in the area and already had serious criminal records. Most of the kids I got to know were quite a bit older than me. Kids my age were at school and not free to roam wherever the fancy took them.

These friendships were disastrous, of course. I went with them when they smashed jewellers' windows and snatched rings and necklaces and belted off with them. One of these was a jeweller's shop next door to a police station, of all places. I stood next to the lad who had smashed the window with a brick, nervous but not particularly frightened, taking the stuff from him as he dipped his hand in and out of the hole, emptying the display. I was no longer shocked by the idea of being involved in this kind of crime. I didn't want to get caught, though, and my stomach was churning. 'Get a move on!' I said to this lad.

'I don't want to cut my bleeding arm off, do I?' he spat back. He'd only been able to make a hole the size of the brick he'd used to smash in the laminated-glass window, and he was right, he had to be careful.

I can't even excuse what I did by saying crimes like these were spur-of-the-moment events. In this case we had already walked round the area and worked out our escape route. We ran across the road, through a graveyard, down another road and into an alley, where we waited for a while until everything seemed quiet. I'd been told about a scrap metal dealer in Earlsfield who would buy certain things off the local kids if they were discreet about approaching him. I started taking power tools and lawnmowers to him that I'd taken from gardens and sheds in the area. The day after our smash-and-grab raid he even took this jewellery from us. He didn't pay big money, of course, but we didn't argue. We took what he offered and went looking for something else to nick.

Stealing to get money was something I saw as a necessity. But I was a teenager now, and I wanted a bit more than survival. I wanted thrills. My new friends now showed me how to do what I'd seen boys in the West End doing a few years before. Not breaking into a car to steal what was in it, but to steal the car itself. I wasn't quite up to driving yet, but more and more often I went with other kids in stolen cars on countless joy-rides as they tried to find a breaker's yard that might buy them, but mostly just for the excitement of leaving London in a car. I had hardly ever ridden in a car before. It was fantastic.

These kids weren't just stealing cars. I persuaded one of

them to get on a train with me one day. My idea was to go to the West End for a bit of a wander around, maybe to see if we could get into one of the pubs, and perhaps impress this kid with how well I knew that patch. He sat opposite me on the train, next to a woman who had put her bag on the seat beside her. Fortunately we hadn't spoken to each other at any point after we'd stepped aboard, because a couple of stations up the line, just as the train was about to pull out, he snatched her bag and leaped out of the door. He was gone. I sat there stunned by what he'd done and the speed he'd done it with, and by the hysteria of the woman who was right in front of me and screaming her head off. Fortunately it was a slow train and it stopped at another station a few minutes later. By now the woman was sobbing and a few of the other passengers were comforting her. I got off as casually as I could amid all the kerfuffle and got the hell away from there. I might not have cared much at that time about how dishonest I was, but I didn't want to be caught.

This particular kid lived in a children's home near Putney. Now this place was a revelation to me. I had met kids from children's homes before, when I'd been hanging about the West End with Dave, my dump-yard mate, but I'd never been in one. If I imagined what these places were like, I suppose I thought they were a bit like my old home, dilapidated, run-down, maybe a bit cleaner and not as smelly, but full of mad kids sleeping four or five to a room with no more privacy or peace than I'd ever had. This home in Putney was beautiful. It had lovely blue carpets everywhere, curtains at all the windows, nice furniture, and it had a flowery smell about it that hit your nostrils as you walked through the door which must have come from cleaning fluid or polish. Most of the boys had their own rooms, with beds and wardrobes and a desk for them to sit and work at. Not that they did a lot of that, of course, but I was very impressed. It looked like a proper home, which I suppose said a lot about how many proper homes I'd seen. But there was order there and calmness, everyone seemed to have their place, and there was always a grown-up around who seemed to care about what was going on.

'How do I get in here?' I asked one of the staff when I was there one day, invited in by one of the lads to watch telly. They had a big lounge full of comfortable chairs and everyone was sitting down quietly watching the box. They could go to the kitchen and help themselves to drinks and biscuits when they wanted.

'You have to be someone who has no parents,' said this man. He looked quite surprised.

I was keen to qualify. 'My dad's dead. My mum isn't, but she doesn't want me around.'

'I'm sorry, son, it doesn't quite work like that. Have a biscuit.'

I was actually jealous of these kids who didn't have parents. That was silly, really, because although I didn't yet know anyone myself who did anything as bad as breaking into people's houses to steal, my friend had said that the kids who lived here were always at it, so they were hardly on the fast track to the good life.

I couldn't understand it. 'Why would they be doing

that when they have a place like this to live?' I asked. 'They ought to stay in and enjoy it. They shouldn't be going out stealing all the time.' He thought I was soft. I thought that I'd never steal again if I had a home like this. I couldn't see why I would need to, but I guess I was seeing the place through rose-tinted glasses. I was cadging a floor to sleep on every night if I could manage it. Mates in the council flats would persuade their mothers to let me stay a few nights, but I could always tell when I was outstaying my welcome and would have to move on. Sometimes friends would smuggle me into their children's home. I even dossed down in probation hostels. Anywhere, rather than go home to get beaten up and then sleep in the living room.

It was a sad state to be in. It made me miss a real opportunity that could have pulled me out of the hole I was in. I had found another sanctuary that was a good deal better for me than any of the friends I was hanging around with. There was a snooker hall in Earlsfield, and through that place I heard about another near Clapham Junction, both places where people like Jimmy White and Tony Meo had learned their skills.

If I went to these places late at night, I discovered, the guys who were serious about their snooker would still be playing into the early hours and I could hang around waiting for one of them to send me to the counter for a cup of tea for them. 'And get something, a cheese roll or whatever, for yourself,' they'd say.

I could even curl up in a corner and get some sleep and no-one would tell me to get up and get out. They were smoky, dimly lit dens, surprisingly free of the boozy stench that had always hung around Dad, and for a noise-hater like me a blissful oasis of low voices and concentration. There was a taxi driver who hung around these places, Bob Davis – no relation to Steve – who people said had encouraged a lot of good players in their early days. He picked me out. He set up a table, showed me a few techniques, and it turned out that I was quite good at it. I didn't think of it as anything other than a bit of entertainment to pass the time. I didn't have the opportunity to watch a lot of telly and had no idea that some people made good money playing this game. I was starting to get better at it and Bob suddenly seemed to be very interested in me.

'Do you do odd jobs, Pete?' he asked me one evening.

'Yeah, I do odd jobs,' I said. 'I wash cars, that kind of thing. I can do anything.'

What he was asking sounded innocent enough, but my stomach was beginning to churn as fear and suspicion took hold. I didn't like this kind of interest coming from a middle-aged man I didn't know too well. My experience told me that middle-aged men who were interested in what young boys liked to do with their spare time were not to be trusted.

'Do you do any other kinds of odd jobs, Pete?'

'Like what?' I said, suddenly aggressive. Before he had a chance to answer, I was on his case. 'You're a fucking nonce, aren't you? You leave me alone, nonce. I don't have nothing to do with the likes of you.'

I threw the cue down and walked out of the pool

hall. I went back again, of course, because I didn't have anywhere else to go much of the time, but Bob and I gave each other a wide berth from then on. A lot of the regular players kept me at arm's length too after that. I can't blame them. No-one wanted to risk having that kind of accusation made against them by a teenager who didn't seem to have a home to go to and appeared to be slightly off his trolley.

Years later, when I bumped into Jimmy White and had a chat about the old days in Clapham and Earlsfield, I asked if he knew whether Bob had been the kind of man who had an unhealthy interest in young boys. Jimmy had spent a lot of time around Bob himself when he was a youngster and he said he'd never seen any sign of that kind of thing in him. So there it was. It was another mistake I made, and I felt really sorry about it, for me and for Bob. Perhaps at any other age I might not have been so hard on him and so quick to jump to conclusions, but the fact was that I had arrived at that age where sex was the huge, all-consuming mystery of life.

An enduring suspicion of all middle-aged men had been put into me by people like Jim, the Lambeth pervert, and Leo, the father-figure who I met after Dad's death and who had befriended me and then sexually assaulted me. Now I was having to cope with the overwhelming urge I suddenly felt to get to know girls, and at the same time being frightened to death of letting my guard down enough to be able to do that. It doesn't matter who you are, where you grow up, what your life is like: hormones and puberty get to us all, and in that sense at least I was no different to any other fourteen-year-old boy. I badly wanted to have a real girlfriend and I couldn't see how it would ever be possible. My clothes, the smell, my lack of money, and a home that I would never dream of inviting a girl to visit – all these things were problems with no solution, but what really churned me up inside was the business of getting physically close to someone. My hormones were screaming at me to find a girl who wouldn't mind if I tried to hold her hand, but the gut fear of any physical contact that had plagued me since I was a small child couldn't contemplate it for a moment.

There had been a girl at school that I'd had a crush on. Caroline. She was absolutely gorgeous. Other boys I knew had girlfriends even if they were just holding hands with them on the way home after school, but I was so ashamed of myself that I couldn't imagine I would ever have the nerve to even speak to a girl. I saw Caroline again in the centre of Wandsworth some months after I'd been expelled. I was in the Arndale Centre thinking about doing a bit of shoplifting. That didn't help me feel any less ashamed when I came face to face with her. She'd seen me first and she'd come over to speak to me. She stood in front of me and smiled.

I didn't smile back. My heart was beating like a mad thing and I turned my head away and walked straight past her, telling myself that there was no way she wanted to speak to a kid like me even though it was obvious that she did. You might say that my interpersonal skills were, to say the least, not good. It was difficult to know what I would say if I did have a conversation with a girl. Other kids could talk about their ambitions, even if they had crazy ambitions like wanting to be a pilot. I didn't have any. All I wanted to do was survive, be clean and have food. I did know that I wanted to be happy too, and that I wanted to be normal, to have a family and a future like other people. But how could I say that to a girl?

'So, Pete, what do you do with yourself?'

'Me? I survive.'

'And what do you want to do when you grow up, Pete?'

'Oh, I want to be normal.'

That wasn't going to work, was it?

My brothers, always quick to sense a weakness, cottoned on to these fears, and whenever I did turn up at the house, Terence in particular liked to give me some stick.

'Out all night again, Dwarf? Not with a girl, though, I bet. Are you queer? You're still a virgin, aren't you, Dwarf? Always will be a virgin. You should think about the priesthood.'

Yet for some reason Terence decided that he should take me under his wing. Now and again, if I was around when he was heading off to a party with some of his mates – his friends were only a little older than the people I knew, but they were generally a more steady crowd from the nicer side of Wandsworth – he'd offer to take me with him.

'We can't have you a virgin all your life, little brother. Here you are, borrow this jacket, come and meet some girls.'

God only knows what I looked like in this blazer of

Terry's with the sleeves tucked up so that they didn't cover my knuckles. I reckoned I looked like a right idiot, but to everyone's surprise, especially Terry's, that wasn't what several of the girls thought at all.

'Christ, you look like David Essex,' one of them said to me, stroking the black curly hair that I had only ever thought of as an extra bit of scruffiness that I couldn't get under control. David Essex was every girl's pin-up at the time, a singer *and* a film star. And *I* looked like him . . .

The pleasure this gave me didn't last long. Embarrassment wiped it out. One of the girls came over to where I was sitting and sat herself on my knee. She started wrapping herself around me, stroking my hair. I panicked, like I had just about managed not to do when Bernie's mum had come to kiss me goodnight back in North Lambeth.

'Get off me,' I shouted, standing up and pitching her onto the floor. 'You shouldn't do that kind of thing. You shouldn't. It's not decent.'

Well, that made her very cross and everyone else in the room pissed themselves laughing. It looked like it was never going to happen for me. I was going to sabotage any chance that came my way.

A few days later, when I'd managed to get over the shock of having at last had a girl in close contact with me, I suddenly decided that I needed to see her again. It was much too late, of course, and that girl was never going to speak to me again, but I didn't know that. I ran round the house like a maniac looking for a decent shirt. I found one that no-one else seemed to want, but it was all screwed up, and, ignoring the laughter of all the brothers who happened to be around at the time, I shot into the kitchen and turned on the stove, so I could heat the old hand-iron on the gas flame in the hope I might be able to make the shirt look a bit more presentable.

Mum was in the kitchen.

'What the fuck are you doing, boy?' she yelled.

'He's got a girlfriend, Mum, and he wants to look good for her,' jeered a brother from somewhere behind me.

'A girlfriend?' screeched Mum. She came up behind me and whacked the back of my head with the flat of her hand. She pulled out one of her less charming expressions to cut me down to size. 'What are you doing thinking about girls? You ain't done shitting yellow, boy. I won't have you thinking of girls, you filthy little beast.'

While she whacked me over the head a few more times, I did my best to save the shirt and switch off the stove. The sharp, urgent, adolescent ache of suddenly wanting to put things right with the girl who'd sat on my knee had been replaced by a more usual and more bearable kind of pain, and for once I was quite glad of it. It was a relief. This girl stuff hurt in a way I'd never been hurt before.

In the end, and without any help from Terry, I found my girl. She was the sister of one of my dodgy mates, but he was the only dodgy one in the family. Her parents and her other brother were okay, and she was lovely. I'd first met her at Tiffany's nightclub in Wimbledon. You were supposed to be eighteen to get in, but I was looking a lot older by this time and she was brought along by her brother especially to meet me, and he'd got her in. She was called Clara, and I decided her name was as beautiful as she was. We talked, we liked each other, we met again when I was out with the lads, and then the night came when a big group of us were all going out and I knew that Clara and I almost had a date. Not quite, I knew that, because all these older lads were telling me that it couldn't be a date if I hadn't kissed her.

I was frightened to death but I knew I wanted to do it. For her, I could put all that horror of touching and being touched aside. I practised loads with a mirror and my arm for days beforehand, just like every other teenage boy that ever walked the earth. It took me all night but eventually, egged on by the lads, I kissed her by the hot-dog van just before we went our separate ways at the end of the evening.

'See you tomorrow?' I said, with my hands in my pockets, hoping that I looked cool and not too bothered whether she said yes or no.

'Yes,' she said.

I had a girlfriend. Round the corner, well out of sight, I jumped in the air and whooped. Peter Roche had a girlfriend. How about that?

16. The Road to the Detention Centre

There was a time after I met Clara when I thought of myself as a grown-up, responsible man who had turned a corner. I was sure we would be together for ever and I was going to look after her, I was going to be a provider in a way that my parents had never been. A year after we got together I turned sixteen and I could at last get a proper job. I was mad keen to find one.

Through a friend I heard about a local carpet-fitting firm that was looking for a lad to be a general gofer, sweeping up, helping to carry the rolls of carpet, making sure all the tools were back in the van at the end of job, and doing the tea runs. I was taken on and suddenly I was out on the road in the van every day with a team of four blokes who travelled all over Greater London, fitting carpets in offices. It felt good and I had no trouble turning up on time and being keen. The sad truth was, however, that even faced with a fairly simple job like this, I had trouble concentrating. I was able to do the job in the shop because I was told what needed doing from minute to minute. With the carpet fitters, I had no trouble with the heavy work because after all those years as the Dwarf I was now shooting up fast and turning out to be quite a tall, broad lad. I had certainly inherited my mother's shoulders and arms. If I was told to do something I was smart and quick about doing it. But if I was told to do more than one thing at a time, I was in trouble.

It sounds silly, but the job I found most difficult was the lunch run. I had to hold in my head a long list of the rolls and buns the men had ordered. We were always working in an area I didn't know and by the time I'd found the nearest sandwich shop it was touch and go whether I'd be able to remember it all.

One lunchtime one of the blokes, I swear to God, asked for a salad roll. These blokes were meat-eaters to a man, but salad was the word I heard and I didn't question it because I had no clear idea what a salad roll was. By the time I got to the shop even that had dropped out of my head. It was too far to go back and ask. The blokes would be furious because their lunch break would have come and gone before I could deliver what they wanted. I had a picture of lettuce in my head. It seemed very unlikely, but I didn't know what else to do.

'A lettuce sandwich?' asked the assistant, amazed.

'Yeah,' I said, desperately uncertain, but unable for the life of me to do any better than that.

'It looks a bit bare, son,' said the assistant. 'You sure you don't want anything else on that?'

'Um. Salt?'

'Salt.'

It wasn't as if I knew anything about fresh food. I was okay with fruit but apart from potatoes, vegetables were a mystery to me. I'd seen them in shops but I had no idea what you did with them. When I was buying food for myself, I stuck to pasties and pies and the occasional tin of beans.

When I got back the lads were all sitting round with their flasks, waiting for their rolls. This guy opened his, looked at it as if he could hardly believe his eyes and lifted the top of the roll off.

'This is a fucking piece of lettuce. What the fuck do you call this, you little cunt?' He was angry. He was angrier still when all the other blokes started to laugh. It was kind of funny. The tea boy had brought him a lettuce sandwich, like he was a rabbit.

I knew it wasn't really funny, though. I knew enough about what people did when they looked the way he did to be very worried, but I couldn't see a way out. This bloke was convinced I was taking the mickey out of him and it was obvious nothing would convince him otherwise. He jumped on me, knocking me onto my back and sitting on me while he thumped the hell out of me. I tried to get a few back in, but I was no match for him. The shouting and yells of our brawling brought staff from other parts of the office.

'What the hell is going on?' shouted a posh man in a very smart dark suit.

My attacker got off me, apologized to the man, and the team cut their lunch break short to get the job finished and get out of there. That was fine by me. I hadn't had enough money to get myself something to eat anyway. When we got back to Wandsworth in the van, the salad roll bloke reached across from his seat on the other side of one of his mates to give me a farewell slap across the face. 'Fuck off, then,' he snarled. When I turned up the next morning, on time, the van had already gone.

'Sorry, son,' said the guy at the depot. 'The boss said to tell you that you're finished.'

I'd only lasted a couple of weeks, and I didn't even get paid for that. I was back to 25p a day at the hardware shop and anything else I could get from odd jobs or stealing.

Then, inevitably, I lost the job at the shop too after one of my so-called friends asked if I could get him some Calor gas. This was something else the shop sold and the big blue canisters were stacked in the back yard. The wall had glass and razor wire along the top of it, but I knew how to get over that without too much damage. No problem, I said. Meet me, we'll get it together on Sunday when the shop's closed.

As much as anything, I think I was trying to buy friendship, even a bit of admiration, by going along with this kind of scheme. We were spotted a few streets away by someone who knew me, and knew the shop owner, as we lugged these huge canisters along the road, and the next time I went there to work I was turned away. Nothing was said about the gas, but I knew I'd blown it.

My stealing, and the joy-riding particularly, began to slowly escalate to the level of the seriously, dangerously criminal. Stealing turned into burglary, breaking into offices and garages and selling whatever I could steal, and joy-riding to the outskirts of London turned into high-speed four-hour rallies up and down the motorways of England.

The stuff we were doing with the cars became more and more outrageous. We had a real shock one night after we'd driven a car away and stopped it somewhere quiet to have a good look at what was in it. We found a box full of shotgun cartridges under one of the seats. Someone suggested the gun would be in the boot. Of course, this meant that we now wanted to get in the boot to have a look. I thank God that we weren't able to open it, and our fright at the thought that this might be a gangster's car got the better of our teenage hunger for the thrill of holding a real gun in our hands. We didn't try quite so hard as we might have done to open the boot and eventually walked away, praying that no-one would ever find out we were the ones who had taken it.

A couple of my brothers had had a few brushes with the law, but none of them had gone off the rails in quite the way I was doing. No-one could possibly have known – I don't think I fully understood it myself – that in addition to all the practical problems I faced about finding a safe place to sleep and enough food to eat, I was severely depressed. My anxiety attacks, the ones that felt like heart attacks, were coming almost daily by the time I was sixteen. I was thinking constantly about death, although I told no-one, not even Clara. There was at least one moment in every day when I thought I might easily drop dead the next second. If that didn't happen, I was beginning to think of all sorts of ways I might make it happen. A car crash was my favourite. Quick, not too much time to register pain. Going out to find bad kids, setting out for a block of flats or a probation hostel or a children's home because I had nowhere else to go, hunting for some company and a plan, even if it was a plan to steal something, was a distraction from these thoughts. The thrill of riding in a stolen car particularly seemed to hold the panic attacks at bay. Being in an office I shouldn't be in while taking something that wasn't mine frightened me to death every time, but the fear also blotted out all those other terrible feelings that seemed much worse. It was wrong, it was stupid, but it was such a relief to be free of the mess that my head was in for just a few hours or even a few minutes. And when it occurred to me that the next joy-ride might be the one that killed me, I felt nothing but relief. That would be it, then, it would all be over and there would never be anything that could worry me or hurt me again, and all the hard, hard work of surviving would be finished with.

Being out with Clara was the one pleasure I had and it felt great. She talked to me like no-one had ever talked to me, about feelings and plans, about the future and even the past. No-one ever chatted about the past in my house. The past was too awful. That was why, when Clara asked me about my family, my parents, aunties, uncles and cousins, I could hardly answer a single question. Apart from the faceless crowd of relatives who had made a brief appearance when Dad died and never come near us again, the only family I knew were my parents, brothers and sisters, and I didn't know much about them. I had no idea where Mum and Dad had grown up and I didn't even know where the family had lived before I was born, even though Christine and Raymond, and perhaps even Paul, must have had some memories of those times.

When she asked if she could see some pictures of me when I was little, I was as embarrassed as hell. This had never crossed my mind. I had envied all sorts of normal experiences that other kids took for granted, like holidays and Christmas and birthday parties, but never before had I stopped to think about the family albums we didn't have. But an idea popped into my head.

'The NSPCC might have some,' I said.

Clara looked at me as if I'd lost the plot. 'Why would the NSPCC have baby pictures of you?'

'I dunno. Mum says they helped us a bit when I was little. Before we moved to North Lambeth. There are some pictures, I found some of them when we moved, but they've disappeared.'

Clara thought about this. 'We could find an NSPCC office and ask. Mind you, if it's one of your mum's stories, there's no saying it's true.'

Clara hadn't met my mum. I was still smarting from the attack almost a year earlier, when she'd beaten me up for daring to think about girls, so I was keeping Clara well away from her. But Clara's questions about my family history had made me curious, and from time to time I started to take the risk of asking Mum a few questions, usually on a Saturday morning, when she wanted me to go down to the bookie's to put her bets on. She could always hold her temper in check a little if there was something she wanted me to do for her.

I would report back to Clara any little snippet Mum

was willing to offer, but my girl was a level-headed fifteen-year-old and she often laughed out loud. It was hard not to agree that Mum's stories were odd. She'd never talked to any of us much except to bark orders, but over the years there had been moments when she would launch into some weird story or other, almost as if she was talking to herself, usually about something that had no connection to anything that was going on at the time.

Once, out of the blue, she started talking about a dog her father had when she was a girl. It had swallowed rat poison and dropped down dead. Her father forced the sticky, tarry stuff from the bottom of his pipe down its throat to try to bring it round and when that didn't work he threw the animal in a ditch.

'The next morning the dog came to the door, wagging its tail, like nothing had happened,' she said.

It was obviously true, but there was something a bit mad about the story and about the way she told it. It didn't tell you much about anything one way or the other and certainly didn't add anything to the life that we were living.

A story I had told Clara very soon after we first met was Mum's favourite fantasy, the one about Lord Snowdon.

'That Lord Snowdon, he came to visit us once,' she would say. 'All the neighbours came out on the balcony to look. He was a friend of your father's.'

It was a wonderful idea. About as likely as him knowing Lloyd George, just like in the song the kids used to sing in the playground, unless the Queen's brother-in-law had been a regular at the pub where my father had done most of his drinking when I was a child. Yet, crazy as it seemed that my father and Lord Snowdon could ever have met in any circumstances, this was a story I first heard when I was about six years old and I held on to it.

Well into my teenage years, as I walked the streets, it gave me food for a fantasy of my own about what it might mean if it was true. Perhaps it meant that there was someone out there, rich and normal, who was interested in me or – maybe, you never knew – even related to me. Someone who might turn up one day and get me away from all this, and take me to a place where people were kind, calm and sensible and where you were never hungry because meals happened like night follows day. I knew other people had lives like that. They weren't necessarily rich, I knew that too, but wealth seemed to offer an added guarantee of food, warmth and clothes that looked like everyone else's, not like rags you'd just pulled out of a bin.

One of the Saturday morning stories I got out of her for Clara made us both laugh like drains, although at first I really wanted to believe it.

Tell me about Dad, I said to her, where he came from, who his family were.

'They were farming people, they had land,' she answered.

Where?

'Oh, in Sussex somewhere.'

Somewhere near where Lord Snowdon's family lived?

'Oh, yes, yes, somewhere like that.'

Blimey. Never mind that I knew beyond any doubt

now that Dad had grown up in Ireland. Without trying I could recall his strong southern Irish accent. Maybe, I speculated wildly, Dad and Lord Snowdon used to meet each other out in the fields on the land their dads owned.

'What happened to Dad's dad?' I asked, knowing I was pushing my luck with my mother's patience, but very interested in the idea that I had once had a grandfather with enough money to be a landowner. That would impress Clara.

'Oh, he was a sea captain.'

This didn't match the farming bit too well, but it wouldn't have been a good idea to say so.

'What happened to him?'

'He went down at sea.'

Where?

'Near Scotland.' She finally snapped. 'Will you stop asking fucking stupid questions, and get out of the house and put those bets on,' she yelled.

So when Clara asked about photographs, yet another Mum story had come to mind. There had been some snapshots lying around in a drawer. They had long since disappeared, probably left behind in the move, but one I could recall quite clearly, a picture of a small boy with smartly combed blond hair, sitting on a swing, wearing shorts and what looked like a brand-new duffel coat.

It had been hard to believe this clean, calm, well-dressed boy could be one of us. My hair was jet black and I couldn't remember it having been any other way, but Mum announced one day: 'That Miss Zils took those photos of Peter. She was the NSPCC lady. Miss Zils liked Peter,' she added in a very offhand way, as if there was no accounting for taste.

To me, though, it had mattered. Someone had liked me when I was little, and liked me enough to take pictures of me. The significance of the National Society for the Prevention of Cruelty to Children having had any involvement with my family was lost on me, at the time and even when I was talking to Clara about these pictures later. It was a tiny scrap of feeling special and, like the crazy idea that Lord Snowdon might turn up one day to take me away, I had never forgotten it.

Clara was as determined as she was sensible. She found an address for the NSPCC office closest to where we'd lived in Lambeth and we got on a bus and went there. Our eyes were out on stalks the second we walked through the door. There was a display of children's pictures behind the reception desk and even Clara recognized the picture I'd described of the boy in the duffel coat.

'Blimey, they've still got it pinned up,' I said, more loudly than I'd meant to.

A couple of women were leafing through some paperwork at the desk and they both looked up. One of them looked at the display.

'That's me,' I said, as proud as if it had been a memento from a beautiful baby competition.

They looked doubtful, with good reason since it was hard for them to know how I could be so sure. I couldn't have been much more than three years old in the picture and they must have been thinking that it was a safe bet it hadn't been framed and hung on the wall of any home

I'd lived in. When I mentioned Miss Zils, I could see they were beginning to believe me. They made a phone call. Within a few minutes Miss Zils herself arrived. She was still working for the NSPCC and she seemed genuinely pleased to see me.

'What a fine young man you have grown into, Peter,' she said, shaking my hand. I was managing to keep myself smarter and cleaner now that I had Clara to impress, but I doubt whether I looked fine. Still, I suppose I was a strong-looking, fresh-faced teenager with no obvious health problems. Miss Zils' raven black hair, as I remembered it, was now almost completely white and she seemed very old to me. What I did recognize immediately was her voice, her unusual accent that I now realized was like a German's from a war film.

'So, what are you doing with yourself, Peter?' she asked.

This was the last question I wanted to be asked. I knew that I wasn't doing much with my life at all. I felt very uncomfortable, especially in front of this educated lady who had liked me when I was little, but I didn't show it.

'This and that. I've got a job in a shop,' I replied as casually as I could.

'Oh, that sounds good,' she said. She was very tactful.

'He was a lovely little boy, your Peter,' she told Clara. 'So bright, so intelligent. And so cheeky,' she added, smiling.

'He's still cheeky, I can tell you that,' said Clara, smiling back at her.

Cheeky, but not very intelligent any more. I was beginning to get caught. I was going out joy-riding with my so-called friends so often that I was stacking the odds against myself. I first appeared in court charged with taking and driving away a car when I was a few months short of my fifteenth birthday, but I'd been in dozens of stolen cars by then. Over the next two years I was caught and taken to court for the same offence perhaps eight or nine times, but the truth was that for every charge I faced there were probably half a dozen more joy-riding offences that the police didn't find out about. Because I was a juvenile, still under sixteen, my mother had to be told about every offence I was charged with, and the first couple of times I had to take the usual beatings from her once the police had gone. But by the time it came to the third, fourth and fifth appearances even she and Raymond seemed to give up. I was, in any case, expert in making myself scarce, sleeping at friends' houses until the fuss had died down, and all I would now get when I turned up again was a sour look from both of them, and perhaps a sarcastic 'So what kind of criminal activity have you been up to now, little brother?' from Raymond. There would still be no food and usually only a floor to sleep on, but at least the violence was easing off a bit.

The sentences I was given by the juvenile court magistrates escalated bit by bit, from my first conditional discharge all the way up to a supervision order, which meant that, in theory at least, I would have to report to a youth social worker regularly for the next couple of years and keep out of trouble if I didn't want to end up in a detention centre.

The problem was that I simply didn't believe that there

was anything anyone could do to me that would make life worse than it was. Not prison, not a beating. That sense of self-preservation I'd seemed to have when I was younger had vanished, so when I got a message that Nick, a regular joy-riding companion of mine, had escaped from the place where he was serving his sentence for his last escapade, I didn't think twice about going to meet him and the two of us going on a car-stealing spree that lasted all day and all night.

We ended up in Redhill, a commuter town in Surrey, trying to steal a Curry's lorry full of fridges. It was madness. We had nowhere to put the lorry or the fridges. I was barely fifteen and Nick was only a couple of years older and we weren't in that kind of league. We couldn't get the lorry started, fortunately for us and everyone else on the road, so it was off to look for another car and then back into London. We found some kind of sports car and got it going and Nick drove, speeding along the main roads at maybe 90 miles an hour and, fools that we were, we had no idea that we had been followed for miles, almost all the way back into town, by the police.

Eventually we got to a junction in south London, where we saw a police car waiting for us.

'I can lose the bastard,' shouted Nick like he was James Bond, swerving wildly round the car in front. Up ahead we saw another patrol car, then another. It ended up with three or four police cars behind us and as many in front.

'Christ, Nick, give it up,' I shouted back, but he was convinced he could get out of this. We smashed into one of the patrol cars ahead of us and then he tried to reverse out of trouble and hit one behind. When we finally crunched to a stop, I felt myself practically lifted out of the car by two officers and being smacked around a bit as they did it. I don't complain about this at all. I should think they were very annoyed.

'Hello, it's Batman and Robin again,' said the desk sergeant as we were brought in. It wasn't the first time Nick and I had come into this police station together, and we were getting quite a reputation.

My mate went back to Borstal and I was bailed to face yet another charge of taking and driving away. Another court appearance, as usual with Paul sitting behind me because as a minor I couldn't appear in court without a member of my family there who was over eighteen and I never wanted to ask Mum to come. The result of that was another kind of order, something new they called an Intermediate Order, which was supposed to put me on a programme where I would be taught how to drive, on private land, and how to do some car mechanics. Nothing ever came of this. My youth worker told me there wasn't the money to run the programme.

I didn't think it made much difference to me one way or the other. I no longer cared, not even for Clara's sake, and my next joy-ride very nearly gave me my wish of a quick end to it all.

It was usually Nick who came up with the wildest car-stealing schemes and I should have known better. In the months he'd been inside since the Redhill escapade I had not exactly been a good boy, but the joy-rides I'd been involved in had at least been uneventful. Then Nick was out again and he suggested stealing a car and driving it to Dover.

'I know where the harbour is. It's dead easy to steal boats and we could sail to France. That would be a laugh. Come on, let's do it.'

It never occurred to either of us that we hadn't a clue about the sea or sailing or what the Channel was like, the ferries and tankers steaming up and down it at all hours of the day and night. We thought it would be just like driving another stolen car, but on water instead of on the M2.

We made it to Dover in the middle of the night, found the harbour and found a boat we could get onto. However, for all Nick's bragging, hot-wiring a boat turned out to be nowhere near as straightforward as hot-wiring a car. We couldn't start it, and it was just as well. We'd have drowned. We didn't come out of that night very well as it was.

We'd dumped the car we'd driven down in, more because it was very low on petrol than because we cared about being spotted and pulled over by the police. We went searching for another to get home in and found one near a block of flats close to the famous cliffs. It caught our eye because it was a convertible, a Triumph Stag, one of the sexiest cars on the road at the time. We cut through the roof and got in easily, and soon had it started. Nick drove to the outskirts of the town and then we had a look at what was in the car and discovered a bag full of thousands of lottery tickets in the boot. They weren't the modern Camelot ones; they were old-fashioned sweep-stake tickets with numbers on them already and we knew they might be worth quite a bit of money if we could find someone dishonest enough to take them off our hands. It was about four in the morning and we'd been going for five or six hours by then, and I suggested that we should have a bit of sleep before we drove back. But Nick was keen to get back to London because he was sure he knew someone who would take the tickets off our hands for a tidy sum, he said, but we had to get back fast before anyone knew the tickets had been taken. I fell asleep in the passenger seat.

I woke up at about half past eight in the morning laid out on a piece of tarmac. I heard someone saying: 'Poor love, he'll be dead by the time the ambulance gets here.'

I had enough wits left to know that I was lying in a pool of blood. I was terrified, sure that I was bleeding to death. I became aware that there was a policeman next to me and he was looking over to the side of the road. Nick was standing up, on the pavement, being asked questions by another policeman. He looked quite well compared to how I felt. I tried to push myself up and heard myself screaming: 'I can't feel my legs, I can't feel them.'

I realized there was a man on the other side of me, telling me to be calm, lie still, the ambulance would be there in a moment. As I was being put into the ambulance I heard him tell one of the policemen: 'I'm a Member of Parliament, you can contact me there if you need a witness account of what happened.'

It was all very bizarre. I stared at the ceiling of the ambulance and the face of one of the ambulance crew appeared over me. I was having trouble breathing. 'Is this how I'm going to die?' I asked him. I was a bit surprised to realize that I did care, at least a little bit, about staying alive.

I came out of hospital the next day with stitches in my mouth where I'd bitten through the inside of my lip, a figure-of-eight bandage strapping up a broken collar bone, and several splinted broken fingers. I have no idea how I got off so lightly. I had to go home, even though I hadn't been there for a couple of weeks. I couldn't sleep on a mate's floor or sneak into a probation hostel room in this state. Mum just looked at me and said: 'You got what was fucking coming to you, then.' For once, there was some justice in what she said.

The next day Nick turned up. I could hardly move.

'I know this house we can get into and there's cash in there' was the first thing he said. No apology for falling asleep at the wheel and nearly killing us both. Just an insane attempt to recruit a one-armed teenager who couldn't speak properly, and could barely walk, to take part in a burglary. And I, just as mad, thought seriously about it and agreed. It was the one and only time that I was involved in a break-in at someone's home and I hated myself for it even as I was holding the window open for Nick to climb in. That night, as I sat strapped up and watching the telly, there was a cop programme on and just as the actors made their arrest, the police knocked on our door. I handed them the share of the cash that Nick had given me and limped off to the police car to spend the night in a cell.

Clara told me I was an idiot and wouldn't speak to me for a couple of weeks. Did it make any difference? No. Could I be any more stupid and heedless? Oh, yes, I could.

I was only fined for the burglary, because I had no previous convictions of that kind and the cash had been recovered, and although the shame of it cured me for ever of breaking into any kind of building, house or office, I still had it in my head that there wasn't that much wrong with stealing cars. There they were, parked on the road, and as my dodgy mates always said, the owners were insured. We were just borrowing them.

Not surprisingly the West Midlands police didn't see it like that when they caught up with us on the outskirts of Birmingham in yet another stolen car. Yet again I was Nick's passenger – I rarely tried to drive because that frightened even me too much – and when the police checked my previous convictions, they took me straight to court and had me remanded to a young offender's institution. No bail for me this time.

This was my first taste of any kind of prison, and it really wasn't that bad. I was in a cell with three other youngsters, a year or two younger than me, and I was quite the lad.

'You're funny, Cockney, you're the business,' one of them said as I told story after story about all the cars I'd been in that weren't mine, all the places I'd been to in them. The Dover story, with a few hilarious additions, had them all in stitches. I was there a week before I could go to court again to ask for bail, and I also told them all sorts of stories about London, particularly the West End, that had them hanging on every word I said.

'It's a great place,' I said enthusiastically. 'Best of all is New Year's Eve in Trafalgar Square. It's a great atmosphere, thousands of people all having a good time together, kissing and hugging. Even the coppers are friendly.'

'I've seen it on the telly,' said one of the lads. 'I'd like to do that one day.'

'I tell you what,' I said, 'let's make a pact. We'll all meet up there again this New Year's Eve. At the bottom of Nelson's Column.'

'How will we know each other?' said the kid. 'We might not recognize each other on the outside.'

We had no toilet in the cell, only a big red plastic cup which we had to share.

'I know,' I said. 'We'll all have to carry a red plastic cup. That's how we'll know each other. Who else would take a red cup to Trafalgar Square on New Year's Eve?'

It was a great idea, we agreed. My court hearing for bail was in the morning. Before we turned in for the night, the other lads all kneeled on the floor and prayed for me.

'Please, God, let Peter get bail in the morning. He really needs to go home,' they said.

I was touched by that. I didn't know why they'd done it, but it made me think that perhaps I hadn't been as clever as I thought I was, telling all those stories about London and joy-riding, as if it was the most glamorous thing you could spend your life doing.

I got bail, but only so that I could be remanded to the

juvenile court back in Balham, where I had become a regular attendant over the last two years, and I knew that this time I was going away. The euphoria I'd felt in the remand centre with those lads had evaporated the moment I walked out of the Birmingham court and started the journey back to London, and on the morning of my trial I borrowed a jacket of Laurence's and asked Mum for the first time if she wouldn't mind coming with me. To my surprise, she said yes, without any jibes or abuse. She said hardly a word on the way there and sat through the court hearing, listening to all my previous convictions, looking weary rather than furious. When I was told that I would be spending the next three months in a detention centre and was beckoned to the cell corridor by the prison officer, she stood up. I took Laurence's coat off and handed it to her. She took it without a word, not even to tell me I was getting what was coming to me.

Three months seemed a long time. Three months without seeing Clara. 'You will write to me?' I'd asked her the night before. I had promised her again and again over the last two years that I would never get in another stolen car, and over and over again I'd broken those promises. I knew she was losing patience with me.

'I don't know, Pete. I don't know if I can. I don't see that you're ever going to change, and I don't want to be around you if this is going to be you for the rest of your life, in and out of prison.'

'Just a letter, you can do that. Just a letter now and again.'

'I'll see,' she said. 'I'm not promising anything. I hope

it goes okay tomorrow. Get through tomorrow and then we'll see.'

Within two weeks of arriving at the detention centre in Kent, I knew that she'd made up her mind. I'd written her four letters and none had come back from her. I plunged into the deepest depression I'd ever known, full of regret and remorse for the stupid, wrong things I'd done. It got so bad that I asked if I could see the priest. I sat with him for an hour, confessing to every theft I'd ever committed. I told him about Clara and asked if he thought she might come round.

'I don't know. You've caused her a lot of pain with the life you've been living. You have to be patient and accept whatever she decides,' he said. 'Can you do that?'

'I don't know, Father. I feel as if there's nothing worth going on for.'

An hour later, as I scrubbed the floor, two officers came up behind me.

'Stand up, Roche, you're coming with us.'

Oh, hell, I thought, what have I done now? The regime was strict. I had been disciplined for not scrubbing properly, for talking back to officers, for not having all the buttons on my shirt done up. But this time, I realized, I was heading for the reception area, not for the office where discipline was handed out. What was going on?

An hour after that, I was given my belongings and put on a prison van.

'You are unstable, Roche, and you need treatment,' said the senior officer as he signed me out of the centre.

The priest, I realized, had decided that I had serious

plans to kill myself and he'd alerted the staff. However bad I felt, the idea of going somewhere new was terrifying. What really hurt, though, was that I had poured my heart out to the one person in the world I should have been able to trust, a priest. Yet again, it seemed to me, my trust had been betrayed.

17. Borstal

I had no idea where I was being taken. I felt angry about the priest's betrayal, but perhaps that was better than simply wanting to be dead. I certainly felt dead, had not a trace of hope inside me, and no expectation that where I was being taken would be any better than the detention centre. I was dead right.

I was loaded onto the green prison van when it came into the prison yard, taken in handcuffs to the back of it from the reception area and told to get in and sit down. It had wooden benches on either side and metal rings were welded to the iron supports behind the benches. I was handcuffed to one of these and the van set off on a journey that seemed to take hours, trundling along and stopping off at various places to pick up some prisoners, drop others off. We made a drop at one prison and lots of these guys looked a lot older and harder than me and I had a moment of relief about the handcuffs, knowing there wasn't too much any of these characters could do to each other or me because of them. I was almost the last to be dropped off. There were three of us left in the van by this time, but the other two were taken off to another entrance. I was escorted alone to a different part of this very grim building that looked a bit like a prison for adults. It turned out to be a Borstal, a prison for young offenders, and I was heading for its hospital wing.

It was never explained to me why I'd been sent here. It was a few days before I realized this was supposed to be a hospital wing and I could only assume that it was the only place in the area where a suicidal seventeen-year-old might be 'treated'. This was 1980, but the regime they had there for sick kids like me was horrific. We were treated the way that the Victorians treated lunatics. I was there for almost two months and I never saw anyone who looked like a doctor. I had no medical examination and no-one ever asked me about my health or state of mind.

A lot of the boys on the wing were sedated, but I only ever saw prison officers handing out drugs, usually two of them to one kid at a time, watching closely to make sure that the medication was swallowed and one with his baton out ready to give him some stick if he tried to refuse. Sometimes, with a particularly difficult inmate, they'd dose him the way you see vets dosing animals, one of them pulling the kid's head up and holding his face towards the ceiling by the hair and the jaw while the other rammed the pills into his mouth, slapping his neck until he was forced to swallow them. But drugs were for the violent, aggressive kids. I wasn't one of those. My 'treatment' was different and it began the moment I walked onto the wing. First I was banged up in a cell. It had a sleeping platform with a hard pad on it, one blanket, a small sink and a flush toilet in one corner by the door. Nothing else. A few moments later the door opened again. Walker, one of many warders on the wing, wanted to give me his own personal welcome.

'Come with me,' he ordered.

I followed him meekly up the concrete-floored corridor. He stopped at a cell door at the end of the landing.

'See that,' he said, opening the door and inviting me to look inside. There was nothing in it at all, not even a concrete sleeping platform or a toilet. Just a strait-jacket lying on the floor. 'If I see you moping, that's where you will end up. So no moping.'

'No, sir, no, sir,' I said. If my dad, my mum and my brothers had taught me nothing else, it was to know when submission was the only sensible option. In any case, I was in a terrible state. It wasn't the loss of freedom that was bothering me. What had I lost? A daily struggle for survival, the worry of where to sleep, where to find food to eat, what to do with the days and the nights. I was relieved, in a way, to know that those things were taken care of for a while. The problem was that with all those things taken care of, I had too much time to think about just how hopeless my life was. Whatever else thieving and joy-riding and all that ducking and diving might be, it was also a distraction from the terrible fear I had of life, of other people and what they could do to you, and from the terrible feelings of failure I had. I knew I couldn't relate to other people in any normal way, I couldn't even eat like they did, so there was no way I could hold down a job. I knew that this meant I was trapped in the way of life I had, and I could see no way out of this except by dying.

Walker took me back to my cell. Before he closed the door he told me: 'You'll be in here for a week. If you're good and you don't mope, you can start coming out after that to do some hard work. That'll stop you looking so bloody miserable.'

He banged the black-painted metal door shut. Extra hard, I'm certain, to make sure the sound echoed down the corridor.

Because the cell had a toilet, there wasn't even a reason for me to come out once a day to 'slop out', to take a chamber pot to the toilets and rinse it. Food and drink came through a hatch in the bottom of the door onto the floor. The light was switched on and off from somewhere outside in the morning and at night. It was peaceful, I'll give it that, and the food was regular. I didn't feel any temptation to bang on the door screaming to be let out like I could hear some of the other kids doing. But those were long, long days to be left alone with the thoughts I was having. The only other interruption to those thoughts was a warden opening the hatch in the upper half of the door from time to time to look at me. They didn't speak when they did this, they just looked in and gave me a hard stare. I suppose they were checking to make sure I hadn't tried to top myself.

At the end of the week I was still asleep when the hatch opened and Walker looked in. He slammed the hatch shut and started opening the door and I scrambled to my feet to stand to attention next to the bed.

'Did I just see right, boy?' he bellowed.

'What? What, sir?' I stammered.

'Did you have your shirt on in bed?'

'Yes, sir, I was cold.' I'd been put in the cell in the

short-sleeved cotton shirt I'd arrived in from the detention centre. Apart from that and the blanket, I didn't have anything to wear in bed and there was no heating in the cell.

'You're not coming out today, boy, until you learn how to sleep like a civilized human being. You don't walk around all day in the clothes you've slept in. Not if you have any self-respect,' he roared, and he turned and walked out of the cell, banging the door behind him again.

I spent another week in there, this time shivering through the nights. It would have been exactly like being back home if it hadn't been for the strange idea of being in a place where someone cared what you went to bed in.

The food was delivered by other inmates, the ones who were allowed to work on the wing. After I'd been shut up for a second week a few of them risked a few words of conversation through the hatch.

'Where you from, kid? What are you in for?'

'Fuck, that's rough,' one of these voices said when I said I'd come from a detention centre. 'What the hell did you do to get sent here? You don't seem like a nutter.'

This was how I discovered that I was now in a Borstal, the kind of place where they put kids who had half murdered people, who had done armed robberies or dozens and dozens of burglaries.

'Yeah,' said the voice through the hatch, half laughing. 'And this is the good bit. The hospital wing.'

When I was finally allowed to leave the cell, I was put straight onto the regular regime of the wing. First thing in the morning, at 6 a.m., the door was opened and left ajar. I had to be up, dressed and standing next to my bed when the prison officer opened up and looked in. Then it was out of the cell and into a marching line to collect breakfast from the trolley at the end of the corridor. We had to eat without talking, clear everything away and stack it on the trolley for the inmate who had the responsibility of returning it to the kitchen that day, and then it was out with the buckets and brushes to clean the whole landing from end to end, including the toilet recesses that were there for the few cells, like the strait-jacket cell, that didn't have a toilet in them, and the alcoves that contained the showers and baths for the rest of us. Scrub, wipe, rub, that was what the warder said as we worked.

I was also given the job of delivering the meals of those who were banged up twenty-four hours a day, like I had been, so I had to collect their pots too. Unlike me they usually weren't newcomers and they were always asking me to get things for them, things they were forbidden. Nothing too terrible, usually just a smoke, but even for that I could have been in bad trouble if I'd been caught. I took pity on one lad, the one who was in the strait-jacket cell at the time.

'Yeah, I've got a roll-up but I can't give it to you. I'll get into trouble.'

'Please, man, just one. Just one.'

I knew that he was let out just once, in the mornings, to slop out his chamber pot.

'Look, I'll leave one and a match behind the toilet in the recess for you. If you get caught, it's nothing to do with me.'

The next morning I heard a commotion up at the top of the corridor coming from his cell. He'd managed to pocket the fag and smoke it in his cell at some point during the previous day. The problem was that the warders could still smell the tobacco smoke. I was shaking with fright as I heard them strip-searching him for the evidence, even though I could hear him saying loudly: 'Where could I have got a fag? I haven't got one, honest . . .'

The fuss seemed to die down and no-one came looking for me. When I put his dinner through the hatch, I asked him if everything was okay.

'Yeah,' he whispered. 'Thanks, the smoke was fantastic.'

'What happened to the butt and the match? They didn't find them, then?' I hissed back.

'Nah,' said the kid. 'It's okay. I ate them.'

I knew it was a tough place, and it didn't take long for me to see exactly how tough. One of the twenty-four-hour lock-up inmates started creating on the second morning after my own lock-up had ended. I was scrubbing the section of corridor outside his cell when he began banging on his door and leaning on his cell's bell-push. It sounded like he'd cracked and couldn't stand it any longer. He was calling for Walker, begging him to let him out. Along came Walker and I kept my head down, scrubbing away as if I'd heard and seen nothing. Walker unlocked the cell and walked in, leaving the door open. He hardly broke his stride as he went into the cell and pulled the lad from behind the door and started beating the shit out of him. Walker had the kid's right arm clamped in one fist while the other slammed into his stomach.

I was panicky. It looked to me as if Walker would kill him. I looked down the corridor behind me and saw another warder some distance down it. I half whistled, nodding my head towards the cell at him. He came along almost at a run. I'd had some idea that if another warder was there, Walker might calm down. Instead the other one waded in too. By this time the kid was on the floor, and the newcomer kicked him a couple of times. Then the two of them picked him up and one held him while the other gave him half a dozen more punches for good measure. I felt sick and more guilty than I'd ever felt about anything. I had actually delivered another attacker to him. It was like watching Dad beat Paul in the basement all over again, and like Paul this kid had wet himself. The smell of urine mixed with the nasty aftershave that all the guards seemed to use made me gag.

But I had no choice but to keep scrubbing and screw all my feelings of panic and horror down tight so that I could look as if I'd seen and heard nothing out of the ordinary.

On that wing I was seeing human despair like I'd never seen it before, and that was saying something. There were a lot of kids on the hospital wing and at least half of them had scars or even open wounds on their wrists and up the arm from the wrist to the elbow from various suicide attempts. Many of them had the unmistakeable signs of heroin abuse, blackened veins and needle marks all up their arms. One had red and blue marks round his neck, where he'd tried to hang himself with his trousers and the fly zip had dug into his skin. It was a madhouse. Even to me it was obvious that they should have been getting some kind of help, not being locked up twenty-four hours a day or beaten or made to scrub floors. As ever, I felt sorry for them and yet again was realizing that, bad as things seemed for me, there were people who were having an even worse time.

I also quickly learned that, just as it was when I was with my family, punishment would come whether I had done anything to deserve it or not. After the scrubbing was finished each day, I was sent to work in the kitchens. By comparison with most of the lads on the hospital wing I was in good shape, I suppose.

'You're not sitting about here idle, Roche. Get some hard work done. That'll cheer you up,' said Walker. He laughed at his joke. He thought of himself as a very funny man. They all thought they were funny.

In the kitchen I was working among the regular inmates, the really hard cases. I was serving a detention centre sentence and I shouldn't have been allowed to associate with them, but I had enough sense not to try to protest. I'd have been given a right pasting from both Walker and them if I'd tried. As it turned out, they were okay with me, especially after Walker caught me drinking from the milk churn. Milk for the Borstal arrived in the big metal churns that you see in picture books about farms, and the one that was being used in the kitchen always had a ladle in it. Milk was probably my favourite comfort food or drink, whatever you want to call it – all those bottles stolen from doorsteps to keep me going through my childhood – and I couldn't resist taking a ladleful and having a good go at it. Walker came up behind me.

'Drop that fucking ladle, Roche,' he screamed.

I dropped it.

He unhooked it from the side of the churn. 'Here, Roche, have another, since you like it so much. Here, drink it!'

It was an order. I knew there was something unpleasant coming, but I had to do as he told me. As I bent to the ladle he pulled it up past my face and poured the lot over my head.

'Now leave it, or I'll shove the ladle up your arse next time.' I wasn't able to wash until the regulation ablution time came round later that afternoon, and a sour, cheesy smell clung to me all day, getting stronger and stronger as the hours in the hot kitchen went by until even I could hardly stand it. This was a straightforward piece of humiliation and, apart from the cheesiness, no problem to deal with.

What was much scarier was Walker's own little initiation ceremony. Without any warning one morning during my first week in the kitchen, he came up behind me – he always seemed to be behind us – and locked his arm round my neck, lifting me right off my feet. I had a moment when I thought I was being attacked by one of the hard-core nutters, and my hands flew up to get hold of this arm that seemed to have come from nowhere.

I heard a voice, quite smug, like a doctor's voice when they're telling you that this won't hurt a bit. 'Don't move, Roche, don't struggle,' it said. I had enough time to think:

'This is one of the screws – and I bet I know which one,' and to see the looks on the faces of the two Borstal boys who were with me as they watched what was happening, and then I lost consciousness. Their expressions told me that this was something they had all seen before. I came to on the floor with Walker standing over me. He didn't say anything. He just smiled a nasty smile as if to say: 'That's how easy it is, boys, that's how easy it is to overpower a seventeen-year-old who thinks he's harder than me.' Then he walked off, his point made. A little later he had the audacity to ask me if I was okay. Not as if he cared about whether I was okay or not, but just to check that I was in line. We both knew what he meant. I wasn't going to say a word to anyone. I was going to be obedient. I wanted to get out of there.

This was especially true after I saw what happened to one lad, who seemed to come up to spend a lot of time on the hospital wing. I heard Walker telling him that he was a waster, a hoaxer, and there was nothing fucking wrong with him. Each morning he would declare the guy fit to return, not that I ever saw anyone there who could have offered any kind of professional medical opinion. He would be marched back off the wing. He looked sick to me. Not in a spectacular way that caused anyone any bother, but sort of switched off, and this seemed to drive Walker crazy. I knew a bit about depression by this time, and it seemed obvious to me that he was depressed. I'd tried to talk to the bloke and he told me that he'd had a Dear John from his girlfriend; she'd written to tell him that she didn't want to see him when he got out.

Shortly after I had seen this lad a few times, I saw Walker having some dealings with another inmate on the wing, who seemed to have trouble walking. I hadn't spoken to this kid much. Rumour had it he'd had some kind of accident but there was something about him I just didn't like. I saw Walker give him a half-ounce packet of tobacco. You can recognize a tobacco packet from fifty yards away once you've been in an institution like that for a couple of weeks. An hour or so later I was in the association room, watching television – this was our treat, if we'd been good, for an hour or so each day – and my new mate got up to use the toilet that was in a recess next door. The next thing I heard was screaming from the corridor and I carefully looked out from the association room. The lad who'd had trouble walking and needed help had my mate on the floor. He was beating him over the head with one of the landing sweeping brushes, a huge heavy yard brush with stiff bristles, and giving him a terrible kicking into the bargain.

I took the risk of going in there to try to break it up, but very quickly two officers arrived. I walked out as the officers walked in and left them to sort it out. That was the only sensible thing to do, just in case they all started on me too. This time, however, they did pull the lads apart and didn't do any more damage to my poor mate. But I guessed that the lad with the so-called walking trouble had been 'paid' to make the hospital wing a less attractive place for my poor friend. That also suggested that the warders were well aware that this bully had no trouble walking. From this moment on, any trace of cheeky-chappie Roche that had survived the depression, the anxiety attacks and the shock of being transferred to this hell on earth disappeared. I kept my head down, I did exactly as I was told, and I heard and saw nothing. I kept as far away from everyone as I possibly could.

This was probably the cleanest place I have ever lived in, and I hated the smell of it. It was a vicious kind of cleanliness, and it seemed right that although we cleaned every inch of the floor every day, the cockroaches were still happy to live there. There were thousands of them, especially in the kitchens, and some of the lads liked to crunch them underfoot, but I could never get into that game.

Thanks to the incessant scrubbing, the constant sour aroma of green soap made your nose feel numb inside. We used bars of green soap in the showers and baths too and strangely, instead of overpowering any other smell that came along, it only seemed to magnify them. I had grown up in some of the most evil-smelling rooms anyone could possibly imagine, but my stomach would turn over in the morning after everyone had visited the toilet recesses for their daily sit-down. Even the hardest cases drew the line at doing that bit of their business in their cells if they could help it.

Keeping clean, scrubbing in the shower or the bath until your skin was raw, was something that the warders insisted on. So I don't know how one guy got away with his complete lack of personal hygiene. He was a black guy, a Rastafarian with dreadlocks, and he smelt so bad, a mixture of sharp underarm odour and something a bit like wet dog that came from his hair, that you could almost see flies buzzing round him. It was hard to sit next to him in the association room, but I liked the black kids I'd met around Wandsworth and I was genuinely curious about how he managed to smell like that in this place. He also seemed to be a bit mad, often apparently talking to an empty chair in the association room, and I had a soft spot for anyone who was crazy but obviously harmless. When I got talking to him he told me he was an actor and he had once been in something with Glenda Jackson. I took that with a pinch of salt, of course. I was the kid who told people that Lord Snowdon knew my father. He amused me, though. He told me I could make it in the movies if I fancied it and I should try finding myself an agent when I got out. That made me laugh.

'What do you do when you go down to have a bath?' I eventually asked him, once I'd weighed him up and decided that he wasn't the kind who might turn unpleasant if I asked a question that was out of line.

I knew that he went down every afternoon to the baths, as we were allowed to do once we'd finished the day's work. Every afternoon, regular as clockwork, he'd be down there with his bar of green soap and a towel. I had to clean the baths as one inmate came out and before the next went in, so I'd heard him running the taps with my own ears. But there was never a mark on his bath so it was as clear as day that he wasn't getting into it. God knows what the bath would have looked like if he had.

'Smokin',' he said.

'Smoking?' I was puzzled. 'You can smoke in the association room.'

He looked at me sideways. The penny dropped. He was smoking dope, sitting with his feet up on the side of the bath so that they couldn't be seen below the partition screen. The steam in the air and the green soap fumes everywhere scrubbed out the distinctive herbal smell of it.

The only other scent in the place was the overpowering aftershave on the warders, and when the green-soap fumes and wafts of Hai Karate collided big-time, fear hit me in the stomach like a fist.

This happened one morning when, again, I was on my knees scrubbing a section of corridor on the wing, and I heard the sound of marching feet coming up the stairwell. This was unusual, because it wasn't the right time of day for incoming prisoners or a change of officers' shifts, and there were too many feet making the sound. Usually there would be no more than a couple of inmates and a couple of wardens at a time moving around the wing. Nine uniformed officers appeared at the top of the stairs, led by Walker, and a tidal wave of eau de cologne seemed to come at me.

I couldn't help it. My brush seemed to be stuck to the floor and I gaped at the men in front of me. Walker glanced down and said: 'Association room, Roche, and shut the door.'

This was the only room on the wing, apart from the cells, that had a door. Everywhere else, including the toilets, was protected from general view by a screen that started at about knee level and ended at most people's shoulders. I left my brush where it was, as if the soap and suds had welded it down and it would never move again. I took myself to the association room as fast as I could. I was the only inmate on the wing not locked up in a cell at that moment.

I knew where the officers were heading. A black kid had been brought up the night before and locked in one of the strip cells. We'd heard that he'd had some bother with one of the officers on one of the regular wings and that he'd attacked this officer while he was out with a work party. There was nothing you could do in a place like this that was worse than that. He'd been brought back and put in the hospital wing overnight. He was fine when he arrived, but he would shortly be needing hospital treatment.

In the association room I stood in a corner with my back to the door and my fingers pressed as hard as I could stand it into my ears. The screams as they laid into him were the worst thing I had ever heard, and I never heard anything like it again.

I was still taking meals to the locked-up inmates at the time and I pushed his through the hatch; it was a few days before I realized that when I was going back to collect his tray at the end of mealtimes, his food was still there, untouched on the plate. I saw no sign of medical treatment being offered to him.

I had completely lost track of time. I suppose I had been there for six, perhaps seven weeks, but no-one had talked to me about how long I would have to stay. It seemed to me that no-one would notice if I was forgotten and never released, and I was far too scared to ask about when I might get out or how I could get myself sent back to the detention centre. This was just another way they kept control, never mentioning release dates until the morning came when you were out. Walker opened my door one morning. I was standing to attention by my bed as usual.

'Don't you want to go home?' he sneered. 'Haven't you got your kit together?'

I gawped at him for a split second, and then got to it fast, not that I had much to take with me. I'd been reading the Bible at night. We were locked up each evening at 7.30 sharp and after that the lights stayed on for another hour and a half. There was no library on the wing and nothing else to do, so I used to pick up the Gideon Bible that everyone had in their cell and take a look through it. I'd been awake early that morning and I'd had another glance at it while waiting for the officers to let us out. It was still lying on my bed, where I'd dropped it as I heard Walker coming, as I was marched out. I was halfway down the stairwell, being followed by Walker, when he bellowed: 'Where's your fucking Bible, boy? I've noticed that you like it. Go back and get it. On the double. It might do you some fucking good, God help us.' I turned on my heel, and even as I raced back to the cell to get it, desperate to follow every order to the letter so that I didn't give him any reason to change his mind and lock me up for another week, it still seemed funny that a bastard like Walker was insisting I took a bible home with me. As he handed me over to reception, he had one last shot.

'Don't let me see you back here again, Roche, or you'll really find out how nasty I can be,' he snarled, and off he went.

I was pushed out of the gates with £20 in my pocket, a rail warrant to get me into central London and a kid I'd never met before who, within thirty minutes of our release, invited me to help him rob a post office in Clapton. He was seventeen too. I bought a copy of the *Sun* at the station, and he bought a *Beano*.

I took the smell of Borstal with me, and like any other teenager I had in my head songs I'd heard on the radio during my time there. For years I couldn't hear Kate Bush singing 'Babooshka' without seeing cockroaches scuttling along polished concrete floors. The lyrics of Paul McCartney's 'Waterfalls' did it too, and they seemed quite apt for the frame of mind I was in at the time: stick to the lake and don't jump down waterfalls.

But the song that made me laugh as I listened to the idiot sitting opposite me was one by The Korgis that had been a hit while we were inside. 'Everybody's Got to Learn Sometime'. I hummed it to myself as the train rattled back into London, my home town, where no-one was looking forward to seeing me.

I had served the full three months of my sentence without any remission, because although I hadn't once been formally disciplined and I had done my best to keep my nose clean, I had been considered too mentally unstable to stay in a detention centre. More than half my sentence had been served in a Borstal. I was going home to the address I'd given, to Mum and Raymond's house, because I had no other to give. I knew they wouldn't want me there, but if I'd told the reception warders that, they would have banged me up again until a probation hostel place could be found for me, and I couldn't face that. I hadn't had a single reply to any of the scores of letters I'd written to Clara, and I half guessed what she would say to me when I did see her again.

What exactly was it that everyone had to learn sometime? I couldn't see that I'd learned anything except that the people who are supposed to look after you are the ones who will always do you the most damage, and that was nothing new to me.

I wasn't quite as quick off the mark as my *Beano*-reading companion hoped to be, but within weeks I was joy-riding again.

18. The Good Guys

I arrived in Wandsworth very early on the day I was released from Borstal. As I turned into our road, it was about half past eight in the morning. I'd travelled in the opposite direction to the crowds of commuters. I was heading out to the suburbs of south London as they went off towards the centre to work. The one house in the suburbs I knew would not be empty was ours. Most of my brothers were having no more luck than I'd had holding down a steady job. Laurence was the only exception, safely away now with the Army. Since he was the only one of us who you could rely on not to start a fight unless he was certain he could win, this seemed quite funny. But none of it was funny, not really. It didn't have much to do with the fact that in 1980 Britain's unemployment rate was sky-high. We all had trouble getting on with other people and dealing with real life, even Laurence, and the Army was his escape from those problems as much as joy-riding was mine. Even Raymond, who had been in his own way the self-control champion of the family and had seemed to be working his way towards a normal life after sticking with the hotel job he got when he was fifteen.

Paul, driven out by Raymond, had vanished from sight. We had occasional news of him living with a girl who he'd had a child with and then, after that relationship ended, from people who thought they'd seen him sleeping rough in various parts of London, but he never made contact with us. Terence was just hanging about, doing nothing in particular, although he had fallen in with a bunch of students who were living in a squat in the area and was starting to get himself some education, doing A-levels at a further education college and talking about going to university to do a degree. This impressed Mum. Raymond was her substitute for Dad, but Terence was now definitely the golden boy, the one who was going to show the world what the Roches were capable of. That left Francis, still mentally out to lunch much of the time, but busy adding to his own criminal record, mostly for petty theft. And, of course, me.

When I walked into the house Raymond, the man of the house, and Terence, the eternal stirrer, were sitting there.

'Hello,' said Raymond, hardly looking up. 'Back then? You start with any more of your criminal crap and you'll be out of this house on your arse. You're not upsetting Mum like that again.'

Terence, as always, had a grin on his face. 'I went to a party last weekend in Baker Street. I saw your Clara there. She was with some bloke. Good-looking bloke, tall, blond hair. She disappeared with him into one of the bedrooms.'

Fantastic. Just the welcome I needed. Certainly no more or less than the welcome I'd expected.

I put my bag down and walked out of the house and towards the street where Clara's mum and dad lived. If there had been one thing that had kept me going through the past three months, it was the thought of seeing her again. Deep down I knew that it was over because I'd heard nothing from her, but I had prayed that I was wrong. The joy of being out of the Borstal had briefly lifted the grey cloud of hopelessness I'd been lost in since being sent down. Even so, I found myself thinking: 'Dear God, Roche, you're always hoping, even after seventeen years of no evidence that it does any good. How stupid are you?'

Clara's house was empty. I walked half a mile to the shop where her mum worked, but she wasn't there either. I walked round and round in circles for an hour until at last, when I knocked on her door, Clara answered it. She was okay with me. She didn't slam the door in my face, but she stood on the step and didn't ask me in or say how pleased she was to see me.

'I'm sorry, Peter. I didn't write to you because I didn't want to do a Dear John on you while you were in there, and I didn't want to lie to you. You just keep getting into trouble, and I can't hack it any more. Nothing makes any difference. You get out of one lot of bother, and then it's something else. I've moved on. You've got to move on too.'

I knew it was coming, but it still devastated me. I didn't try to argue with her because I didn't trust myself to speak. I walked off, back towards my house. I couldn't understand how it was that my legs could still move and I seemed to be still alive, still breathing. When I got home, through the door and out of sight of the street, I did something I hadn't done since I was a small child in the North Lambeth house. I cried. I cried in front of my brothers and for once, just for once, neither of them tried to make me feel worse than I already did.

The worst thing was that Clara was right. What girl worth being with would want to be with someone like me? For the next few days I was like a zombie. I didn't speak and, because I was hurting inside so badly, I wasn't even hungry. My insides seemed to have frozen solid.

With Paul and Laurence gone, there was a bed in the house that I could call my own, although I still had to share a room with Francis when he turned up. He was doing as much dossing down with mates as I had been doing before I'd been sentenced, so that wasn't very often. Raymond seemed to have a campaign under way to get everyone out of the house except for himself and Mum, although he seemed to be able to tolerate having Terence around. Now there was just Francis and me to deal with. Yet surprisingly no-one challenged me when I went upstairs and made that bed my own. I call it a bed, but of course, as ever in our house, it was a mattress on the floor. Still, it was warm and dry, and not as dirty as it would have been in North Lambeth. Since we were all technically grown-ups, there were even times when the bedding got taken to the launderette, but this bedroom was still fairly sordid. There were no sheets or pillow cases and the pillows and blankets were ancient and stained, and a musty smell hung in the air that opening the window couldn't get rid of. It was more like a students' dive than a family home containing a mother and her grown-up sons, but even so it was a lot more cosy than a Borstal cell.

In the old days I would have been given all sorts of aggravation about not having earned a bed, and just to ram the point home I would probably have been forced to sleep on the sofa, even though there was space for me upstairs. I would have gone along with it too, after giving Raymond and Terence and Mum a bit of cheek, as much as I could get away with without a full-scale beating, but I would have given in after the first slap round the head. This time something was different. I was different. It was as if, now I'd been in prison, everyone had suddenly noticed that I wasn't the Dwarf any more. I was every inch as tall as Raymond and quite fit and nifty with it. More than that, though, after the experiences I'd had inside and then Clara's rejection of me, I must have had an expression in my eyes that warned off anyone who came near me. The message they sent out, for a while at least, was 'Don't even think about it.' So they left me alone and I was dimly aware how strange this seemed, because inside I felt utterly beaten.

I had one last attempt to persuade Clara to change her mind. After a week or so I got together enough courage to ask her to meet me for a drink, just for a chat. I have to admit that I thought that if I could get a few drinks inside her and maybe persuade her to make love with me, I'd get her back. Instead, after one drink during which she told me that she still loved me, but that she couldn't waste her life on a no-hoper like me, her new boyfriend arrived on his motorbike to pick her up and she was gone.

So that was that, and I had enough sense to know that the honeymoon period at home would never last. They would soon be back to the old habit of laying into me one way or another, and it would be sooner rather than later once the novelty of my reappearance had worn off. I wanted no more of that bullying. If nothing else, I was beginning to be quite afraid of what I might do to them if they tried it. Strange as it may seem, despite all the wounds and bruises and pain Mum had dished out to me for as long as I could remember, I had never raised my fist to her, and I didn't ever want to be pushed so far that I might lose control and hit her back. That morality – that you didn't hit women, and particularly a woman who was your mother – had stuck with me. But the stint in Borstal had instilled such loathing and anger in me that my anxiety attacks seemed to be coming every half-hour, and often with them came uncontrollable feelings of anger. I wondered if I might be about to be sent into a psychiatric hospital. Another institution, another kind of prison, the last thing I could face. Finding somewhere else to live, another way to live, was suddenly vital.

When one of my old joy-riding friends turned up on the doorstep, saying he'd heard I was out, and that he'd heard Clara had dumped me, I was pleased to see him, even though I was well aware that I shouldn't be. I didn't ever want to go back to prison, and I knew that hanging round with friends like him was the fastest and surest way to end up there. Yet I was even more pleased when he told me he was living in a probation hostel in Coventry. Common sense told me this meant he was in with a bad crowd up there. But it was a long way from London and I liked that idea.

'Come back with me,' said Neville. 'It's really easy to find places to live up there. Much easier than London. Come on, I know I can find you a place to live, no problem. We can have fun.'

It sounded good. Get away from the house, away from Clara. Out we went, nicked a car, and drove ninety miles up the M1 to Coventry. I was still on licence, and if I'd been caught, that would have been me straight back to the tender mercies of Mr Walker, or someone very like him.

We got away with it that time. We set about having fun and we actually did have some, and for once not much of it involved stealing or joy-riding. It has to be said that the quality of the company Neville introduced me to in the Midlands was not much better than anything I'd known in London and his idea of how easy it was to find a place to live turned out to be how easy it was to persuade someone to let you sleep on their floor. They were all people who were into drugs or theft of some kind, but at least that meant they didn't care about my record. I was getting used to the idea that I deserved no better.

One floor I found in a council estate on the outskirts of Birmingham cured me of any fantasy I had that life was better outside London. That place, to me, was real poverty. The estate reminded me of an abandoned town in the Wild West, only built out of bricks and concrete. If I'd seen tumbleweed coming down the bleak wide streets, with their scabby grass verges littered with rubbish, old washing machines, burnt-out cars, bent prams and bicycle frames, it wouldn't have surprised me a bit. I'd known some rough places but I'd never seen anything like this, whole districts of filthy-looking crumbling houses with stinking bin bags strewn around them. In London you walked from one poor street into a millionaire's row just round the corner and took it for granted that this was how it was. Here groups of hungry-looking kids hung about as night fell and I wondered who or what they could possibly find to prey on. I knew as soon as I looked at them that they were kids like the kid I had been, out looking for an angle, a chink of opportunity that might get them some money or a thrill, but for the life of me I couldn't see anyone or anything that would provide them with either. Everyone around them was as dirt poor as they were. The town centre, any kind of shopping centre, was miles and miles away and there never seemed to be any buses. There was no Underground ticket machine to con with a lead button to get them around fast, away from their own patch, and no West End, heaving with fat-pursed tourists, for them to go begging or thieving in. It frightened me to think what life would be like for a kid with parents like mine in a place like this.

Fortunately I wasn't a kid. I was almost a grown-up and I was able to hang around with a whole crowd of other almost-grown-up people like me, but they were people who were much wiser than any I'd met so far to the dodges that could be pulled to get enough money to go to the pubs and clubs with. Neville seemed to know a lot of people, especially in Coventry, and it wasn't hard to find someone who would let me sign on from their address so that I could get a weekly unemployment benefit giro.

I missed Clara badly, but she was a good distance away now, and with plenty going on around me and a reasonable bit of floor to call my own on most nights, I was feeling a bit more free of the heartache and even of the anxiety attacks.

Coventry, believe it or not, was an exciting place to be for a youngster in the early 1980s. It was the home town of The Specials, one of the biggest British ska bands who were doing this new kind of multiracial music that everyone seemed to be into in the Midlands, and there were lots of bands like them doing the rounds. I'd never been able to go along with the racism that a lot of young Londoners from my neck of the woods were into at the time. I didn't think very deeply about it, but it seemed too much like the bullying that had made my own life a misery and I wanted no part of it. So I really enjoyed the atmosphere in Coventry pubs and clubs like Mr George's and the Lady Godiva, a lot of kids from all sorts of backgrounds, black, white and Asian, rubbing along together, and there was a lot of energy in the music that seemed to help me get the panic and jumpiness out of my bones. For a while it was a good substitute for the criminal diversions that had been, in their way, my medication. Doctors kept giving me vitamin tonics. This worked better. Quite often, it has to be said, trouble would kick off at these places late at night when the National Front boys turned up looking for aggro, but from my point of view that was just a normal part of life. I rarely got involved myself, not unless I could see that the odds were stacked against some small kid and he needed a bit of help.

It was a new life, it was different, and for a while it was okay. Life took a bit of a dip when the old desperate need to be alone, away from people, began to resurface, and sleeping on strangers' floors was becoming a bit tiresome. My giro had been nicked from the house where it was being sent to and I didn't have any money at all, and begging didn't work in Coventry. But it was more than that. This fear of people was now a fixed part of me, even though I was almost eighteen and I'd managed to get a long way away from the people who had made me feel that way. I took myself off for a while and slept rough, spending a few nights sleeping in the outside lavatory of a run-down house on the outskirts of the city. I sat on the floor with my back against the wall and my knees pulled up, my feet braced against the opposite wall. It was early 1981 and I heard someone in the street saying that these were the coldest nights since records began, or something like that. Walking around with chalk on my back from the whitewashed wall of the toilet, freezing almost to death and looking every inch a tramp, I had a vision of being found dead from hypothermia, in Coventry of all places, and that being the end of everything. I decided to pull myself together. I went and found

Neville and told him I wanted to get back to London, where at least I knew my own patch and I knew what to expect. I was, surprisingly, feeling homesick. He sorted me out with some better-looking clothes and told me not to be so soft.

'You need a night out, mate. I know a couple of girls. Come with us tonight, we'll get you cheered up,'

Off we went and I struck up a relationship with one of these girls. It wasn't exactly love, but she was a kind girl and she took a bit of the sting out of losing Clara. The only problem was that she lived in Birmingham, and although it wasn't that far away, it was far enough to be too expensive for me to get on the train to see her. A few nights later Neville came up with the bright idea of stealing a car and going to see her and some of her mates. Of course I went along with it. I was almost eighteen, but I was still an idiot.

We went to Birmingham, picked up my new girlfriend and two of her friends, and went back to Coventry for a night out. At the end of the night, at two in the morning, we got ourselves another car and set off to take them back home. Neville took the motorway, and that was definitely a mistake. We were coming up to a service station and he started to pull onto the slip road that led to it.

'What are you doing, for fuck's sake?' I asked him. 'We need to get these girls back. We haven't got the money for a coffee.'

'Um. Yeah, well, the police are behind us,' said Neville, who had lost his usual cockiness. 'We'll just park up and very calmly go into the cafeteria.'

There were very few people in there at that time in the morning. If Neville had thought we might lose our police friends here, there wasn't a chance of it. Like the teenage idiots we were, we still hoped that we could get away with this. The two officers were now watching us from the other end of the cafeteria. We sat at a table, with one cup of coffee between us, listening to Neville's new plan. The girls were looking really worried.

'My dad's going to kill me,' said one of my girlfriend's mates.

'If they stop us, we just say the car's nothing to do with us,' said Neville. 'They can't prove it was us in it. We're nowhere near it now and we're not going anywhere near it again.'

'How the fuck are we going to get home, then?' demanded the friend, now almost about to start crying.

'We'll call a taxi!' said Neville, grinning suddenly, because this bright idea had come to him out of nowhere and it seemed like a master plan.

We did call a taxi. It took a while to arrive but we saw it pull up outside the cafeteria. We all got up and went out to it. Perhaps a dozen officers came out of the darkness and jumped on us.

'You Londoners think you're quite the lads, don't you?' said the enormous detective who came into the interview room at Coventry police station at five o'clock that morning, clearly ready to give me a hard time. 'We're not pansies up here, you know, whatever you might have heard. I'm still playing rugby, son, and I'm past forty. So wipe that attitude off your face and be sensible. We need a statement from you, and if you give it to us and tell us the truth, it'll go a lot better for you. If you want it hard, I can make it hard.'

I really wasn't trying to be the cocky Londoner. I was knotted up with fright inside. I knew that this little escapade would put me straight back in a detention centre or, if I was very unlucky, back into Borstal. Not on the hospital wing this time, either. I knew the system had a way of making sure that you generally got sent back to where you'd been before just so that you could see all those old faces again and think to yourself: 'God, why was I so stupid?'

But this detective, with his swagger and his talk of rugby-playing, made my hackles rise. I was thinking: 'Yeah, I've seen this all before, you fucking bully. You have no idea how many times I've seen this before. The next thing's a beating. I know. Well, do your worst, you arsehole. There's much worse coming where I'm going to, and I can take that too.'

'Come on, son. You look like you need a cup of tea. Do you drink tea?'

Tea? I looked at him in silence, not sure if he was taking the piss.

'How many sugars? A lad like you always takes sugar. I've a boy your age, he likes two sugars in his. Good and strong, and sweet. What do you say?'

If this was a nice cop routine, I didn't care any more. I was tired, frightened and suddenly hungry.

'Two. Please.'

After that, he even let me talk to Neville alone. I told

him that I'd been fingerprinted and they'd found my prints in the car.

'At the end of the day, mate, they've got me by the short and curlies. There's nothing I can do about it. They're going to send me back to the detention centre whatever I do. I might at least get a shorter sentence if I just make a statement.'

'Yeah,' said Neville. He knew that he was heading back to a jail of some kind too, probably an adult prison, because he was more than a year older than me, just turned nineteen. I was on licence, but he was still on probation, and committing a crime while on probation was viewed much more severely by the courts.

'I bet the girls have spilled the beans anyway. Let's get it over with.'

The huge detective took my statement and when it was all done, he looked me in the eye.

'Okay, son, sign it and I'll let you go as soon as you've appeared in court this morning.'

'No, you won't,' I said, suddenly pissed off with him again. He didn't need to lie like that. I knew what the score was with a record like mine, and given that I was ninety miles from the address I should have been living at while I was on licence, I'd never get bail.

'Don't worry, you will get bail,' he said calmly. 'I'll make sure of that. And afterwards, when the court breaks for lunch, meet me in the Dog and Trumpet and I'll buy you a drink.'

I had no idea what to make of all this. None at all. I asked him if Neville would get bail too.

'I'll sign it if you let him go too,' I said, as if I had the bargaining power of the United States behind me.

He smiled. 'Don't be silly, son. You know that's never going to happen. He's a year older than you and living in a probation hostel. And his previous is a list so long that it stretches from here to the Smoke.'

By this time my own previous convictions, which included numerous car thefts, being carried in a stolen car, a couple of petty thefts of property from sheds and gardens, and one burglary, was not exactly a short list. I did what I was told and hoped for the best, but expected nothing.

In court Neville's convictions were put before the magistrates and he was sent off to a remand centre to await trial for the previous night's car theft. When my turn came, it seemed the policeman who was giving the prosecution its information hadn't been able to find any previous matters against my name.

'I don't do that for everyone,' said the big detective in the pub as he handed me a pint of lager. I had left the court on bail, as he had promised, and at first I'd headed out into the centre of Coventry as far away from the court as I could get. I had wandered around a bit, realizing that with Neville gone I was a bit lost. I saw a clock on a tower in the distance. Almost noon. I might as well get that drink, I thought.

'There's something about you that tells me you could make a go of it if you made a decision to keep out of trouble, and to keep your hands off other people's property. This is probably the only chance you'll ever get. Your previous convictions will never again somehow not quite make it to the court. I'll make sure that your previous isn't there when your trial for this car theft comes up. You needed a break, and I've given you one. Try to make the most of it.'

I wanted to break down and cry. Instead, being me, I pointed out that I was not quite eighteen and he'd just bought me a drink in a pub. 'You could get done for that,' I said, as cheerful as I could manage to be. 'Can I have another?'

He gave me what they call an old-fashioned look, his chin down and his eyebrows up as he looked over his pint at me, and just the hint of a smile. 'I think that one pint will do you, son.'

Whether I liked it or not, I had to admit that I had met a good guy, a good policeman, someone who wanted to help me and who probably shouldn't have helped me as much as he did. It made a difference. When things went well for me because I'd been offered help of the kind that didn't ask for anything in return, I could still respond to it. Not straight away, of course. I was still a teenager with a messed-up mind, still human, and still a youngster with little education and a criminal record that was going to make any attempt at living a normal life hard for me.

I had to stay in the area to make sure I could be in court for the car theft trial and any hearings leading up to it. I couldn't risk going back to London and finding that I couldn't get back, or missing a hearing because a letter hadn't got to me. I would have been arrested and then it would have been back in prison on remand for certain, and there would have been nothing my good copper could have done to help me.

Amazingly my girlfriend and her family offered to let me stay with them. Her stepmother, I discovered, was at least grateful that Neville and I had insisted the girls had no idea the car was stolen. That was a ludicrous idea, of course, but I suspect the big detective also had a hand in keeping the girls out of it and none of them were charged.

They weren't bad people and they tried to live a normal, decent life, and I think those few weeks did me good. Staying there meant that I had an address where I would be certain to get the letters that told me when to turn up at court, and it also meant that Mum and Raymond didn't have to know that I'd been caught again.

I managed to get to every hearing on time, except for the day when the full trial was heard. On that day everyone in the house had gone out early and I had no money to get from there to Coventry. I got on the train at Birmingham without a ticket and although it was a short journey, I was found out by the ticket inspector. He got off with me at Coventry and called the police to charge me with evading the fare. I begged him to let me go. All I could think about was getting to that court, and although I told him what the problem was, he wasn't in the mood to take pity on me. In frustration and panic I pushed him out of the way and ran for it. It was a ridiculous thing to do, if only because I'd told him where I was heading.

The full trial for the car theft went ahead and my convictions weren't disclosed to the court. I came out of that with a supervision order but straight into the arms of the inspector and the police, this time to be charged with fare evasion and, worse, common assault.

This was the mildest kind of assault, the kind that deals with a shove or a push that causes no injury but which is still a criminal offence, but I was deeply ashamed. I had that strange moral code that a lot of kids I knew lived by. It was okay to take other people's property, but damaging people was well out of order.

This time my convictions were read out. Fortunately for me the court accepted that violence was not one of my vices, and I was put on probation. Neville, of course, was sent to prison for his part in the car theft and for several other offences he'd committed while he'd been in the Coventry probation hostel.

I walked free, grateful not to be locked up, but lost without his company and knowing that I couldn't stay with my Birmingham girlfriend any longer. I didn't care that much about her and it wasn't fair. For a little while longer I lived rough in the area again, but it was a cold, cold early spring in Coventry that year and I soon had sores on my legs and chilblains on my feet, and my stomach was growling fiercely with the old familiar hunger.

I walked to the station deciding that I would dice with British Rail's ticket inspectors just once more. If I was going to make a relatively normal life for myself, it would have to be back in London, on my own patch. Running away was not the answer.

19. Love, Marriage and Betrayal

Back in London, and briefly back in Wandsworth with Mum and Raymond, I was in a terrible state, too ill both physically and mentally at first to notice that Mum had lost a lot of her fight. The house was almost empty, just the two of them rubbing along together apart from the occasional appearance of Terry, who had done what he said he was going to do and made it to university. He was definitely the clever one. From time to time I wondered whether that beating that he thought had damaged his hearing all those years ago had frightened even Mum and Dad enough to make them lay off him to some extent while he was growing up. I certainly wondered, when I ran my fingers through my hair and encountered the dozens of bumpy scars on my scalp, whether I was a bit brain-damaged from all the batterings and hammerings my head had taken down the years from Dad's fists and Mum's yard brooms and plates, not to mention my brother's mate head-butting me to find out how hard my skull was. Often my head just didn't seem to work properly.

The others were all gone: Paul out on the streets somewhere, Laurence in the Army, and Francis was living with his girlfriend and their child in a council flat to the north of Wandsworth. Although there was plenty of room at Mum's, there was nothing but sourness in the way she and Raymond treated me. Raymond wanted no company. He lived like a hermit, rarely going out, keeping the place as neat as possible. It was quite strange, seeing Mum in a neat house. Raymond didn't want anyone else there messing it up. Mum, it seemed to me, just wasn't interested in me. Well, she never had been. Francis took pity on me, saying that I could sign on for unemployment benefit from his place and stay there from time to time when I needed to. It meant that I was getting some money to keep me away from stealing, and I had somewhere to sleep if I was ever tempted to think that there was no alternative but to look up my old, bad associates, the ones who were still burglars and car thieves when they weren't in prison. Thanks to the big detective in Coventry I had come back determined to keep away from trouble if I could.

I decided that since I was almost a man, I would try to behave like one. I found an employment agency and signed on with them, like a real grown-up. It went well. They sent me for two days' work here, three days' work there, mostly unskilled labouring jobs, but I seemed to cope well with them. Then the agency people told me they had a job that could easily turn into a permanent position. They sent me off to a factory in Croydon, on the edge of south London, that made parts for engines. A bloke called Noel met me on the factory floor with a metal bar that must have been ten feet long.

'This is for you, boy, and what you have to do with it is go over there and clean those buggers out, scrape any bits you can see off the roof and the sides.'

He pointed to a row of furnaces at the end of the workshop, things the size of a phone box and all roaring red-hot. Ha, ha, I thought. Get a rise out of the new boy.

But that was exactly what I was there to do, it turned out. There were a lot of West Indian guys working there, and one of them showed me where to get one of the fire-resistant protective all-in-one suits they were wearing. This job frightened the life out of me. I could only just about lift the bar, it was so heavy. Then, to get any leverage on it, I had to get a lot closer to the furnace than I liked. It was obvious that any slip-up would burn my hands right off in a matter of moments. The heat was tremendous and inside the suit I was wet through. It was obvious why no-one else in the place wanted the job. The blokes there told me that no-one lasted long doing it and I was the third lad who'd been sent there in three months.

I tried hard to stick it, though. It was the first promise of a permanent job I'd had since I had been taken on by the carpet-fitting firm, but it really took its toll on me. One of the West Indian guys led me away from the furnaces for a few minutes.

'You're not looking well, man. It makes you sweat, this job. You've got to keep topping up your salt. Get a bag of crisps and a drink of water.'

I had very little idea about how the human body worked. After suffering so much bodily abuse, I was accustomed to not thinking about my body at all. I had no idea what he meant about salt and sweating. I didn't have the money to buy crisps, and anyway eating was something I didn't do. Obviously I did eat from time to time, but hunger was something I could forget about for long periods of time. I had trained myself well in that way, at least. When other people were sitting down eating in the factory, I'd walk away and wander the streets for half an hour. I might have a pie or a pasty if I could find a shop and had a bit of money on me, or I might not bother. With little food and no understanding of what it meant to look after my health, it was no wonder the job made me ill.

Worse than the physical hardship of it was what it did to my mind. The severity of my anxiety attacks had been racking up since a few months before I'd left Coventry and now they became unbearable. Feeling sick and panicky, sure that I was on the verge of a heart attack, after a few weeks I told the factory I couldn't stay. Back at the agency, they refused to keep me on their books. I'd walked out on a good job and they couldn't trust me enough to send me anywhere else, they said.

I had made a new friend from the area where Francis lived, a decent guy of my own age called Barry, who wasn't interested in being a criminal and who made me laugh. He reminded me a bit of Dave from the dump yard, the friend I'd lost when I was nine. Just as I was giving up the factory job he joined the Royal Marines.

'Maybe I should join the Navy,' I thought to myself. Why the Navy? I have no idea. I did know that I didn't want to fight anyone. So into my head popped the idea that the merchant marine service would be the thing for me. There was no chance of any of the armed forces taking me anyway, not with my previous convictions. I asked a few people how to get into the merchant navy but no-one seemed to know. What I did know from my Soho days was that on the far side of Trafalgar Square there was a thing called Admiralty Arch and I'd often seen sailors in uniform round there. That was where I went.

A sailor was in the hallway area of the building cleaning the floor. I instantly thought of Borstal. Still, I was determined to give it a go.

'Where do I join the merchant navy?' I asked him.

He looked up, leaning on his scrubbing brush. 'This is the Royal Navy, mate,' he said. When I looked a bit blank he added: 'You know, the military lot, the ones that have guns on the ships.'

'Yeah, but I must be able to join the ones that don't have guns somewhere round here?'

This sailor was starting to get a 'here we go' look on his face. He sighed.

'This is HMS' – something or other, I can't remember exactly what he said the name was – 'and there is no-one here from the merchant navy.'

I got argumentative. I thought he was winding me up. I knew what HMS meant.

'This ain't a ship,' I said suspiciously. 'You must know where I can join the merchant navy. That's all I want to know. Where is it?'

'Now look, kid, this isn't the merchant navy. I don't know where the bleeding merchant navy is. This is a Royal Navy ship' – he gave me a very hard look – 'and it is in port. Now fuck off.'

I went ashore and walked up Pall Mall. The sun was shining, all the tourists were out in their holiday clothes with video cameras slung over their shoulders, eating ice cream, and I felt as if the clear blue sky was trying to suck me up into it. I was close to tears, but then I was close to tears a lot these days. My heart was beating funny and I couldn't ever seem to get rid of the knot of anxiety in my stomach. Thank God, I said to myself, that my mind is sound. But there's something terribly wrong with my body.

The doctor sent me to St George's Hospital in Tooting to be looked over by a bunch of head-doctors, and at about the same time I was there Mum was being prodded and tested and X-rayed in Fulham. My doctors did proper medical tests on me because I insisted that my heart was where the trouble was – and, in a way, it was – but every result said that physically I was in quite good shape. I felt guilty that I'd wasted their time, and when I was asked to come and talk to some kind of specialist I didn't want to put them to any more trouble. I never went back.

Mum had lung cancer, Francis told me, when I turned up at his place looking for a floor to sleep on for a few nights. All those years of endless fags had caught up with her. I thought now about how grey her skin had looked when I came back from Coventry, how she had seemed weaker and less belligerent than she ever had been, but I'd assumed she was just getting old. In fact she was only fifty-nine, hardly ancient. She was having radiotherapy, chemotherapy, drugs, the lot, said Francis, and she didn't look good. I was surprised that I cared as much as I did, and I went over to Fulham to see her. It was the first time ever that I'd looked at her and thought she looked little. Even when I'd grown enough to be taller than her in my early teens, she had still looked enormous to me. The broad shoulders and powerful arms had vanished. She looked like she'd been shrunk in the wash and, at the same time, the sweet musty smell that had always hung around her was much stronger.

'You all right, Mum? Francis told me you weren't well.'

'I'm all right, boy,' she said, offhand, reaching for her fags. She didn't really look at me; she was looking round the room and out of the window as if she was guilty of something. I had only seen her look frightened once before, on the day we'd moved out of the house in North Lambeth and heard Dad's voice, and I wondered if that was the unfamiliar thing I could see behind the weakness and frailty that had suddenly overtaken her. I felt sorry for her, even though that was more than she'd ever done for me.

Raymond was there to look after her, at least, and for me the struggle to survive was still going on. I was managing to stay away from thieving, but it was hard to keep going since I didn't seem able to hang on to any kind of job for very long. Concentration was still the same problem it had always been for me, but more and more I was finding it difficult to be around people, the same people, that is, day in and day out. I could be happy in crowds of strangers, though, and when I had a bit of money from my giro or some odd job I'd been able to pick up, I started going into central London with Barry when he was on leave. On one of these trips we bumped into two girls outside the Empire in Leicester Square. One of them, a short, very dark-haired girl who looked almost Maltese, was someone I liked the look of a lot. I told her I was coming up to nineteen, and she said she was nineteen too. The four of us hung about together a bit that afternoon and then the girls said they had to get to work. They worked in a nightclub, they said.

'Do you want to meet up again tomorrow? I've got the night off,' the dark-haired girl asked me.

I definitely did.

'That bench in Leicester Square. Same place. About two o'clock.'

Off she went with her friend, and I slept happily in a corner of the Earlsfield snooker club, looking forward to seeing her again. I had started going back to the club because it was the one warm, dry, safe place I knew that had nothing to do with crime. I was older now and, outwardly at least, calmer. Most of the blokes, if they remembered my argument with Bob Davis, the taxi driver I had accused of being a paedophile, had put it aside and accepted me as part of the furniture. The next day the girl didn't turn up, but her friend did.

'Where's Jackie?' I asked, and this girl must have been able to read the disappointment written all over my face. She was pissed off that I wasn't pleased to see her.

'Her name's not Jackie. She told you the false name she's using at the strip club.'

'Strip club?' I echoed, like an idiot.

'Yeah, pal, she works at a strip club. And, since you're asking, she's not nineteen. She's fifteen.' She looked pleased with herself when she saw the look on my face. It wouldn't have mattered to a lot of the lads I knew, but it mattered to me. I wasn't going to take advantage of a girl who wasn't even old enough, in the eyes of the law, to be at work.

'Which strip club?' I asked. Maybe this girl thought I was going to give her mate a hard time and was quite pleased about it, since I'd shown no interest in her. She told me.

I was feeling that old urge returning that made me want to protect, to fight if necessary, to get someone else out of trouble, just like I'd done in the playground sometimes when I'd seen a reflection of myself in some other poor kid being picked on by the bullies. Never mind that I couldn't defend myself. Now here I was, barely getting by, but determined to be this girl's knight in shining armour and maybe even get her home to her parents.

I asked Barry to come with me and off we went to the club. There was Jackie, or whatever her name was, on the door in a tacky, sexy little costume. She'd obviously been put there to pull the punters in. She saw me coming and disappeared inside. A big guy came out to meet us.

'I want to see that girl,' I said.

'And who are you?'

'I need to talk to her. And you shouldn't be letting her work here. She's only fifteen,' I told him. 'I'm coming back in an hour and if I don't see her then, I'm bringing the Vice Squad down here and getting this place closed up.'

An hour later I pushed my way into the club past a big bloke who had a baseball bat in his hand and saw her standing just inside the club between two very, very big blokes. I pulled back for a moment, not quite sure what was going on. She suddenly ran forward, grabbed my hand and shouted 'Run!'

A few hours later, safely away, we were at Barry's house. I'd persuaded him to ask his mum to give her a bed for the night. Even if my mum had been well I couldn't have taken her to my family's house. Sally, as she really was, admitted that she was only fifteen. It turned out she was sharing some dive in Clapham with the other girl, who was a stripper at the club and, into the bargain, a heroin addict. She couldn't go back there in case the strip club guys wanted to find her. Young as she was, she was worth good money to them. She said she'd run away from some trouble at home, forty miles away in Hampshire, but she agreed that she'd had enough of London and would let me take her back there. Next morning I borrowed some money off Barry and we both got on the train and I delivered her back to her parents' house. They were suspicious of me, at first, and that wasn't surprising, this young Cockney turning up on the doorstep out of the blue with their daughter, but they thawed out eventually and her dad gave me the money to get back to London.

Before I left, I gave Sally the number of the snooker

hall. I had half an idea that she would be off again at some point, and I told her to leave me a message there if she ever needed help. As it turned out she was on the first train back to London after she turned sixteen. Within a few months we were together and living in a squat on the same estate where Francis and his girlfriend were living.

I wasn't very happy about this squatting lark. It felt too much like burglary, even though it involved breaking into council flats that had been empty for months and had nothing at all in them apart from the fixtures and fittings. On the other hand, what I needed more than anything else at the time was a home to call my own, especially now I was with Sally. She was wild, not the level-headed girl that my first love Clara had been, but she just did it for me. I was head over heels in love and I felt like I'd rejoined the human race after a long time away. Strangely, although she was so young, she was the one who was wise to the squatting business and to all the ways we could sign on and get our giros without having to admit that we were living in a flat that wasn't legally ours. She'd learned a lot during her first brief stint in London. Then she'd been using someone else's National Insurance number to get the dole – she couldn't do it in her own name because she was underage – and she had also discovered that if you claimed to be living at an unsafe address where a cheque might be stolen, you could ask at the benefit office for a giro to be handed to you over the counter rather than posted.

It wasn't exactly the high life, but it was a more stable

life than anything I had ever known: going shopping, having food in the cupboards, keeping whatever place we were living in clean, and having someone around who liked my company and wanted to talk to me. It was like a dream come true. I was almost surprised by how much I liked living in a clean place. At one point a couple we knew joined us in the two-bedroom flat we'd recently moved into without the council's permission. They brought their own bedding and made a place for themselves in the empty bedroom, but they brought a dog with them too. It did its business one time too many in the hall and I told them they had to either take the dog for a walk as often as it needed or find another place. As long as I lived I might not ever be rich, but I was never again going to live in the kind of filth that my parents had made me live in.

Sally came back to the flat one afternoon with a funny look on her face.

'Guess where I've been?' she said.

I had no idea.

'I've been to the doctor's. I'm not right. I had to find out what was going on.'

This was news to me. My first thought was of Mum's illness, and I had a bad moment when I wondered if Sal had cancer.

'It's good news and it's sort of bad news,' she said. 'I'm pregnant. That's the good bit.'

I gasped and felt panicky. What was the bad bit?

'The bad bit, sort of, is that there's two of them.'

'Two of what?' I asked, mystified, alarmed, confused.

'Two babies. It's twins.'

God almighty. But never for a moment did I consider anything other than sitting tight, making sure she was okay, and forcing myself to get used to the idea that I was going to be a father. With two children. And this time, things were going to be different. My children weren't going to be treated the way I had been. I would make sure of it.

Mum died a couple of weeks after Sal told me about the twins. Francis had got a message to me that she was in the Royal Marsden Hospital, very ill, and not likely now to come out. The doctors thought she didn't have a lot of time left. I went down to the hospital to see her. She looked like someone else's mum, not mine.

'I need to see Paul,' she said. 'It's been so many years, will I ever see him again? I just want to see him again.'

It was peculiar hearing this kind of regret from her. She'd never been kind to him when he was around and she'd done nothing to stop him going. Still, I promised her I would do my best to find him and send him to her if I could. Just in case I imagined there had been some change in her, there was a flash of the old Bridget Roche, the one who had given birth to me and dragged me up in pain and misery.

She was being given a lot of morphine and she was rambling a bit, going on and on about wanting to be at home, sure that this was just another part of her treatment and she'd be out once she'd got over it. It was obvious that she would be leaving that ward feet first.

'When am I going home?' she suddenly demanded,

looking at me with the old fierceness in those dark brown eyes, the only part of her that didn't look as if every bit of colour had been drained out.

'I don't know, Mum. In a couple of days.'

'Don't you lie to me, boy,' she said, the last words she ever said to me. It should have been a bark, like the old days, but it was faint, crackly, with none of the terrifying power of the old days. Even so I couldn't help myself. I took a step back from the bed. I'd had enough of this, and I was a total coward about it.

'I have to go to the toilet, Mum,' I said. 'I'll be back in a minute.'

I walked straight out of the hospital. Just for this one time in my life, the only time, I thanked God I had brothers. I knew for certain that Raymond and Terry, and possibly Francis and Laurence, would go on visiting her but I knew I couldn't go there again.

I'd recently heard from one of the Wandsworth lads that he'd seen Paul near one of the mainline stations, so I went looking for him instead. It felt like something I could do for her, but I didn't find him, and Mum died at four o'clock the next morning. I went down to the house when I heard, meaning to say sorry, or something like that, to Raymond, because I thought he'd be feeling the worst of all of us. He'd hardly left her side for years. He opened the door and stood on the step and said I couldn't come in.

'You won't be excluded from the funeral, though,' he added in the odd, formal way he had of speaking these days. 'I will keep you informed of the arrangements.'

That day I went out with two friends in a car and crashed near Tower Bridge. I did some fairly serious damage to myself, because I had to be pulled from the wreckage by a bloke who happened to be passing. My so-called friends had legged it, leaving me unconscious over the driving wheel. In hospital I was visited by the police, who thought I must have been drink-driving. Funnily enough that was about the only motoring crime I hadn't committed – apart, that is, from stealing the car. No, this was a car I'd bought for £60 from some bloke I knew from the snooker hall with the idea that since I was becoming a family man, I needed some transport. I really had given up stealing cars. On the other hand, there was the small matter of the car having no tax, no MOT and no insurance, and me having no driving licence. I was still an idiot, but at least not the kind who couldn't keep his hands off other people's property.

I was out of hospital in time to go to the funeral parlour to say goodbye to Mum with my brothers. Not Paul, because still no-one had been able to find him. We all stood around the coffin, unsure of what to say or do. It wasn't scary this time, not like it had been when we'd gone to see Dad in his coffin thirteen years ago. We were all grown-up and we all had lives of our own, fragile though they were, and we would go our separate ways when we left. I wondered what we had in common. Our surnames. This woman in front of us in the coffin. The fact that the way she and Dad had raised us meant that not one of us trusted any of the others as far as we could throw them.

The only one who showed any emotion was Raymond, who was choked up, as I had suspected he would be. He asked if someone could say the Lord's Prayer. I looked at the others. No-one else seemed to be up for it, so I did it. When I'd finished, Francis spoke.

'Nice curtains,' he said, looking at the windows of the funeral parlour.

The court let me off very, very lightly. I went there full of guilt about how stupid I'd been. On the day in question, as they say, I had by now realized that I should hardly have been allowed to get on a bus, let alone drive a car. It was something like what had happened to me after Dad died. Up front, my mind said that I felt nothing, but in the back seat all sorts of emotions were raging away, so terrible and destructive that I couldn't begin to risk letting them loose. Grief, anger, bitterness, confusion, all those things, and a kind of despair in realizing that now I would always be someone who had never felt loved by his mother. There had been no purpose to the trip in the car with those lads. It had been an attempt at the same kind of running away from what was going on inside me that joy-riding had been when I was a young teenager. I was grateful that it was, in some ways, only a feeble echo of the things I had done then. I was gutted to think that I could have killed myself before my children had been born, and worse, I could easily have taken some innocent bystander with me. I told the court that this idea was haunting me and I was more sorry than I could say for that, as grateful as a human being could be that I hadn't killed anyone. I told them about my mother, the anxiety, my pregnant girlfriend.

Yet again I was lucky, so lucky, not to get locked up.

'That will be a £300 fine, Mr Roche. And don't go anywhere near a car again until you have a licence, and make sure the car is safe and legal.'

My response? An incredulous 'How much?'

There were sniggers all round the court. Oh, thanks, I thought. Laugh at me, make the judge really cross. I didn't mean it to come out like that. I was grateful, I really was – it just seemed a lot of money.

'You can go to prison if you prefer, Mr Roche.'

'No, your honour, thank you. Thank you very much. I'm very grateful. Thank you.'

I backed out of there before he changed his mind. I went down to the nearest Underground station and there, on the pavement outside, looking as rough as any tramp I'd ever seen, was Paul. It must have been getting on for six years since I'd last seen him. But I knew it was him all right. He was in his mid-twenties, but in his rags he looked like a bigger version of the boy he'd been when we'd lived in North Lambeth. It was a shock to be taken back in time like that.

I think that's why my first words to him were 'Hello, Paul. Mum's dead.'

Sal decided she wanted to go home to have her babies, so, with me out from under the threat of prison for the last time in my life, we went to Hampshire and the twins were born there while we were living in a hostel for homeless families. Very soon after they were born we married in the local register office with a borrowed ring, and in time we got a council place of our own. The twins were three when a third child came along, and it was so far, so good.

Life wasn't perfect. I tried hard to provide for my family but I usually didn't last more than a couple of months in any job. The longest I managed was a year on the railways as a ticket inspector, funnily enough. For a while it was okay, because it was obviously a job full of strangers. I didn't have to see the same faces every day and for a while this was comforting. I didn't have to worry about what they thought of me, because they were gone as quickly as they arrived. I didn't have to worry about what their angle might be. They wanted to ride on a train, that was all. I didn't have to find a way of not having to eat in front of them. Then one morning some madman thumped a passenger on the platform and I had to help restrain him until the police arrived. The job seemed to be poisoned for me after that. The anxiety and depression returned and I started to hate the crowds of people. I was overwhelmed by that old dump-yard feeling of just wanting to get away from everyone and everything. I went sick and eventually I resigned, rather than waiting to get the sack.

Sal and I must have moved a dozen times in ten years. Into London, back out to Hampshire again, back in again, one council exchange after another. She still had the runaway in her that had taken her to London when she was fifteen, and I was running away from what was going on inside me, although what we told each other each time was that another move would make things better, there'd be better jobs to be had for me in the next place, something I could do without it scrambling my mind. Another three children came along, and we always seemed to have debts and no money.

Even so we had created something very few other members of my family seemed to have managed, a stable family. The children were everything to me, even though I worried myself sick about feeding them and clothing them. One way or another, we managed it. None of them ever went to school without decent clothes and shoes on or without breakfast inside them. I knew where they were at night – safe in bed. I knew where they were during the day too. I never, ever raised a hand to them.

Still stuck with that insane feeling of responsibility that had been born in me so long ago, I always did what I could to help if any of my brothers turned up. Although Terry had got his degree, he didn't seem to have done much with it and didn't seem able to settle. He turned up one day saying he had nowhere else to stay.

He'd been with us a couple of months when I came home one afternoon, walking through the front door to find him and Sal standing in the hall. Something was wrong, I knew it right away. I had no idea what it was. I wondered if someone was dead.

'I'm leaving you, Pete,' said Sal. I saw the bag on the floor next to her and our youngest child, hardly more than a baby, in her arms. Terry was slightly behind her and he had half a smile on his face.

I knew that smile. I'd seen it hundreds of times. It was the one he always had on his face when someone else was about to get a hiding. The time I remembered now was the Sunday morning when Dad was dying behind the bedroom door, although none of us knew that, and Terry had reached past me to knock on the door a second time to wind him up, ready to leg it up the stairs if Dad brought his belt out to me.

You bastard, I thought. You fucking bastard. All this time gone by, and it should be over now, surely to God it should be over. But no, as if my fucking brothers hadn't done enough to me over the years, you're taking my wife away from me and their mother away from my children. You complete fucking bastard.

20. Answers

The struggle with the social workers was terrible. Five of the children were still with me, and no-one could say that I didn't love them or that I treated them badly, but my mental state was so fragile that everyone, including me, was frightened that I would neglect them because I was so ill.

'You are a good father, Peter, a very good father,' said the psychiatrist my doctor had sent me to. 'You must hold on to that and trust yourself.'

I had first been given anti-depressants when I was in my mid-twenties, after years of pestering GPs with my fears of a heart attack. The anxiety had returned with a vengeance while I was working on the railway, and it seemed to get totally beyond control whenever Sal was pregnant again. One doctor even told me that I should find a way of getting relief from panic attacks that didn't involve producing babies.

I found it almost impossible to accept that I needed that kind of medication. It said to me that I wasn't a man, that I couldn't cope. Mental illness wasn't something that a working-class man like me should have. To have something wrong with your mind was a weakness, and I couldn't afford to be weak. I had a wife and children who depended on me and I had to be strong for them.

After Sal and Terry left I couldn't keep up the pretence any longer. I had to admit that my mind was in a terrible mess. Even so, I insisted that what had caused this illness was the betrayal of my wife and my brother, nothing else.

'I don't know, Peter,' said the psychiatrist. 'I feel this is about something else too, about your life before this happened. Perhaps about things that happened when you were a child.'

No. That was over. I had survived. I had got away. It was over and it had nothing to do with what was going on now, I was sure of that. I told him none of it.

'Well, what I want to tell you is that I have never seen symptoms like yours before in a man whose wife has left him,' said the psychiatrist, 'and I have seen men whose wives have left them for their oldest and dearest friends. You don't talk about your brother as if he had ever been that kind of friend to you. Your condition reminds me most of people I have seen who have been caught up in terrible disasters, witnessed terrible scenes, cruelties more horrible than usual human experience. Train crashes, wars, mass murders, that kind of thing. We call it post-traumatic stress disorder.'

And even then the penny didn't drop. I didn't come anywhere near accepting that I was still living with the consequences of my childhood until five or six years later, when my life had at last turned a corner.

During the time that I was struggling to keep everything together for the children after Sal had gone, her parents and family had done all they could to help me. Of course, they couldn't turn their backs on her, but they didn't shut me out either, and it was a lesson to me that family could be something different, something good, in a way that my own had never been.

A young relative of Sal's lived close by. Lisa had been left by her partner, and she started coming round regularly to look after the children, see them off to school, make sure they had a meal to come home to, helping me to get them ready for bed. It began as something she wanted to do for the kids and ended with her moving in with me. Five years on we were settled together in a way I never had been with Sal. For the first time in my life I began to talk to another human being about some of the things that had happened to me when I was a child, and she listened. She was sympathetic, but she was practical too.

Like my first love, Clara, she was the kind of person who wondered what I'd looked like when I was a boy and I'd told her the same story about Miss Zils and her camera.

'And what were the NSPCC doing at your house?' she asked.

This was a question that had begun to bother me too. All the thinking I'd done about why Terry had done what he did, *how* he could have done it, had stirred up an awful lot of questions. Whether I wanted to or not, his betrayal had forced me back to remembering the boys we'd been. At first the memories came back out of pure bitterness as I remembered every snide remark he'd made to get me a hiding from Dad or Mum. The bitterness faded a bit with time, thankfully.

What bothered me so badly was how he could have

seduced my wife without considering what this might do to my children, to his own nieces and nephews. Why didn't he have the same driving need I had to make sure, after all we had suffered, that the next generation knew nothing about childhood suffering? That led, in the end, to a very simple question that lurked right at the bottom of it all. If the NSPCC had known about my family when I was two, why had any of us had to suffer at all beyond that time?

'Find out,' said Lisa, very simply.

It took me a while, of course, and Lisa didn't nag, and yet she didn't give up. Find out. Ring the NSPCC. The number's in the phone book. Miss Zils isn't a common name, someone will remember her. Maybe she's still alive. Find out.

Miss Zils phoned me back no more than half an hour after I'd spoken to the man who had answered the phone at the NSPCC's head office.

'Come and see me, Peter. I always hoped you would get in touch again. I'm retired now, but I would love to see you again.'

I rang the doorbell for her first-floor flat in a quiet Victorian terraced street in south London. She led me upstairs and as she showed me into her living room, the first thing she pointed out was a large framed photograph that was hanging right in the middle of her living room wall. It was of a toddler with curly hair looking up towards whoever was taking the picture, rubbing one eye with his hand, and he appeared to be standing in a gloomy place, almost in the dark. He was wearing some kind of flannel jacket pinned together with a big nappy pin over a vest and a pair of wellingtons. He looked dirty and very sad. The expression on his face made my stomach turn over and my eyes filled with tears. I felt I would cry if I didn't control myself. I am certain that I had never set eyes on it before that day, yet I felt as though I knew it well. Even so, what Miss Zils said as she pointed at it felt like being hit over the head with a brick.

'That,' said Miss Zils, 'is the picture Lord Snowdon took of you.'

It says a lot about my mother, I think, that she could have translated what happened on the day in 1965 when that picture was taken into a story that ran along the lines of 'Lord Snowdon was a friend of your father's.' All the unpleasantness behind it, particularly what that day said about her as a mother and about my father as a father, had simply been wiped clean out of her strange, lopsided, pathetic version of it.

This is the story as I pieced it together over the next few months after meeting Miss Zils again. I was two years old in the May of 1965, the year that marked the twentieth anniversary of the end of the Second World War and also of the founding of the welfare state. The NSPCC decided to get a big fund-raising publicity campaign underway. Britain was supposed to be a brave new world, a country where there was a safety net to catch all the unfortunate people who had been dealt a bad hand in life. A pension for the elderly, money for the unemployed, support for the sick and disabled, free health care for everyone. And, for children who were being neglected or ill-treated, eagle-eyed social services watching over them.

But the NSPCC knew that there were still thousands of children living in conditions as squalid and brutal as any that Charles Dickens had written about a hundred years earlier, and they wanted to let the world know this. I can understand that they had work to do and they needed money to do it, and they couldn't let the public get carried away with the idea that the bad old days were over now and that charities like the NSPCC didn't need their support or their donations any more.

The NSPCC's patron was the Queen. Lord Snowdon had married the Queen's sister, Princess Margaret, in 1960, and for a while after I discovered this picture of me existed I assumed that was how he had come to be the photographer who took it, invited to do so because of his close connection to the charity's royal patron.

I was to find out, however, that there was another twist to the tale. He had been a highly regarded photographer before he joined the Royal Family and afterwards he was the most famous photographer in Britain, but he didn't exactly have a job. I read somewhere that a life with no job to do drove him crazy, and I thought to myself that this at least was one experience that Peter Roche and Lord Snowdon would one day have in common. When the *Sunday Times Magazine*, the first colour magazine ever to be published with a British newspaper, was launched, he started working for it.

So it wasn't just that the NSPCC wanted show-stopping pictures for their own magazine or posters. The plan from the start was to have them published in one of the most influential publications of the day. As it happened, they told Miss Zils to take care of Lord Snowdon on the day he set out to record childhood poverty in south London, and they told her to take him to some of 'her' families. She told me later that she was given no warning. She was simply told to go and meet her boss at Waterloo station. She went there with the bag of clothes she was planning to hand out to various families on her Lambeth round and her boss came to meet her as she walked up the station concourse. She was dimly aware of several shiny and impressive black cars standing behind him in the road in the middle of the station, normally used by the mail vans as they load and unload at night after the commuters have gone home.

'Lord Snowdon is here,' he told the astonished woman. 'You're going to go in his car with him and take him to see the families you visit. Give him all the help he needs.'

I got the impression that Miss Zils wasn't very happy about this, either at the time or later, when she was telling me about it when we were both adults. It wasn't the idea of Lord Snowdon that bothered her, but whether it was right or fair to take any photographer with her when the families had been given no warning; however, she did as she was told. Even very educated people like her did in those days.

So she took him to our place in Lambeth, where Davie and Bridget Roche were living in a three-bedroomed flat with nine children and a lodger. I can easily believe that my mother was right, that all the neighbours did come out onto their balconies to see what was going on as the fleet of shiny black cars pulled into the service road behind them. Royalty in Lambeth. The word would have spread round the estate in minutes.

The NSPCC pictures from that day are still in Lord Snowdon's archive. He used up twenty old-fashioned rolls of film that day, thirty-six pictures on each roll, and the Roche family got a whole roll to itself. These are the only thirty-six photographs that anyone ever took in any house that we lived in. There are pictures of the mantelpiece, of some of my brothers – although I can't quite work out who is who because no other pictures of us when we were young exist – some of Miss Zils examining us, and some with the posh lady reporter who came with Lord Snowdon standing in the background with her coat and gloves on and a handbag over her arm, looking as if she's the Queen herself. There are some of a woman sitting in a room that's too full of tatty furniture, strewn with clothes and blankets, and she's wearing a torn jacket that looks like it might be the best bit of clothing she has, smoking. Who she is is a mystery to me. My mother would have been in her early forties by then, and this woman, though she looks like she's had a hard life, doesn't look anywhere near that old. Our oldest sister Kathleen would have been about in her early twenties, but I'm sure she wasn't living with us. My best guess is that she is John-John's mother, our neighbour. There's one that has my dad standing in the background, wearing his usual suit and tie. But almost half the film, one picture after another, is of me on my own. There are sixteen pictures of me, sometimes looking up, sometimes looking away. There was something about the way I looked that he wanted to catch on film.

When I went to see Miss Zils all those years later, she showed me the picture, but she didn't let me in on the whole secret of how that picture had been used. She did tell me that it had been used 'well', as she put it, and that it had touched the hearts of a lot of people.

Miss Zils had been born in Germany and had come to Britain as a refugee during the war, she told me. She talked a little about how she and her mother and sister had been forced to walk hundreds of miles to get out of Germany and escape the Nazis. To me she looked rather like Marlene Dietrich and talked like her too, and she was obviously educated and quite intellectual. She said that she had artist friends in Germany who had been so taken with the photograph that they had painted their own versions of it. To me this was bewildering.

'It brought in a lot of donations from the people who saw it, one big donation in particular from a retired British army colonel who came in person to our office after seeing the picture,' said Miss Zils. 'He had a copy of it with him. He wanted to meet the boy in the picture, he wanted to meet you and your family so that he could help you directly. I had to tell him that it wasn't our policy to allow the public to meet the children in photographs of this kind. But even so he was very generous. When he died he left his entire estate to the NSPCC.'

That was when I finally cried. The shock of seeing the picture hadn't made me crack up and I'd held myself together through the story about Lord Snowdon. But being told that there had been someone who wanted to help and they'd been kept away from me was more than I could stand. I felt turned over, used. It had been a publicity stunt – I had been a publicity stunt – and it had worked well. Somehow, out of the 700 pictures Lord Snowdon had taken that day to illustrate the suffering that children were still being put through in 1965, somebody had picked that picture of me, and it had worked great for the NSPCC. It hadn't worked great for me. Pride made me choke back the tears as much as I could and I said nothing of this to Miss Zils. I didn't want to upset her.

Miss Zils explained that she began to bring her camera with her when she visited us in Lambeth because her boss wanted to follow up the 'story' of Lord Snowdon's little lost child. I was quite full of myself, she remembered, and after a few visits I knew where she wanted to take me and I would lead the way to the swings.

Back home with Lisa, the first thing I said to her as I walked through the door was 'I've seen a picture that Lord Snowdon took of me.'

Lisa looked at me. 'Yes, Peter,' she said, smiling.

I had no-one to blame for her disbelief but myself. I was always larking about, teasing her, thinking of some outrageous thing to say to see if I could get her going or make her laugh.

'I have, really. It was on Miss Zils' living room wall. A huge picture, just me, about two years old.'

'How do you know it's you?'

'Because she told me. It's how she knew who I was when the NSPCC rang her and told her that I wanted to speak to her. She's never forgotten my name. The picture's been on her wall ever since 1965.'

Lisa looked at me for a long, long time.

'I'd like to see that picture,' she said.

When I rang the NSPCC and was put through to their archivist, he knew right away what picture I was talking about.

'A very famous picture,' he said. 'Very famous indeed. Can I ask what your interest is in it?'

'It's me. The boy in the picture is me.'

'Is it really? That's amazing.'

He promised to send me some copies of the *Child's Guardian*, a magazine that he explained the NSPCC had published for its subscribers and donors during the 1960s, with stories about the children the charity had helped and the work that was being done.

'You'll find them interesting,' he promised.

They were. There was more than one story about me. In one picture I was on a swing wearing the smart check duffel coat. In another I was holding a teddy bear. In another, I had on the hat I was given at the big building in central London that Miss Zils took me to on the bus. This had been the head office of the NSPCC, I discovered. These pictures of me scrubbed up, looking like any other happy, well-cared-for child, made me feel as if at the time I must have been abducted by aliens who knew nothing about what my life was really like.

But Miss Zils had told me that she did know something

about my life. 'I know that coat I gave you was taken away from you and given to one of your brothers,' she had said.

But readers of the *Child's Guardian* could never have suspected this. What they saw was Lord Snowdon's picture next to Miss Zils' snapshots. The story they told was: 'This is that boy then and this is him now. Look how we've transformed his life.'

There was even a line in one of these stories that the NSPCC had taken this boy's big brothers and sisters for a day out at the zoo. A copy of the *Child's Guardian* from 1966 carried a little story about me and my family. It didn't name us, and the way the story was told probably wasn't anything out of the ordinary for an era when attitudes towards families like ours were patronizing and demeaning, but I felt humiliated by it.

'We have found his father a job and we have bought his mother a shopping trolley because she has a weak heart and can't carry the family groceries on her own,' it says. I didn't know about the trolley and I couldn't recall Mum having a weak heart. Dad's job, of course, was one of my many sources of childhood shame. I should have felt grateful for it – at least he had a job – but I had never been able to while the kids ran after me calling me bogbrush.

I still didn't understand how a photograph published in this little charity magazine could be so famous, but under the picture of the two-year-old me rubbing my eye was a sentence in small type: 'Courtesy of Lord Snowdon and the *Sunday Times*'.

I went to London again, egged on by Lisa, this time to the newspaper library at Colindale in north London. I got copies of the *Sunday Times* for 1965 out of the archives on microfiche rolls, clipped them into the reading machine and began to scroll through them.

Seeing my picture on the front cover of what was then the most famous colour magazine in the country made my heart stand still. In August 1965 the *Sunday Times Magazine* had run a story called 'Some of Our Children' illustrated by its famous chief photographer. His sequence of pictures catalogued the abuse, poverty and neglect still being suffered in the mid-1960s by children in Britain, and I was the star of the show. There I was on the cover, and inside there was the picture of my bruises. The picture that was taken – I assume while she was signing a form giving her permission for what was going on – shows something my mother probably hasn't fully understood the meaning of. I am guessing that when the remarkable visitors arrived, I was dressed only in a vest and Mum quickly put me into wellingtons and pinned one of my brother's shirts round me. It would have been seen, I'm sure, only as making me decent.

As I sat in the Colindale library looking at the pictures I felt close to tears. To be honest, I felt disgusted. It was disgusting that they had taken that picture of me, disgusting that they had used me like that. The most disgusting thing, though, was that then they went away and never came back except to take more fund-raising pictures.

I don't blame Lord Snowdon at all. I don't even blame

the NSPCC. I know that they were well-meaning and that they were only trying to raise money in order to help more children. I do understand that people saw things differently in 1965 and I have since seen for myself how the work the NSPCC does has moved on since those days. I know that they would never now use a child the way they used me. But it was hard to look at those pictures at the age of thirty, knowing what I knew about how that child had suffered through all the years that followed.

I had gone to Miss Zils as an adult intending to ask some hard questions. At that time, recovering from the worst kind of crisis in my personal life, I was desperate for some answers. Why had no-one noticed what my brothers and sisters and I were going through when we were children? Why hadn't we been rescued?

When I asked, the charity discovered that none of the paper records from the office where Miss Zils worked had survived the arrival of the computer age. They didn't think there would have been any record of us anyway, because in those days they had only kept records when a case of child cruelty was taken to court. But well-meaning people who followed the work of the NSPCC, including, I assume, my army colonel, were led to believe that my life had improved, when in fact I had been left with a family that treated me worse than most people treat their dogs.

I never did ask Miss Zils any of my questions. She was an old lady and she obviously felt she had done some good with her life, and possibly that she had even done me some good, and I didn't want to be rude or hurt her feelings.

'You were a lovely boy but you were left to run wild. I would have liked to have done more for you but my boss wouldn't let me,' said Miss Zils.

I don't know why, she didn't explain why, and I didn't feel it was right to ask. I had the idea that it might kill her if I told her what my life, my brothers' lives, had really been like after we'd left the Lambeth flat and she lost contact with us.

I try to take some comfort from the fact that Miss Zils, after all that time, still had my picture on her wall in her living room. After her death in 2002 one of her friends said that it had hung there for thirty-seven years, from shortly after the day it was taken at our flat in Lambeth until the day she died. I don't believe she had it there only because it was a picture taken by one of the most famous photographers in Britain. There's nothing very cheery about it; it's not a picture you can look at and think: 'That's beautiful.' I feel sure she was never the kind of person who could have pointed it out to people as if she was proud of it, proud of having found that child for Lord Snowdon's camera, proud of the fact that she'd had to leave me and my family to our fate.

I try to think of it as proof that although she could do nothing for me, she really did care and didn't forget me. Perhaps keeping the picture in front of her was a way of reminding herself of what she had done with her life, of the children she had been able to save without forgetting the ones she hadn't. I could be wrong, but I like to feel that it was a sort of keeping in touch with me and hoping for the best for me. I hope that's true.

21. Epilogue

The social workers eventually declared that I was a good father and fit to look after my children. There have been moments since when I have thought that it was almost worth the hell I went through after Sal and Terry left to get that official seal of approval. After the childhood I'd had, it mattered more than anything to me that I could look in the mirror and not see my father or mother staring back, not to have to think: 'You're as much of a bastard as they were.'

That was why, even if I felt ready to kill Terry at times, I decided that the only thing I could do, for the sake of my children, was to be on the best terms I could possibly manage with both him and Sally. I wanted to be a million miles away from the pair of them, but once they had a house of their own it seemed to me that our children, particularly our girls, needed to be with their mother, and I agreed that the children could go and live with them. But because I was determined to be there for my kids as much as was humanly possible, it meant I had to make up my mind to live in the same neighbourhood as the wife and brother who had betrayed me so bitterly.

It was hard. All I will say is that I forced myself to be as civil to Terry as I could. I begged him: 'Whatever else you do, please, please, do right by my kids. They're your nieces and nephews too. Remember our childhood, and don't put them through any of that.'

I married Lisa some years ago and we now have four children. She has supported every inch of the way my determination to be the best father I could be to the children I shared with Sally, even when it seemed to both of us that we would be a lot happier if we put a lot of distance between that old life and our new family. Thanks to her determination and courage, I have never been more than a few miles away from any of them at any time in their lives. It isn't the way I would have wanted it to be when they were born, but since the choice was taken out of my hands I count it as one of my successes.

There isn't a day that goes by when I don't wonder what would have become of me if I hadn't met Lisa. She is the steadiness my life has always lacked, kind and compassionate, understanding and tolerant, the one thing in my life that I know will never fail me, let me down, betray my trust in her. I don't know what I ever did to deserve her. But there is no easy way out of a childhood like ours, and the truth is that there have been few happy endings in our family. There has been a lot of failure to face, and not just for me. I am not the only Roche child who has had to deal with separation and divorce. Apart from Kathleen, the eldest, who died in Australia when she was in her early forties, and Raymond, who has never married or had children, every one of us has struggled at some point in our lives to make lasting relationships. Not one of us, I believe, is to blame. Affection is something you have to learn about as a small child and none of us were given that chance.

Several of my brothers live within thirty miles of my home, but I rarely have any contact with them. I find that even now, after all the brutality of our childhood has faded, I can't quite feel easy in their company. I don't blame them for the way they treated me, because I understand better than anyone alive what made them do it, but the old habits of mistrust and fear die hard. I have never been able to get a firm hold on what most people would call normal life. The kind of concentration and emotional stability that a steady job requires has never come easily to me and I have spent a lot of my adult life being kept on an even keel by anti-depressants.

I now have the ambitions I lacked when I was a teenager. They are very simple. When I grow up, I want to be able to live without being pursued from moment to moment by depression and anxiety. I want to go to work like everyone else. And that's it.

I try hard to count my successes instead of dwelling on my failures. I have never hit my children, never called them the names I was called by my parents, never abused or taken advantage of their weakness. My children go to school with food in their stomachs. They go on school trips with money and packed lunches. They go out in shoes without holes and that fit them, in clean clothes, in clean underwear. I know where they are, and if I don't know, I find out fast. I like to live in a clean house, wear clean clothes and have food in my cupboards. I have a valid driving licence, and my car has insurance, road tax and an MOT. There has been no joy-riding and no thieving since the day I got back from Coventry after my big detective took pity on me and saved me from a second stint in prison.

I do worry that my children will one day turn round to me and say: 'You can't tell us what to do. You weren't perfect.' I have to hope that even if I can't claim to be perfect, I can at least say that I'm an expert on where all the bad things a teenager can do lead to, and none of those destinations are good. I can hope that this account of my life will help them understand a little of how I came to be that teenager. I also hope they will feel able to talk to me about their fears and problems, and let me offer them the help and guidance that I never had.

Like all children who have known themselves to be unwanted and unloved, even now I find myself wishing that I could talk to my own parents and get them to talk to me, to explain it all, in the hope that I might begin to understand why they treated me the way they did. It's a hopeless wish and it would be hopeless even if they were still alive. They would never have known how to have that kind of conversation. But a child goes on hoping when all hope is gone, and none of us are ever really able to leave behind the child we once were. I certainly haven't been able to.

This story begins and ends with a photograph taken when I was two years old. Finding it was like discovering that I really did exist after all. It was as if someone was saying: 'No, it wasn't all in your imagination, that childhood really did happen, and it happened to you.'

Once I knew it existed, I knew I would never be happy until I had told the story of what had happened to that child after the picture was taken. Since I discovered I was the child in the picture, I have often been told that it remains one of the most striking images of Britain in the twentieth century and is the kind of picture that will be seen again and again, always in some archive somewhere, always being exhibited or republished, known all over the world from New York to Sydney. Limited-edition prints of it sell for £2,000, ironically in a West End gallery in one of the streets where I used to walk as a penniless, hungry child in rags.

I could never have been happy while there was a possibility that people would look at it and assume that because it was so famous, and because Lord Snowdon had taken it, life had been better for that child afterwards. I wanted people who had seen it, who might see it in the future, to know exactly what life was like on my side of the camera lens.